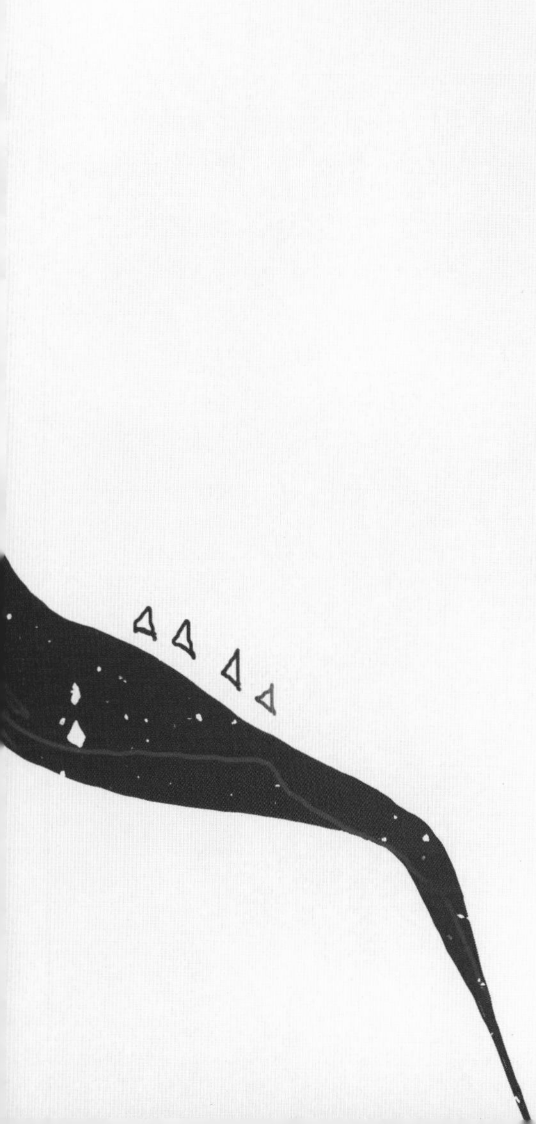

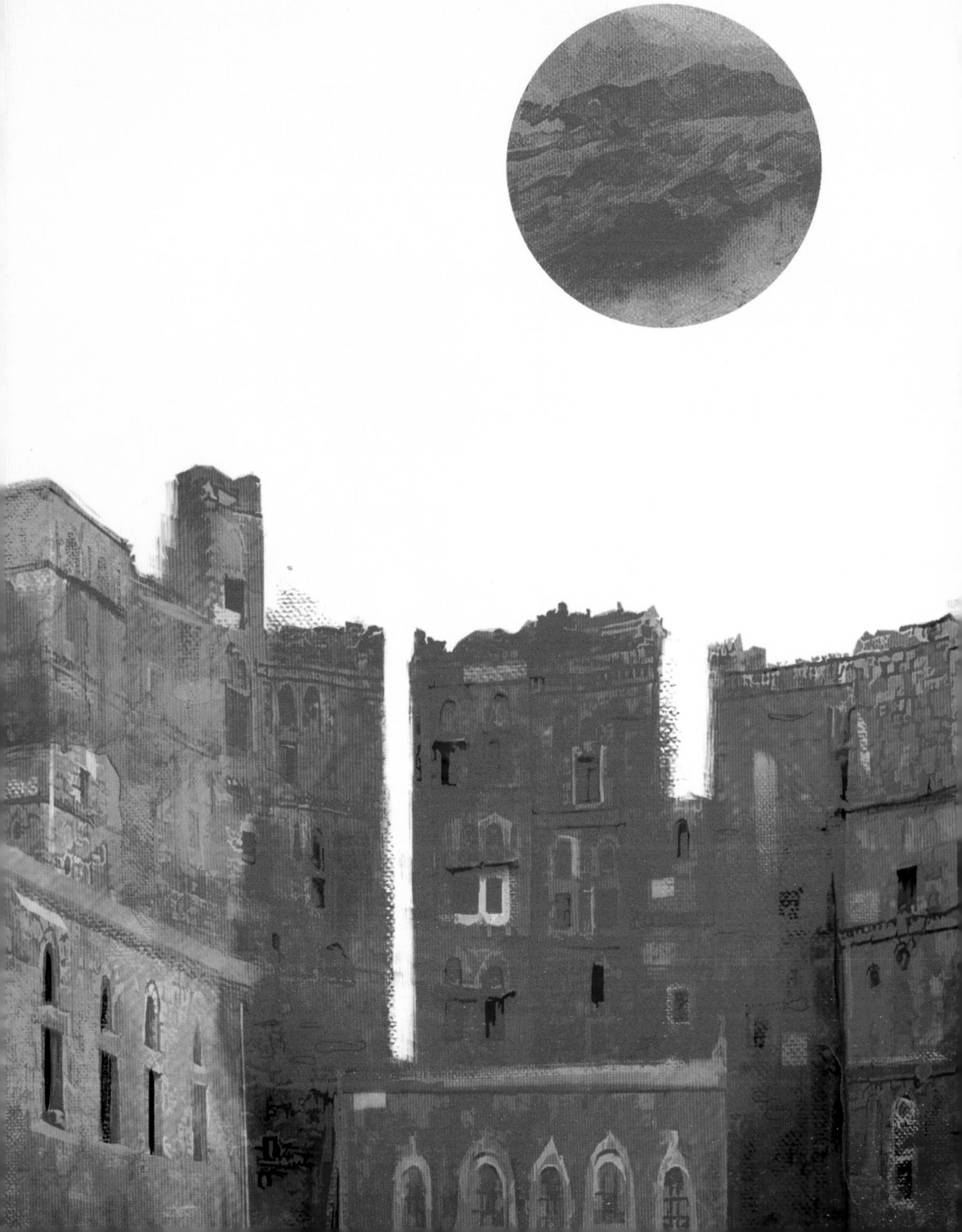

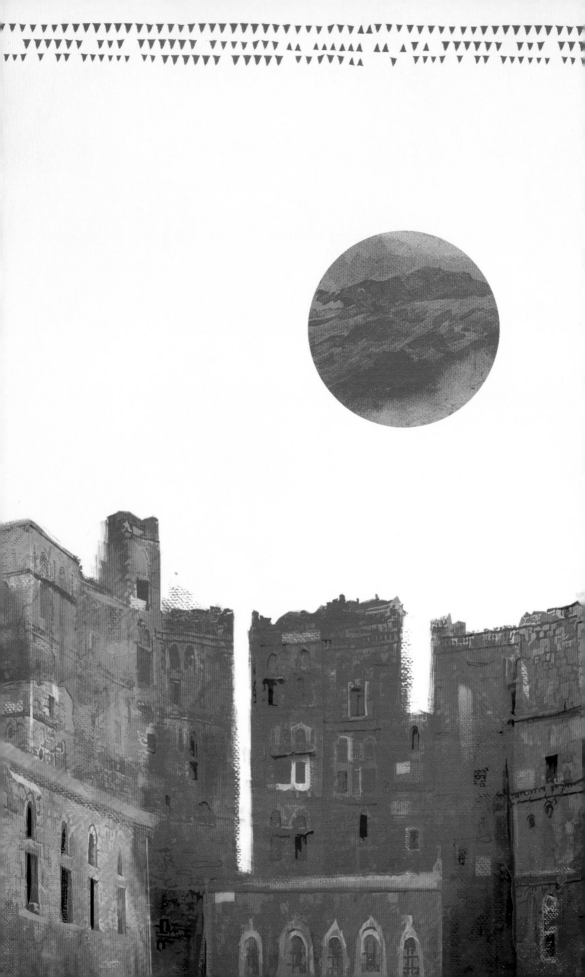

The Cloud

K.I. Zachopoulos & Vincenzo Balzano

Published by
ARCHAIA™

THE CLOUD, July 2016. Published by Archaia, a division of Boom Entertainment, Inc. The Cloud is ™ and © 2016 Kostas Zachopoulos & Vincenzo Balzano. All Rights Reserved. Archaia™ and the Archaia logo are trademarks of Boom Entertainment, Inc., registered in various countries and categories. All characters, events, and institutions depicted herein are fictional. Any similarity between any of the names, characters, persons, events, and/or institutions in this publication to actual names, characters, and persons, whether living or dead, events, and/or institutions is unintended and purely coincidental.

BOOM! Studios, 5670 Wilshire Boulevard, Suite 450, Los Angeles, CA 90036-5679. Printed in China. First Printing.

ISBN: 978-1-60886-725-7, eISBN: 978-1-61398-396-6

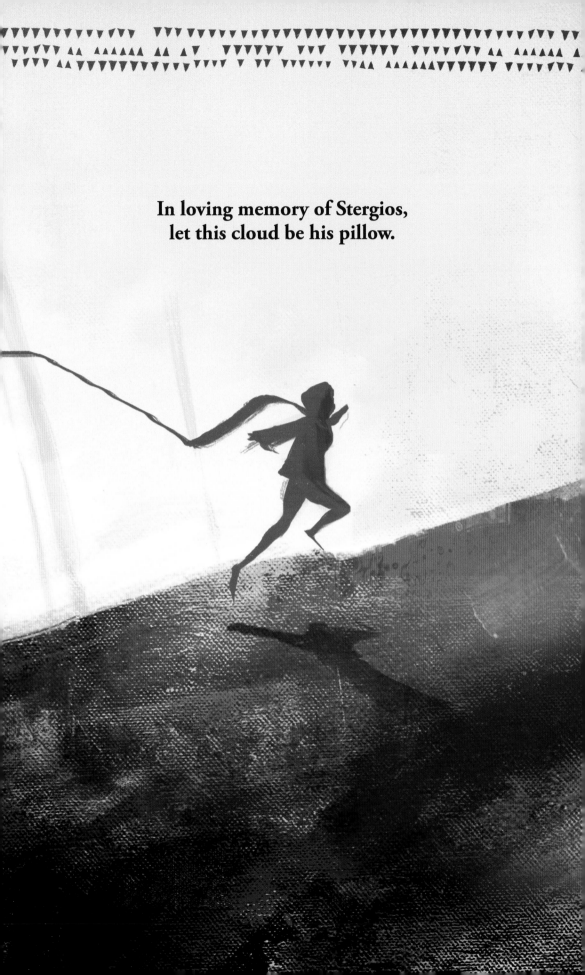

In loving memory of Stergios,
let this cloud be his pillow.

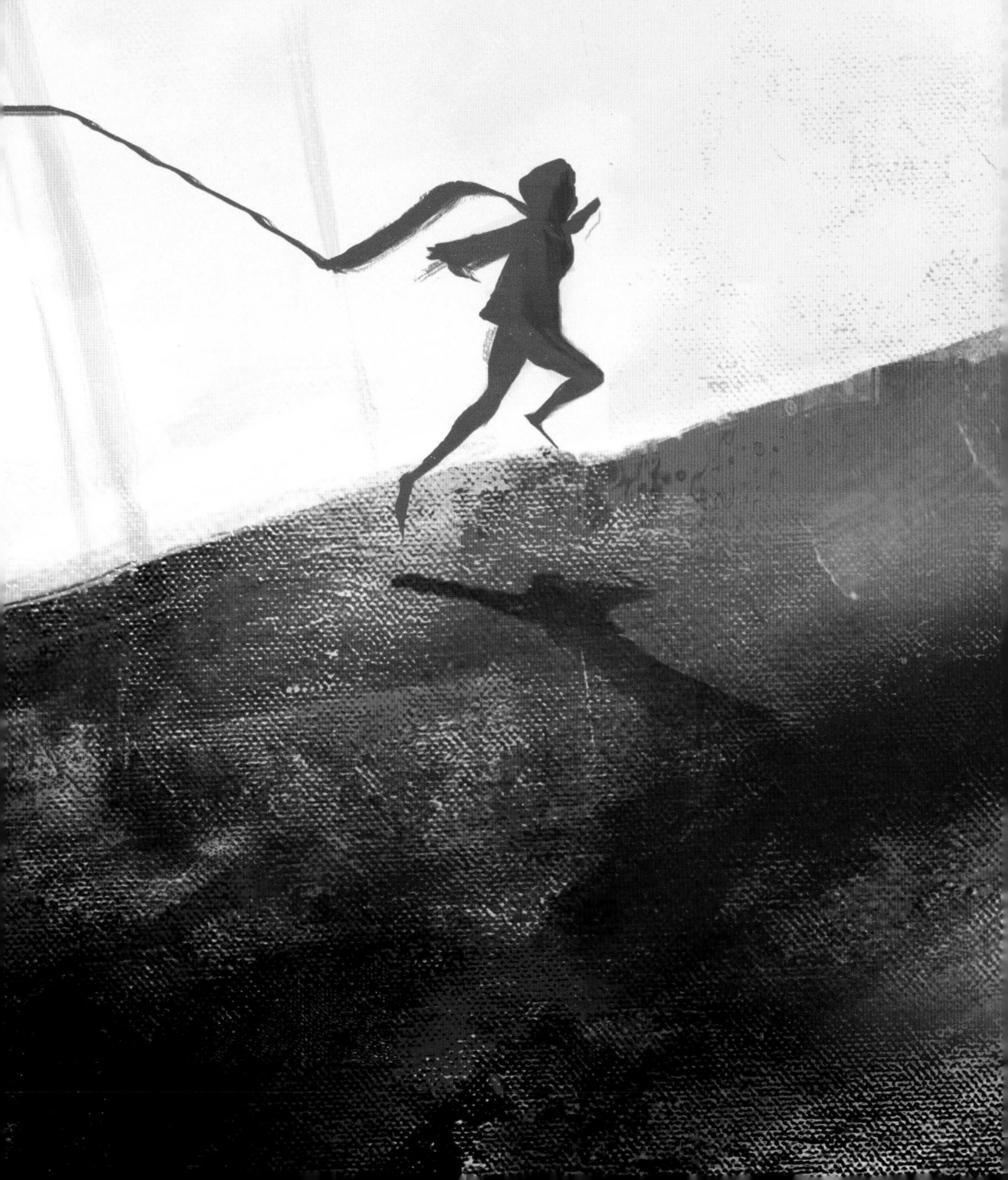

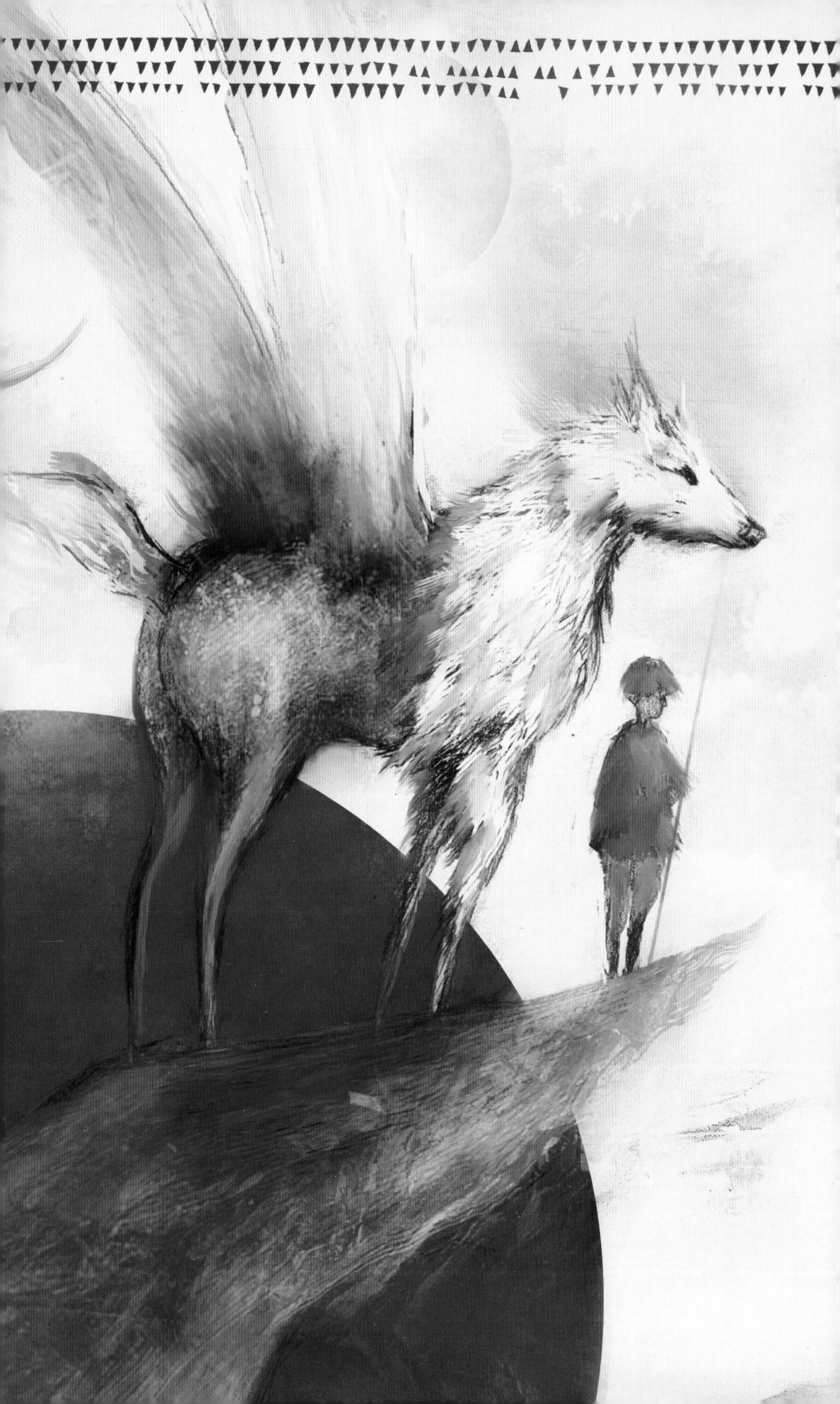

Created by
K.I. Zachopoulos & **Vincenzo Balzano**

Written by
K.I. Zachopoulos

Illustrated by
Vincenzo Balzano

Lettered by
Warren Montgomery

Designer
Scott Newman

Associate Editor
Whitney Leopard

Editor
Sierra Hahn

Special thanks to
Rebecca Taylor

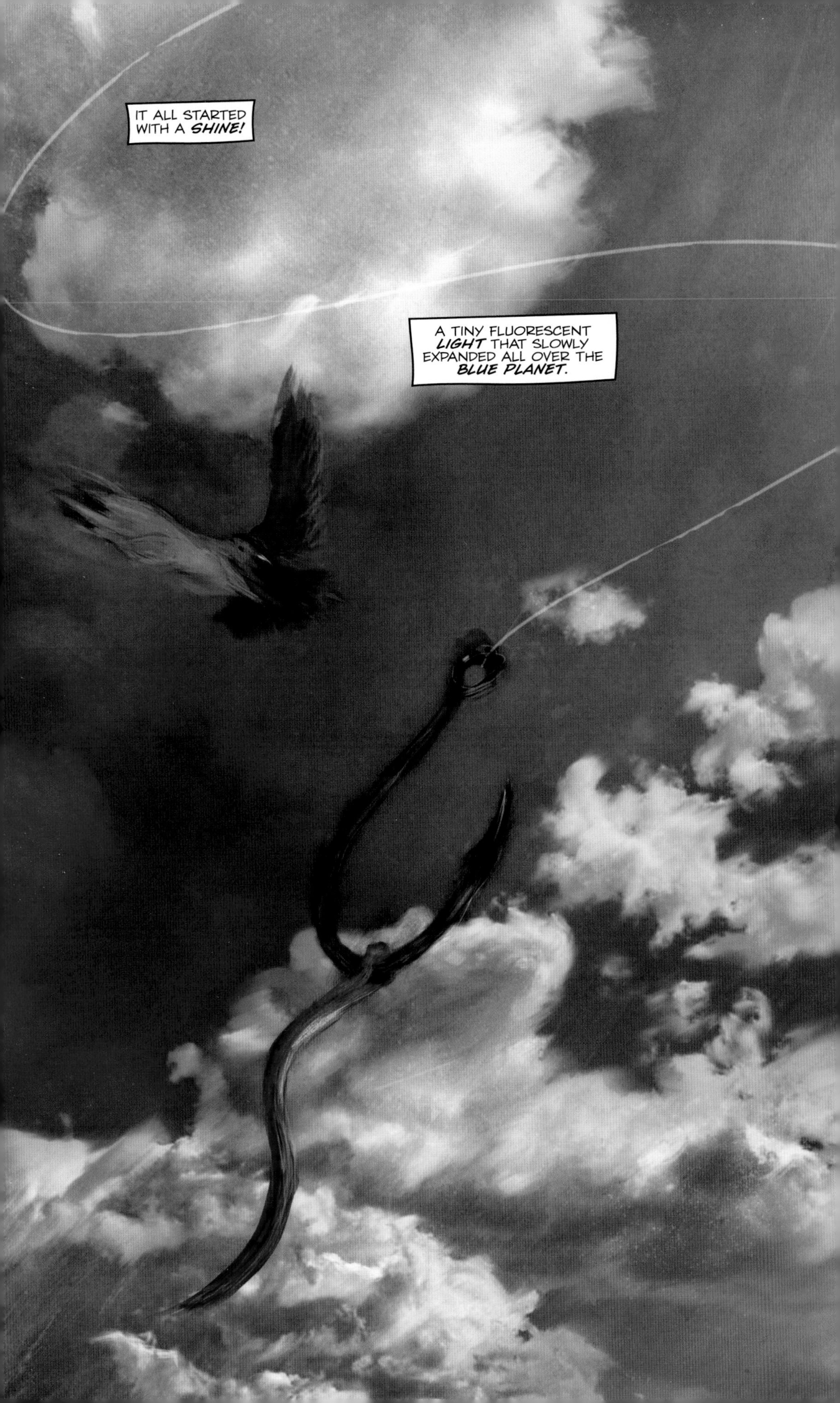
IT ALL STARTED WITH A SHINE!
A TINY FLUORESCENT LIGHT THAT SLOWLY EXPANDED ALL OVER THE BLUE PLANET.

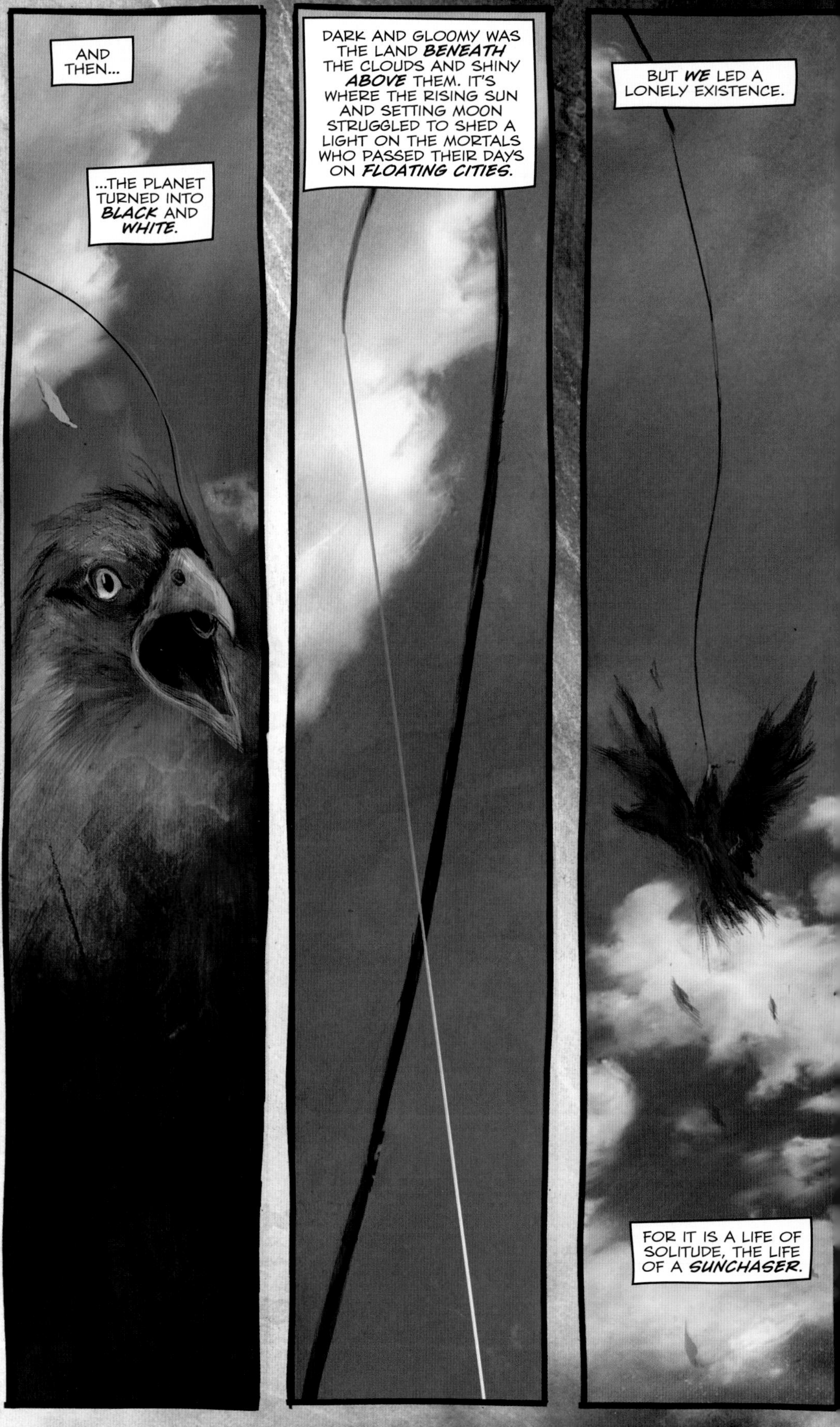
AND THEN...
...THE PLANET TURNED INTO BLACK AND WHITE.
DARK AND GLOOMY WAS THE LAND BENEATH THE CLOUDS AND SHINY ABOVE THEM. IT'S WHERE THE RISING SUN AND SETTING MOON STRUGGLED TO SHED A LIGHT ON THE MORTALS WHO PASSED THEIR DAYS ON FLOATING CITIES.
BUT WE LED A LONELY EXISTENCE.
FOR IT IS A LIFE OF SOLITUDE, THE LIFE OF A SUNCHASER.

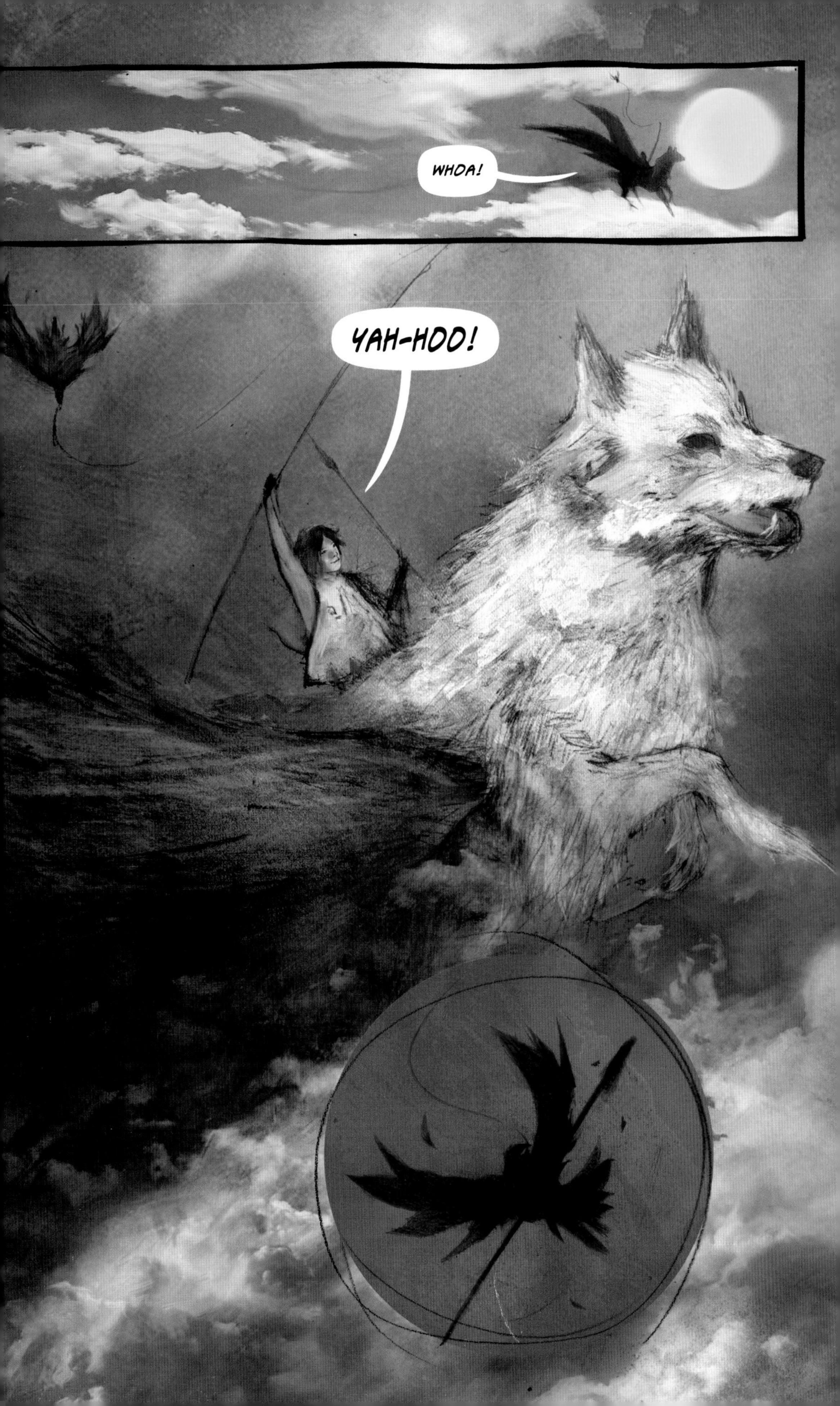
WHOA!
YAH-HOO!

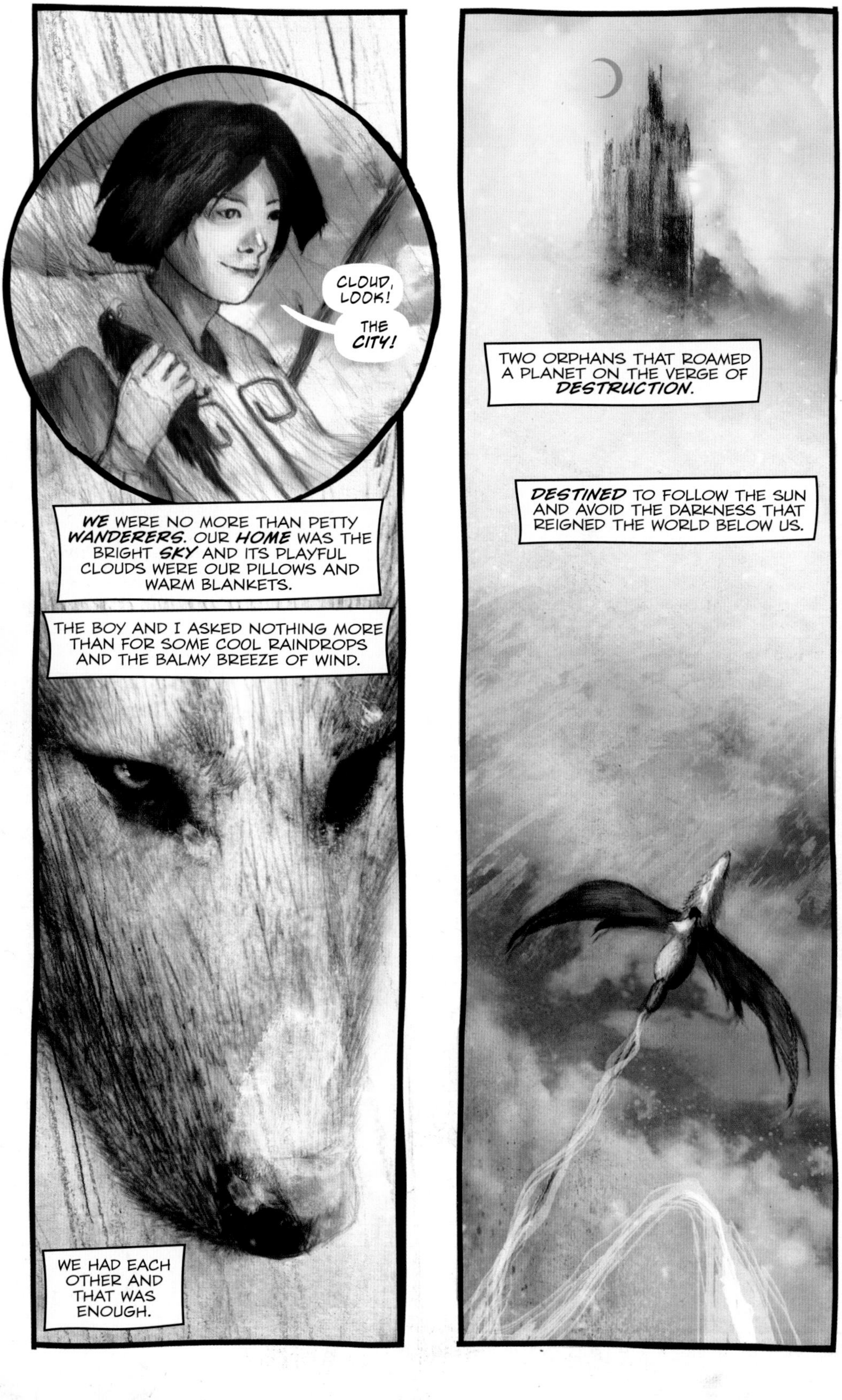
CLOUD, LOOK!
THE CITY!
WE WERE NO MORE THAN PETTY WANDERERS. OUR HOME WAS THE BRIGHT SKY AND ITS PLAYFUL CLOUDS WERE OUR PILLOWS AND WARM BLANKETS.
THE BOY AND I ASKED NOTHING MORE THAN FOR SOME COOL RAINDROPS AND THE BALMY BREEZE OF WIND.
WE HAD EACH OTHER AND THAT WAS ENOUGH.
TWO ORPHANS THAT ROAMED A PLANET ON THE VERGE OF DESTRUCTION.
DESTINED TO FOLLOW THE SUN AND AVOID THE DARKNESS THAT REIGNED THE WORLD BELOW US.

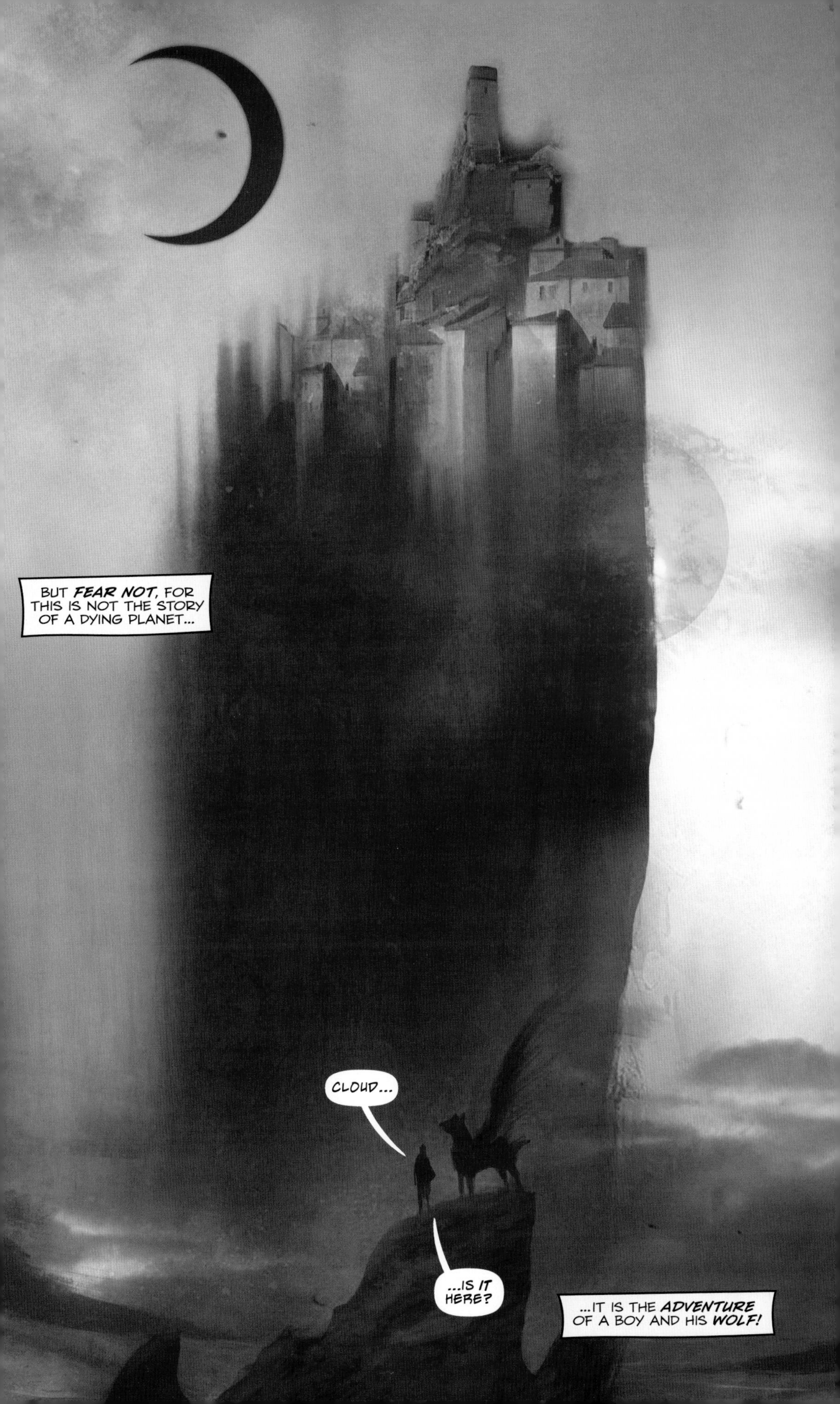
BUT FEAR NOT, FOR THIS IS NOT THE STORY OF A DYING PLANET...
CLOUD...
...IS IT HERE?
...IT IS THE ADVENTURE OF A BOY AND HIS WOLF!

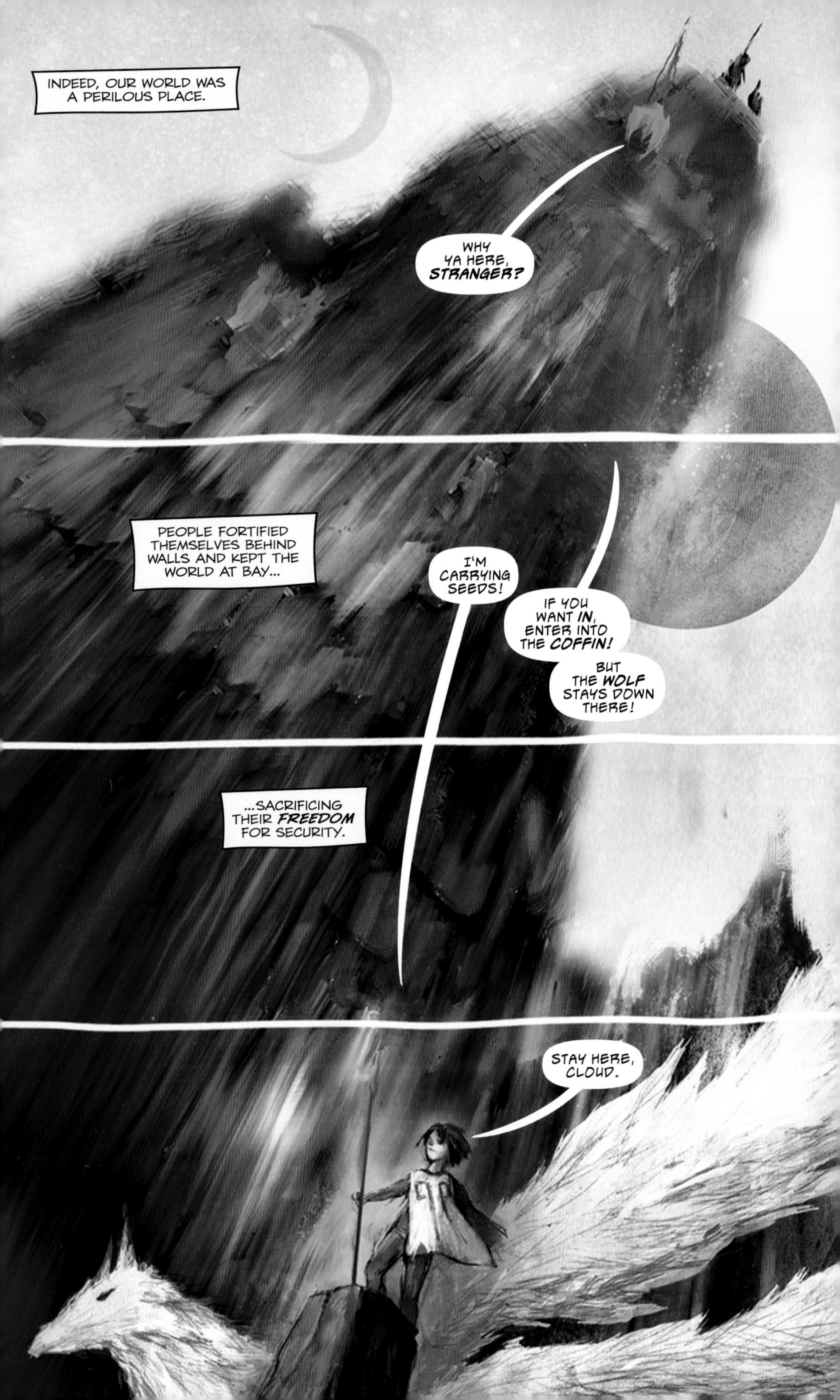
INDEED, OUR WORLD WAS A PERILOUS PLACE.
WHY YA HERE, STRANGER?
PEOPLE FORTIFIED THEMSELVES BEHIND WALLS AND KEPT THE WORLD AT BAY...
I'M CARRYING SEEDS!
IF YOU WANT IN, ENTER INTO THE COFFIN!
BUT THE WOLF STAYS DOWN THERE!
...SACRIFICING THEIR FREEDOM FOR SECURITY.
STAY HERE, CLOUD.

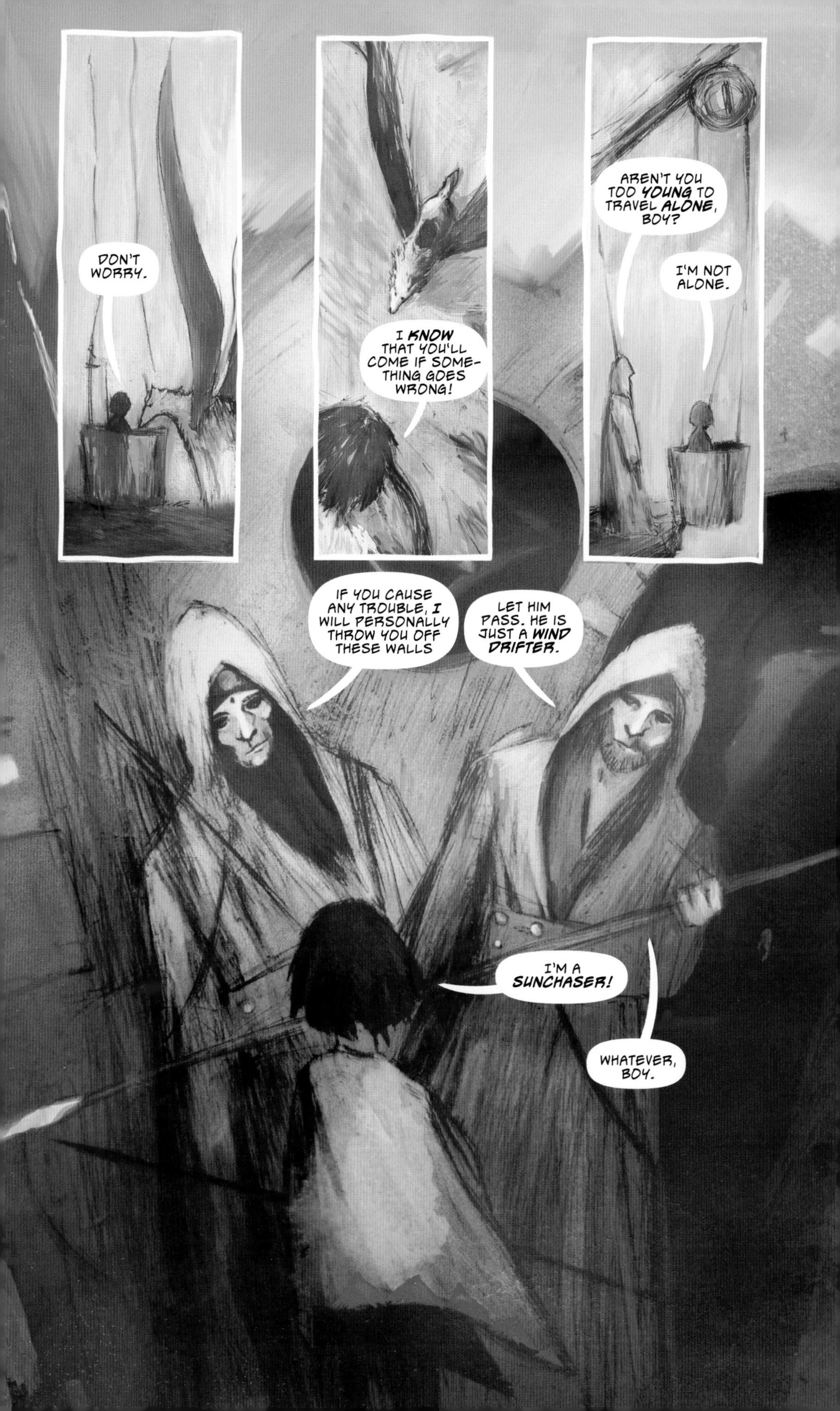
DON'T WORRY.
I KNOW THAT YOU'LL COME IF SOMETHING GOES WRONG!
AREN'T YOU TOO YOUNG TO TRAVEL ALONE, BOY?
I'M NOT ALONE.
IF YOU CAUSE ANY TROUBLE, I WILL PERSONALLY THROW YOU OFF THESE WALLS
LET HIM PASS. HE IS JUST A WIND DRIFTER.
I'M A SUNCHASER!
WHATEVER, BOY.

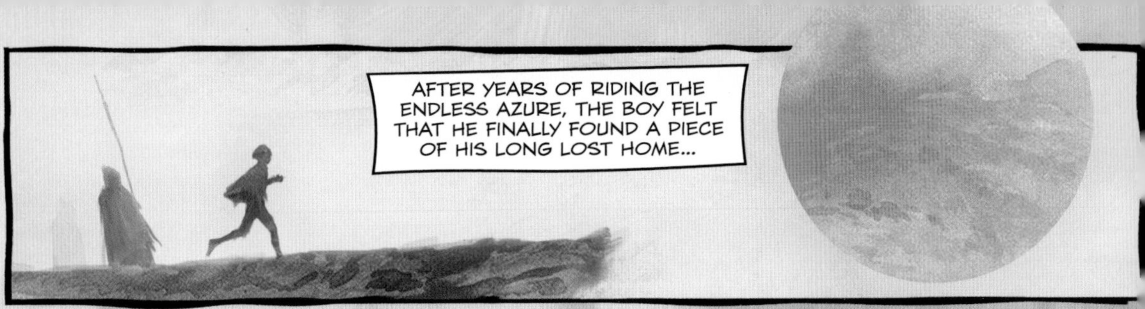
AFTER YEARS OF RIDING THE ENDLESS AZURE, THE BOY FELT THAT HE FINALLY FOUND A PIECE OF HIS LONG LOST HOME...

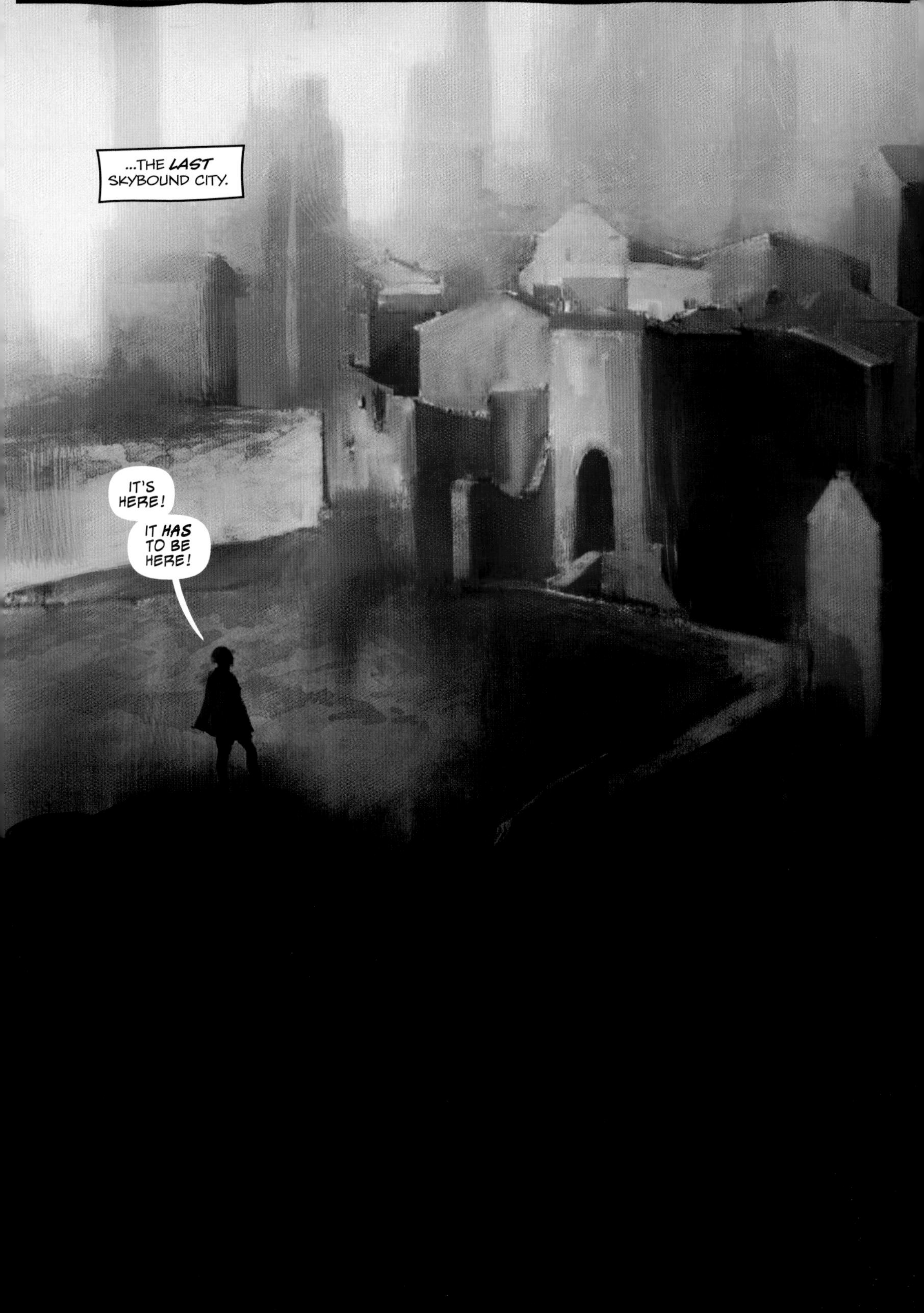
...THE LAST SKYBOUND CITY.
IT'S HERE!
IT HAS TO BE HERE!

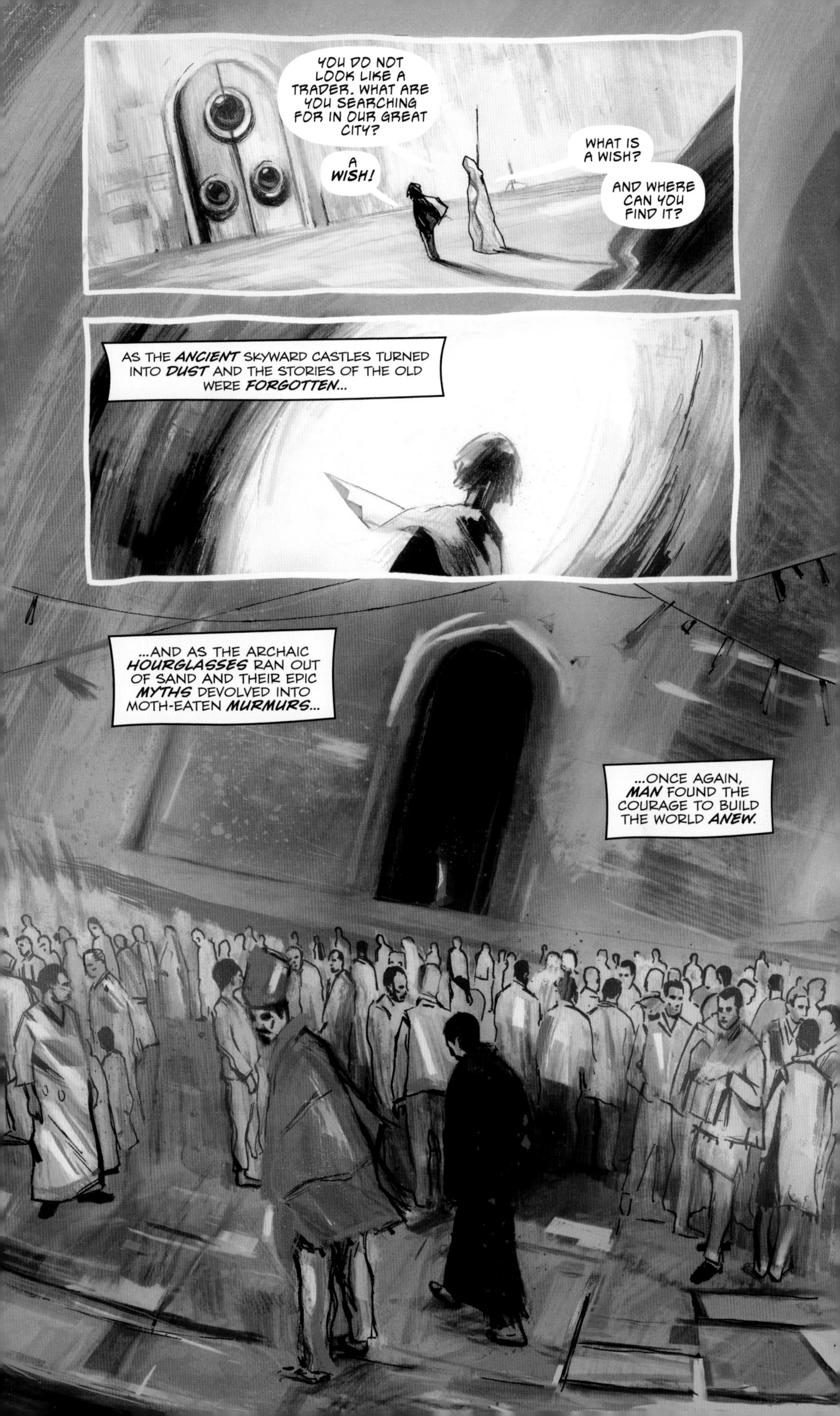
YOU DO NOT LOOK LIKE A TRADER. WHAT ARE YOU SEARCHING FOR IN OUR GREAT CITY?
A WISH!
WHAT IS A WISH?
AND WHERE CAN YOU FIND IT?
AS THE ANCIENT SKYWARD CASTLES TURNED INTO DUST AND THE STORIES OF THE OLD WERE FORGOTTEN...
...AND AS THE ARCHAIC HOURGLASSES RAN OUT OF SAND AND THEIR EPIC MYTHS DEVOLVED INTO MOTH-EATEN MURMURS...
...ONCE AGAIN, MAN FOUND THE COURAGE TO BUILD THE WORLD ANEW.

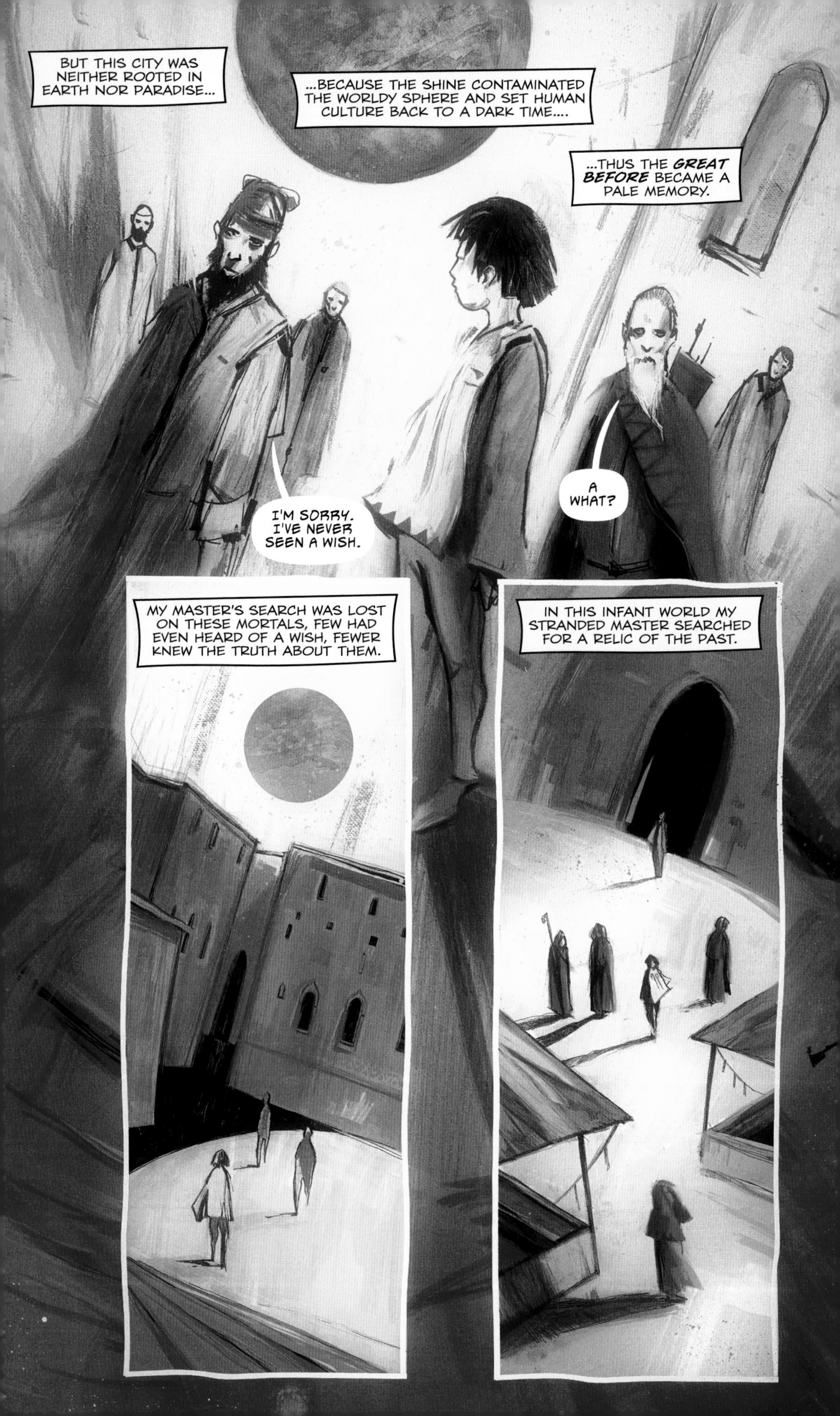
BUT THIS CITY WAS NEITHER ROOTED IN EARTH NOR PARADISE...
...BECAUSE THE SHINE CONTAMINATED THE WORLDY SPHERE AND SET HUMAN CULTURE BACK TO A DARK TIME....
...THUS THE GREAT BEFORE BECAME A PALE MEMORY.
I'M SORRY. I'VE NEVER SEEN A WISH.
A WHAT?
MY MASTER'S SEARCH WAS LOST ON THESE MORTALS, FEW HAD EVEN HEARD OF A WISH, FEWER KNEW THE TRUTH ABOUT THEM.
IN THIS INFANT WORLD MY STRANDED MASTER SEARCHED FOR A RELIC OF THE PAST.

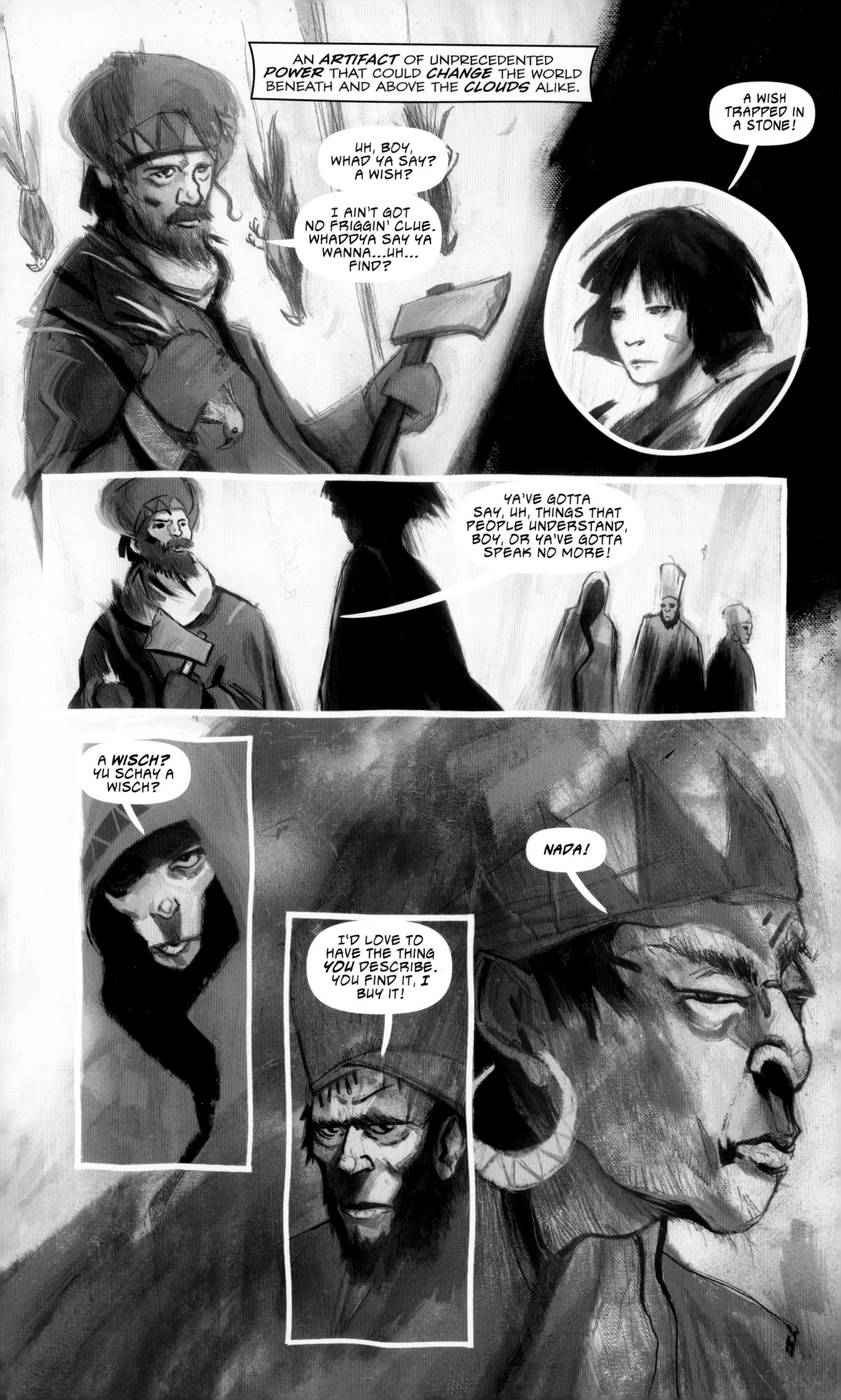
AN ARTIFACT OF UNPRECEDENTED POWER THAT COULD CHANGE THE WORLD BENEATH AND ABOVE THE CLOUDS ALIKE.
UH, BOY, WHAD YA SAY? A WISH?
I AIN'T GOT NO FRIGGIN' CLUE. WHADDYA SAY YA WANNA...UH... FIND?
A WISH TRAPPED IN A STONE!
YA'VE GOTTA SAY, UH, THINGS THAT PEOPLE UNDERSTAND, BOY, OR YA'VE GOTTA SPEAK NO MORE!
A WISCH? YU SCHAY A WISCH?
NADA!
I'D LOVE TO HAVE THE THING YOU DESCRIBE. YOU FIND IT, I BUY IT!

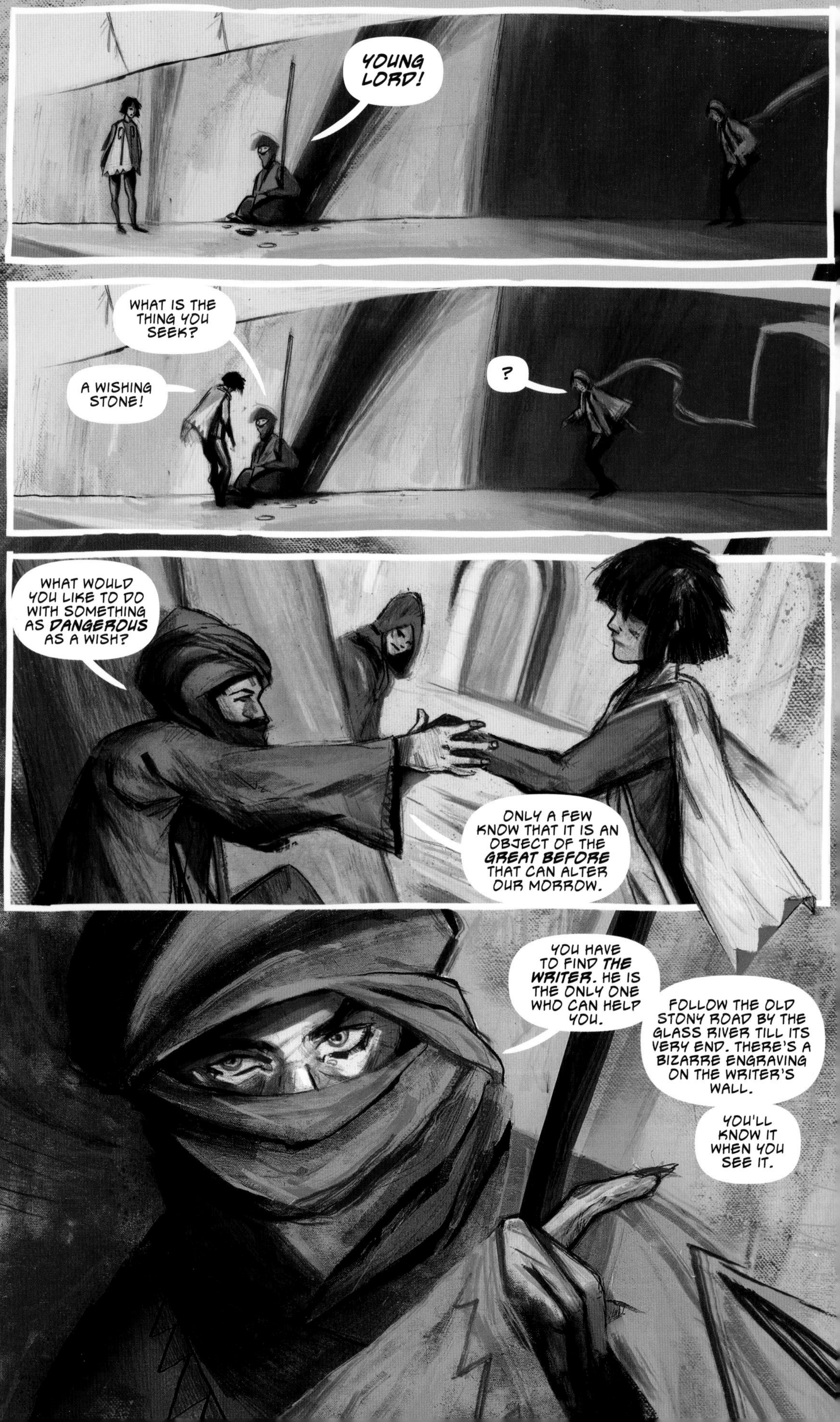
YOUNG LORD!
WHAT IS THE THING YOU SEEK?
A WISHING STONE!
?
WHAT WOULD YOU LIKE TO DO WITH SOMETHING AS DANGEROUS AS A WISH?
ONLY A FEW KNOW THAT IT IS AN OBJECT OF THE GREAT BEFORE THAT CAN ALTER OUR MORROW.
YOU HAVE TO FIND THE WRITER. HE IS THE ONLY ONE WHO CAN HELP YOU.
FOLLOW THE OLD STONY ROAD BY THE GLASS RIVER TILL ITS VERY END. THERE'S A BIZARRE ENGRAVING ON THE WRITER'S WALL.
YOU'LL KNOW IT WHEN YOU SEE IT.

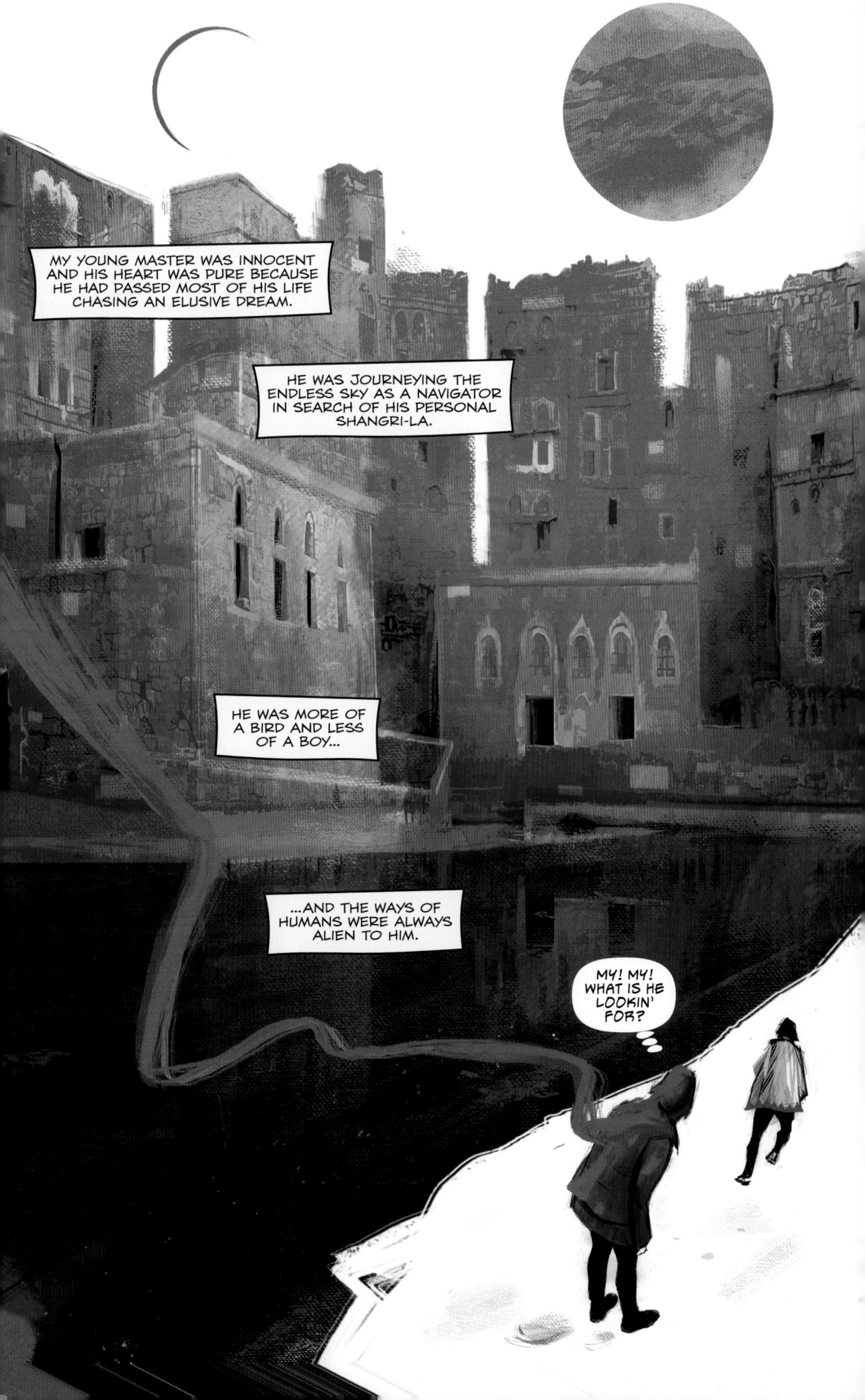
MY YOUNG MASTER WAS INNOCENT AND HIS HEART WAS PURE BECAUSE HE HAD PASSED MOST OF HIS LIFE CHASING AN ELUSIVE DREAM.
HE WAS JOURNEYING THE ENDLESS SKY AS A NAVIGATOR IN SEARCH OF HIS PERSONAL SHANGRI-LA.
HE WAS MORE OF A BIRD AND LESS OF A BOY...
...AND THE WAYS OF HUMANS WERE ALWAYS ALIEN TO HIM.
MY! MY! WHAT IS HE LOOKIN' FOR?

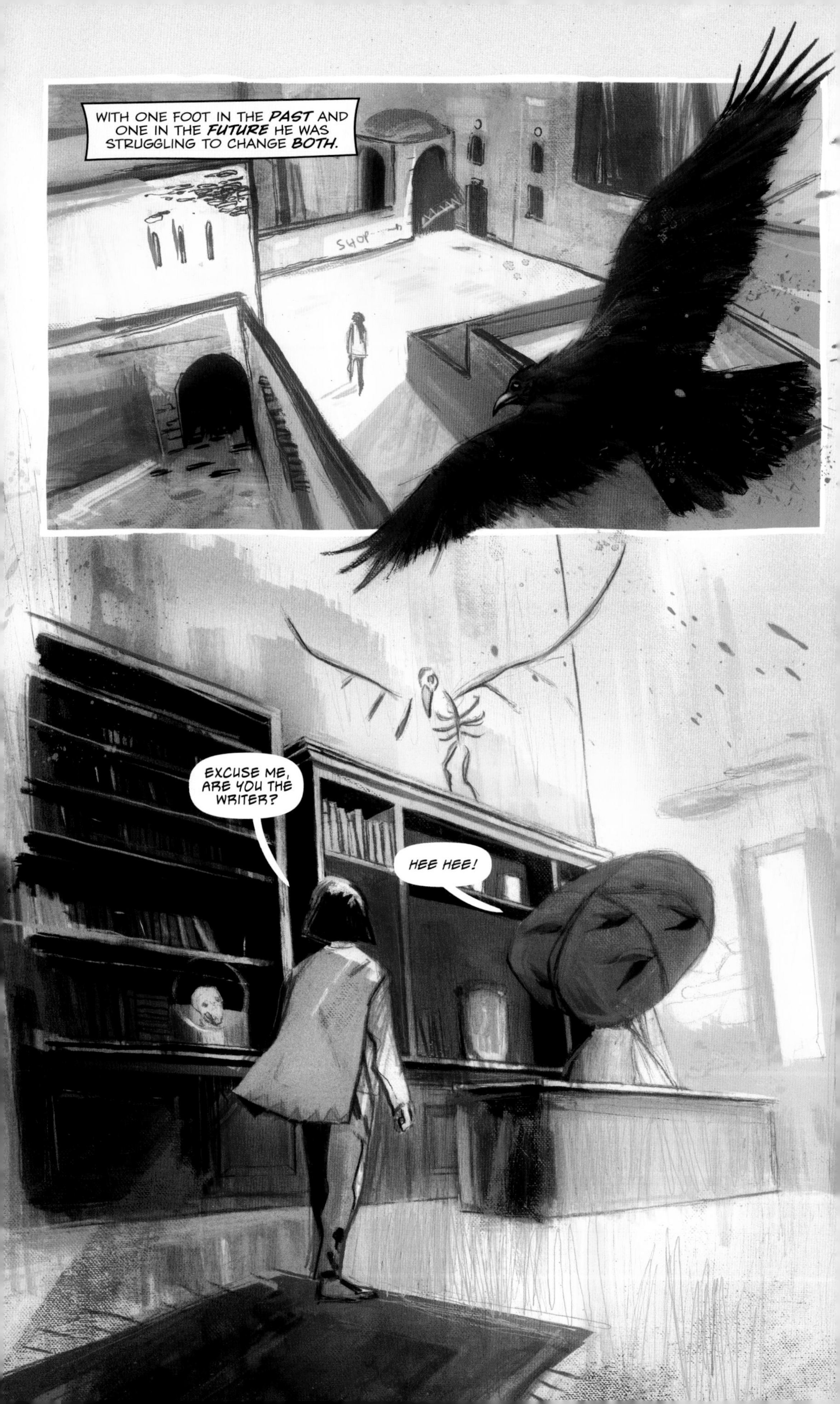
WITH ONE FOOT IN THE *PAST* AND ONE IN THE *FUTURE* HE WAS STRUGGLING TO CHANGE *BOTH*.
SHOP
EXCUSE ME, ARE YOU THE WRITER?
HEE HEE!

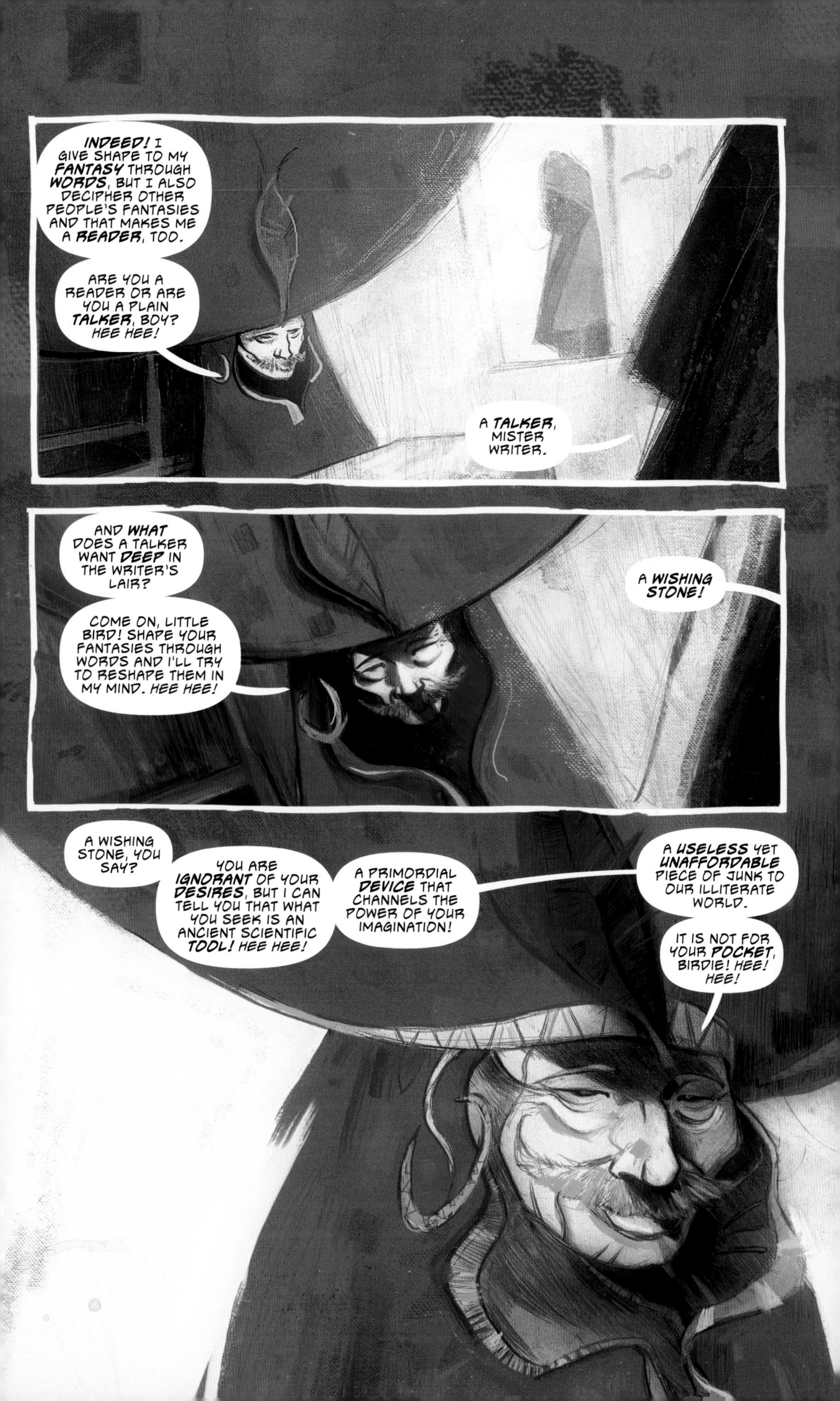

INDEED! I GIVE SHAPE TO MY FANTASY THROUGH WORDS, BUT I ALSO DECIPHER OTHER PEOPLE'S FANTASIES AND THAT MAKES ME A READER, TOO.
ARE YOU A READER OR ARE YOU A PLAIN TALKER, BOY? HEE HEE!
A TALKER, MISTER WRITER.
AND WHAT DOES A TALKER WANT DEEP IN THE WRITER'S LAIR?
COME ON, LITTLE BIRD! SHAPE YOUR FANTASIES THROUGH WORDS AND I'LL TRY TO RESHAPE THEM IN MY MIND. HEE HEE!
A WISHING STONE!
A WISHING STONE, YOU SAY?
YOU ARE IGNORANT OF YOUR DESIRES, BUT I CAN TELL YOU THAT WHAT YOU SEEK IS AN ANCIENT SCIENTIFIC TOOL! HEE HEE!
A PRIMORDIAL DEVICE THAT CHANNELS THE POWER OF YOUR IMAGINATION!
A USELESS YET UNAFFORDABLE PIECE OF JUNK TO OUR ILLITERATE WORLD.
IT IS NOT FOR YOUR POCKET, BIRDIE! HEE! HEE!

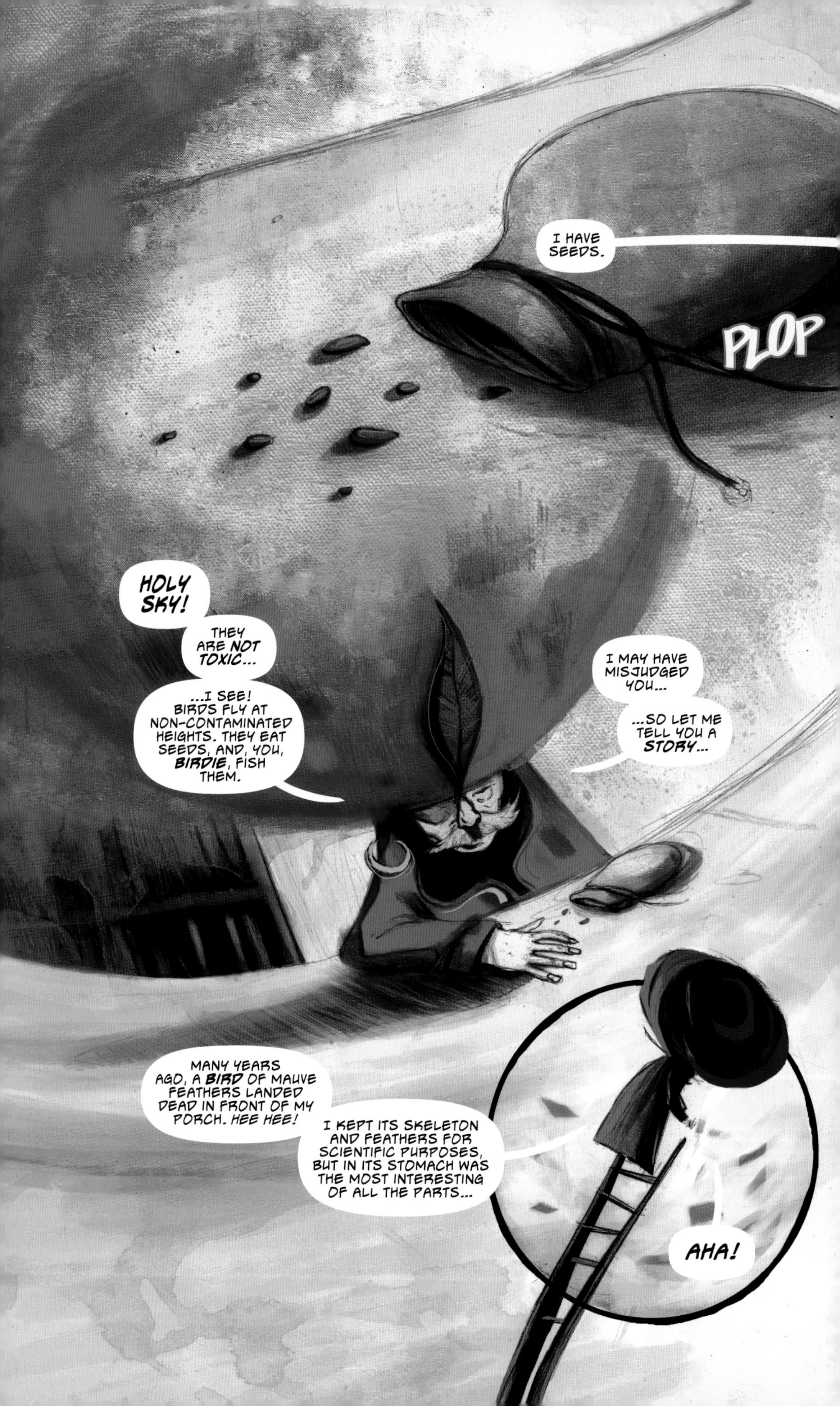
I HAVE SEEDS.
PLOP
HOLY SKY!
THEY ARE NOT TOXIC...
...I SEE! BIRDS FLY AT NON-CONTAMINATED HEIGHTS. THEY EAT SEEDS, AND, YOU, BIRDIE, FISH THEM.
I MAY HAVE MISJUDGED YOU...
...SO LET ME TELL YOU A STORY...
MANY YEARS AGO, A BIRD OF MAUVE FEATHERS LANDED DEAD IN FRONT OF MY PORCH. HEE HEE!
I KEPT ITS SKELETON AND FEATHERS FOR SCIENTIFIC PURPOSES, BUT IN ITS STOMACH WAS THE MOST INTERESTING OF ALL THE PARTS...
AHA!

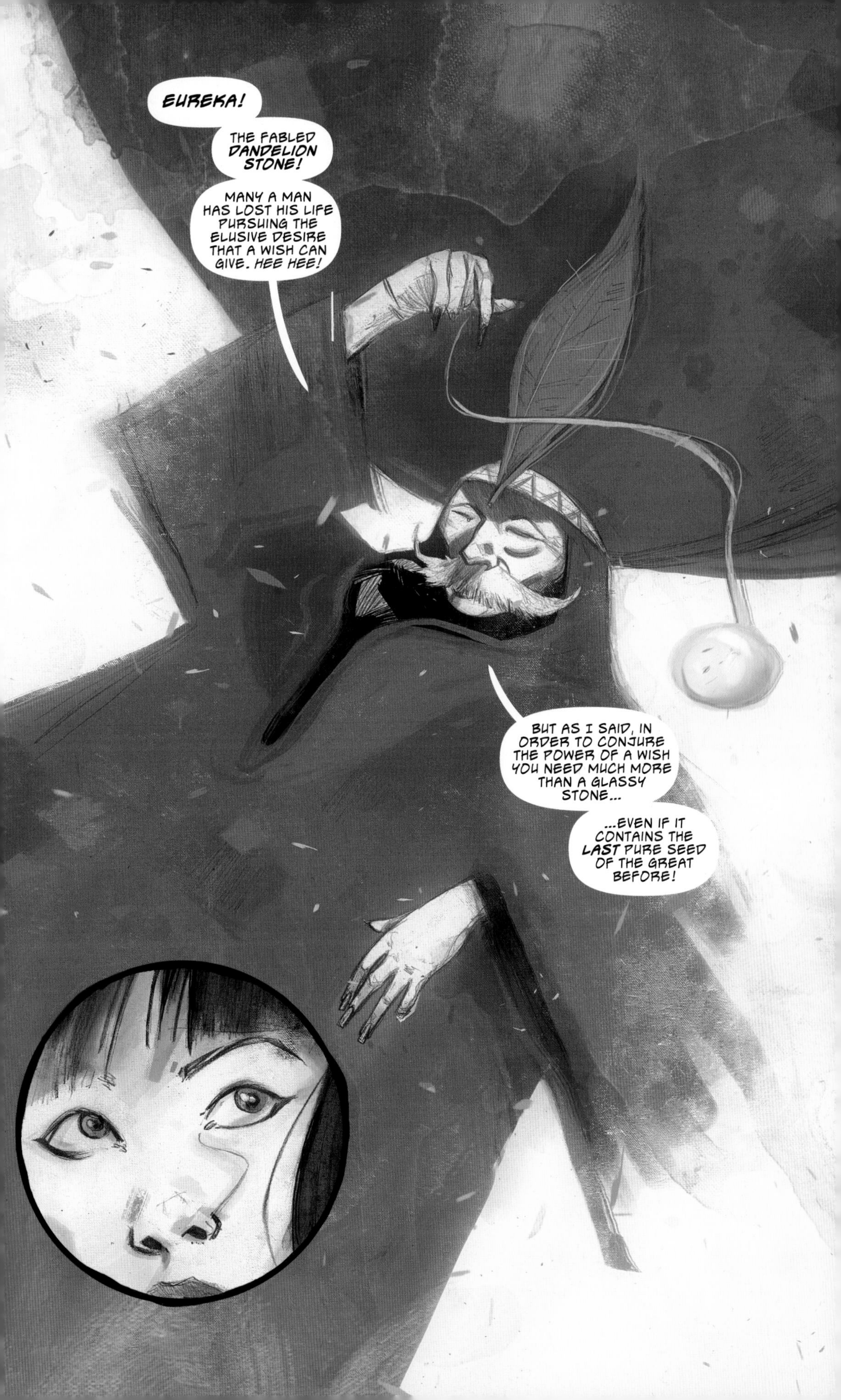

EUREKA!
THE FABLED DANDELION STONE!
MANY A MAN HAS LOST HIS LIFE PURSUING THE ELUSIVE DESIRE THAT A WISH CAN GIVE. HEE HEE!
BUT AS I SAID, IN ORDER TO CONJURE THE POWER OF A WISH YOU NEED MUCH MORE THAN A GLASSY STONE...
...EVEN IF IT CONTAINS THE LAST PURE SEED OF THE GREAT BEFORE!

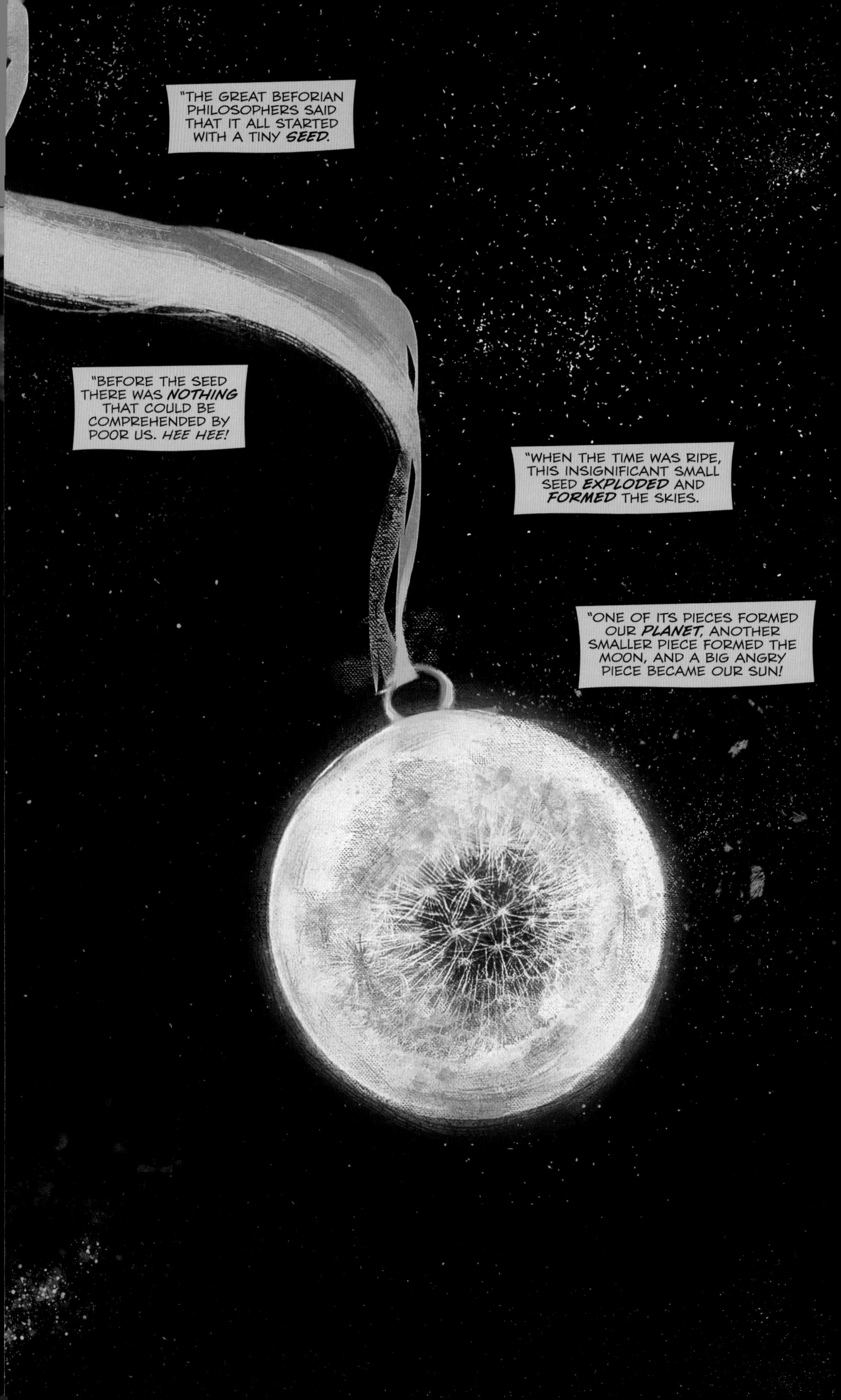
"THE GREAT BEFORIAN PHILOSOPHERS SAID THAT IT ALL STARTED WITH A TINY ***SEED***.
"BEFORE THE SEED THERE WAS ***NOTHING*** THAT COULD BE COMPREHENDED BY POOR US. *HEE HEE!*
"WHEN THE TIME WAS RIPE, THIS INSIGNIFICANT SMALL SEED ***EXPLODED*** AND ***FORMED*** THE SKIES.
"ONE OF ITS PIECES FORMED OUR ***PLANET***, ANOTHER SMALLER PIECE FORMED THE MOON, AND A BIG ANGRY PIECE BECAME OUR SUN!

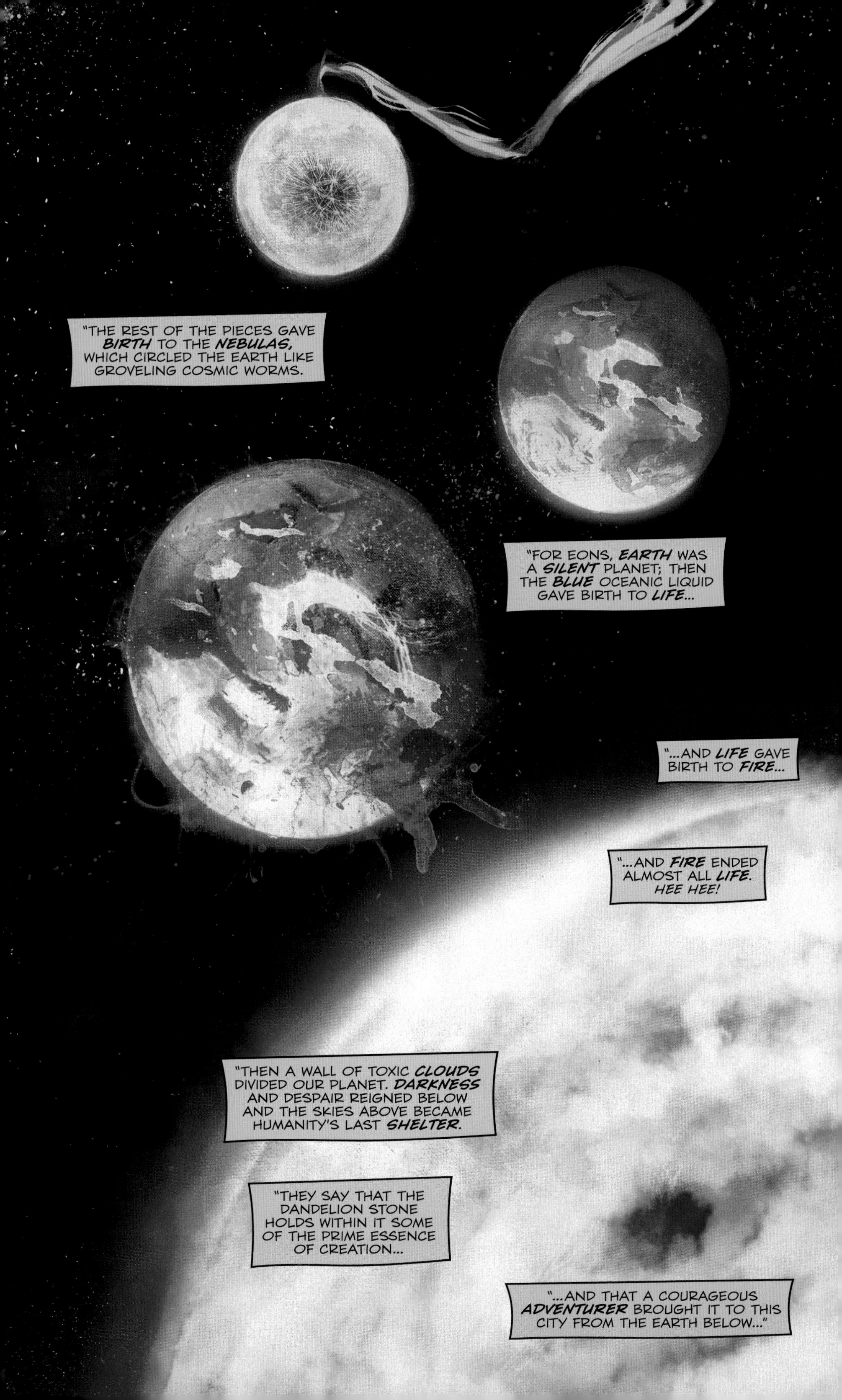
"THE REST OF THE PIECES GAVE *BIRTH* TO THE *NEBULAS,* WHICH CIRCLED THE EARTH LIKE GROVELING COSMIC WORMS.
"FOR EONS, *EARTH* WAS A *SILENT* PLANET; THEN THE *BLUE* OCEANIC LIQUID GAVE BIRTH TO *LIFE*...
"...AND *LIFE* GAVE BIRTH TO *FIRE*...
"...AND *FIRE* ENDED ALMOST ALL *LIFE*. *HEE HEE!*
"THEN A WALL OF TOXIC *CLOUDS* DIVIDED OUR PLANET. *DARKNESS* AND DESPAIR REIGNED BELOW AND THE SKIES ABOVE BECAME HUMANITY'S LAST *SHELTER*.
"THEY SAY THAT THE DANDELION STONE HOLDS WITHIN IT SOME OF THE PRIME ESSENCE OF CREATION...
"...AND THAT A COURAGEOUS *ADVENTURER* BROUGHT IT TO THIS CITY FROM THE EARTH BELOW..."

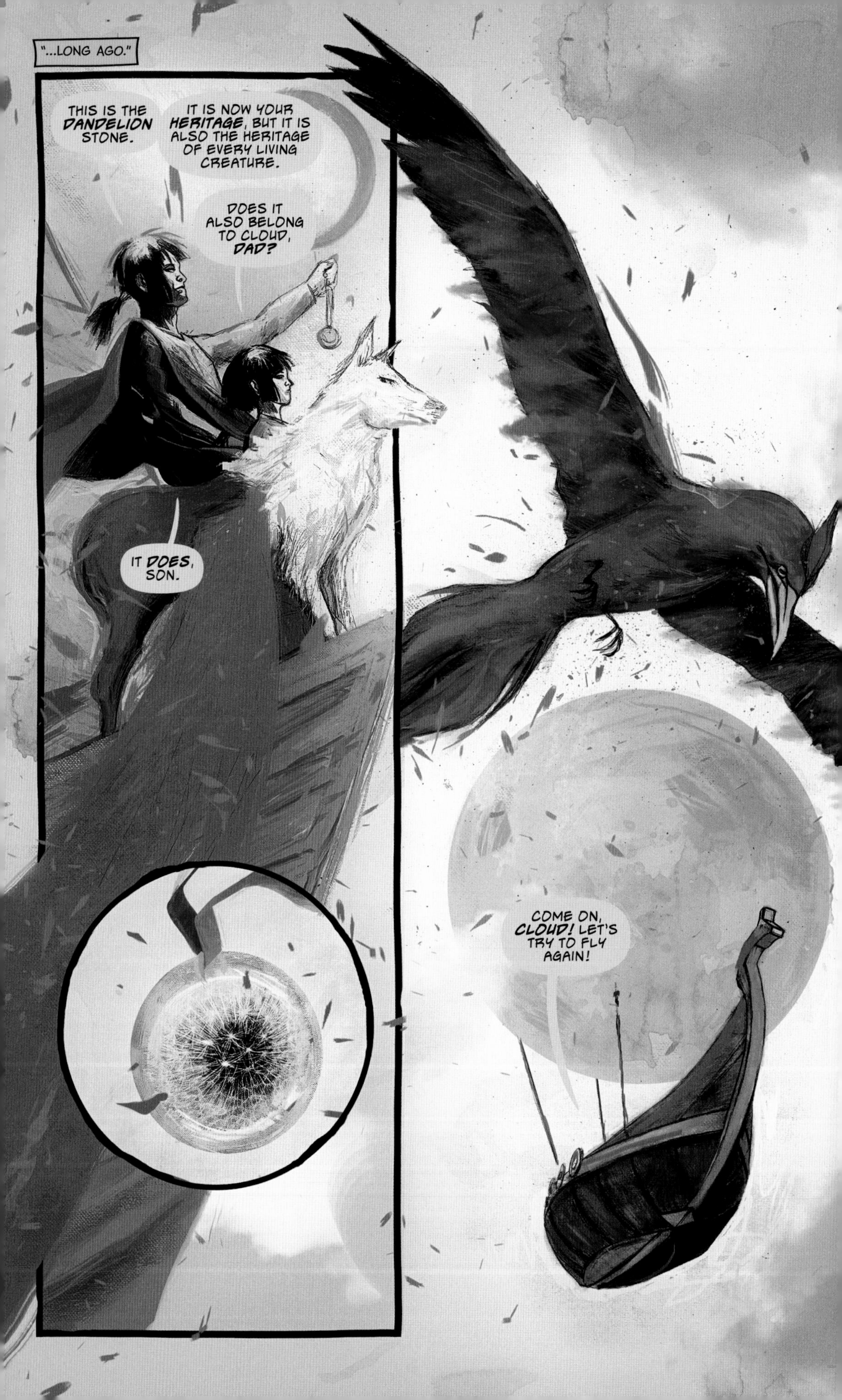
"...LONG AGO."
THIS IS THE DANDELION STONE.
IT IS NOW YOUR HERITAGE, BUT IT IS ALSO THE HERITAGE OF EVERY LIVING CREATURE.
DOES IT ALSO BELONG TO CLOUD, DAD?
IT DOES, SON.
COME ON, CLOUD! LET'S TRY TO FLY AGAIN!

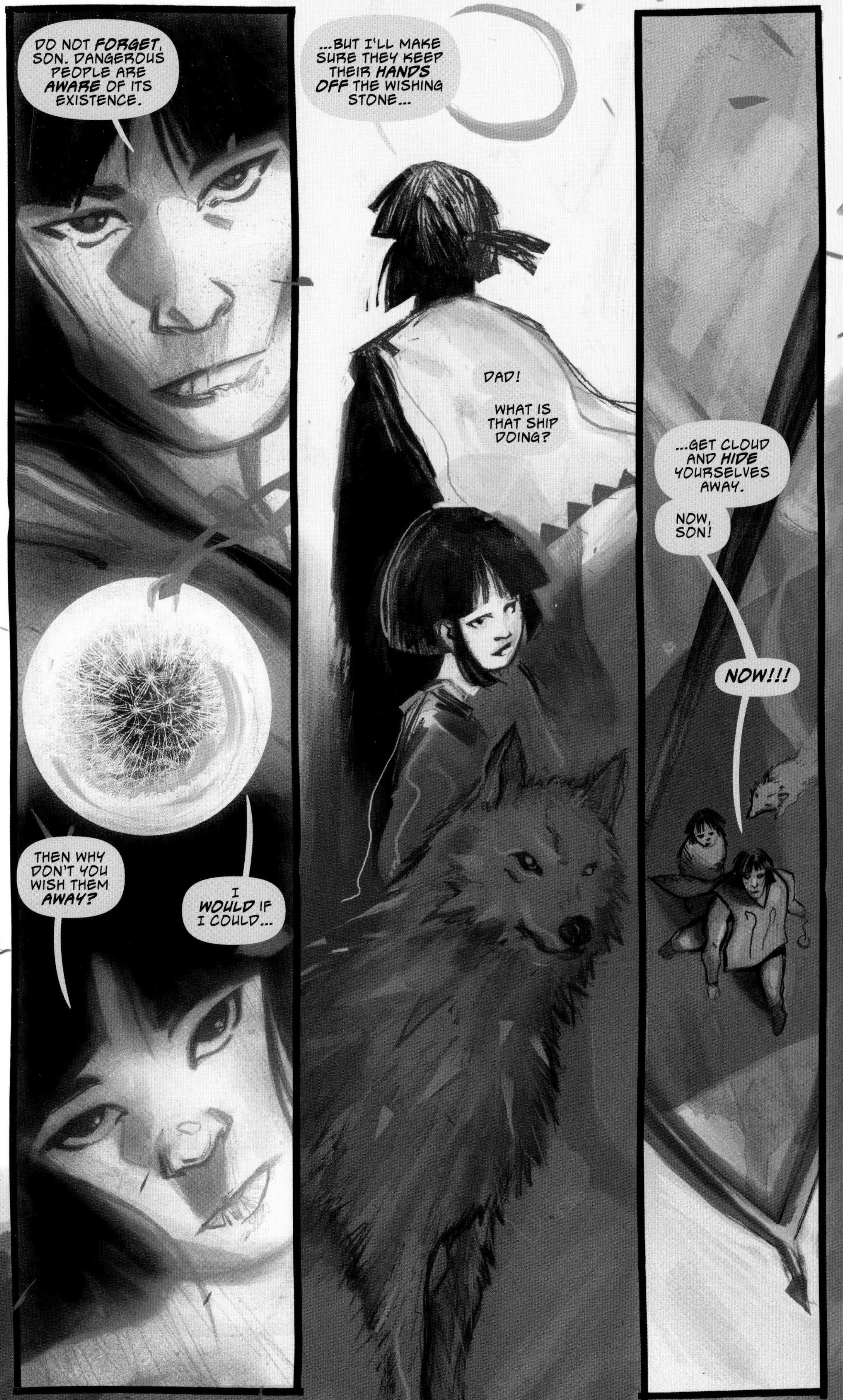
DO NOT FORGET, SON. DANGEROUS PEOPLE ARE AWARE OF ITS EXISTENCE.
THEN WHY DON'T YOU WISH THEM AWAY?
I WOULD IF I COULD...
...BUT I'LL MAKE SURE THEY KEEP THEIR HANDS OFF THE WISHING STONE...
DAD!
WHAT IS THAT SHIP DOING?
...GET CLOUD AND HIDE YOURSELVES AWAY.
NOW, SON!
NOW!!!

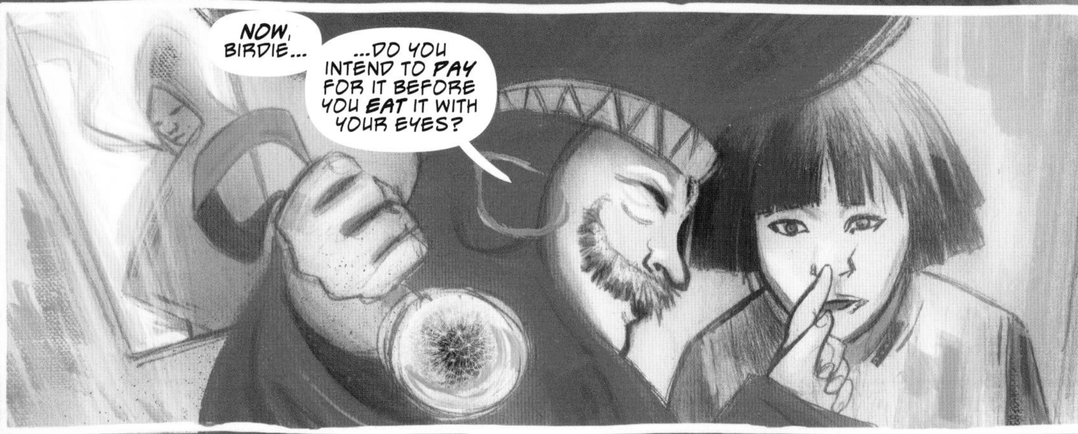
NOW, BIRDIE...
...DO YOU INTEND TO PAY FOR IT BEFORE YOU EAT IT WITH YOUR EYES?

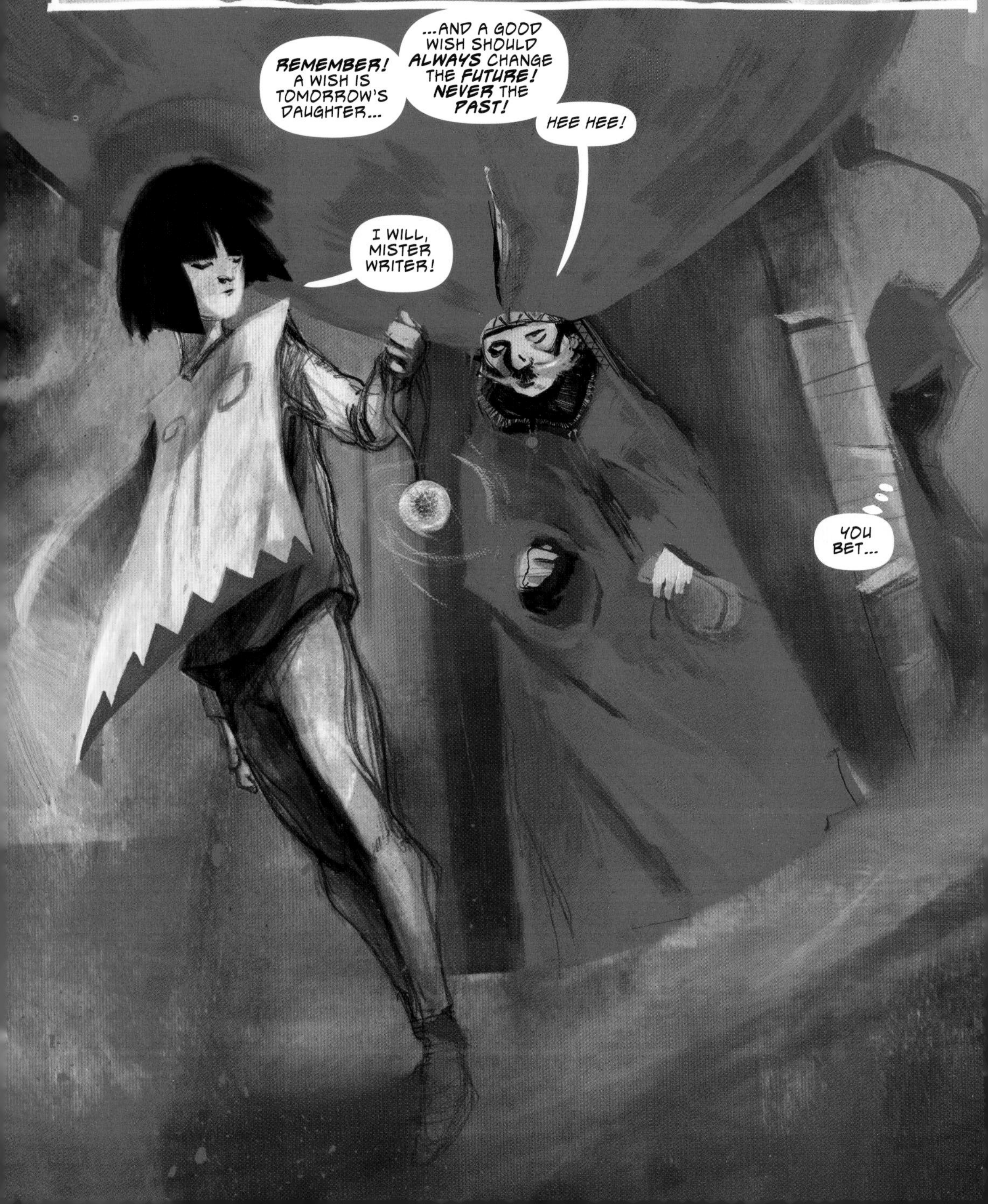
REMEMBER! A WISH IS TOMORROW'S DAUGHTER...
...AND A GOOD WISH SHOULD ALWAYS CHANGE THE FUTURE! NEVER THE PAST!
HEE HEE!
I WILL, MISTER WRITER!
YOU BET...

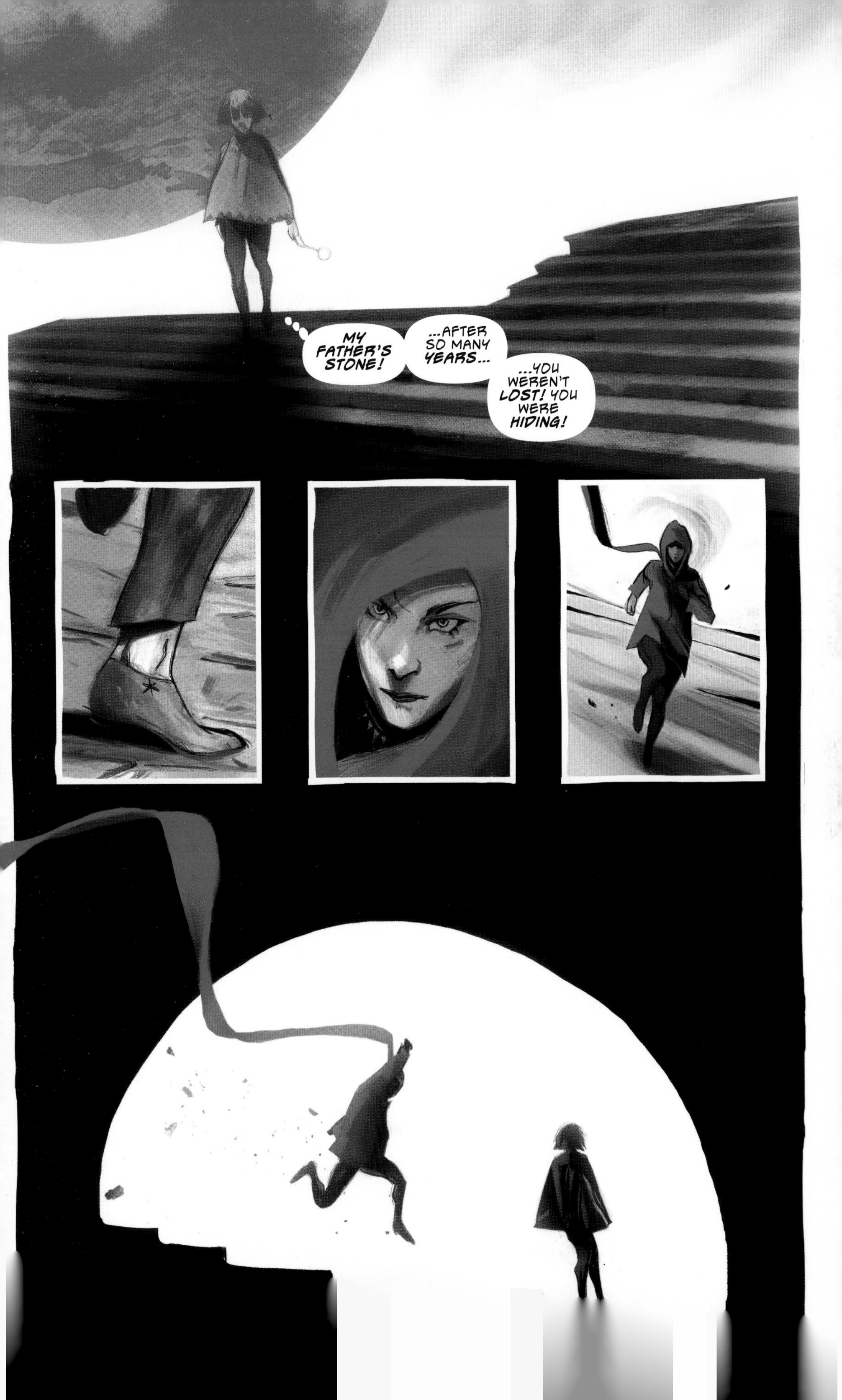
MY FATHER'S STONE!
...AFTER SO MANY YEARS...
...YOU WEREN'T LOST! YOU WERE HIDING!

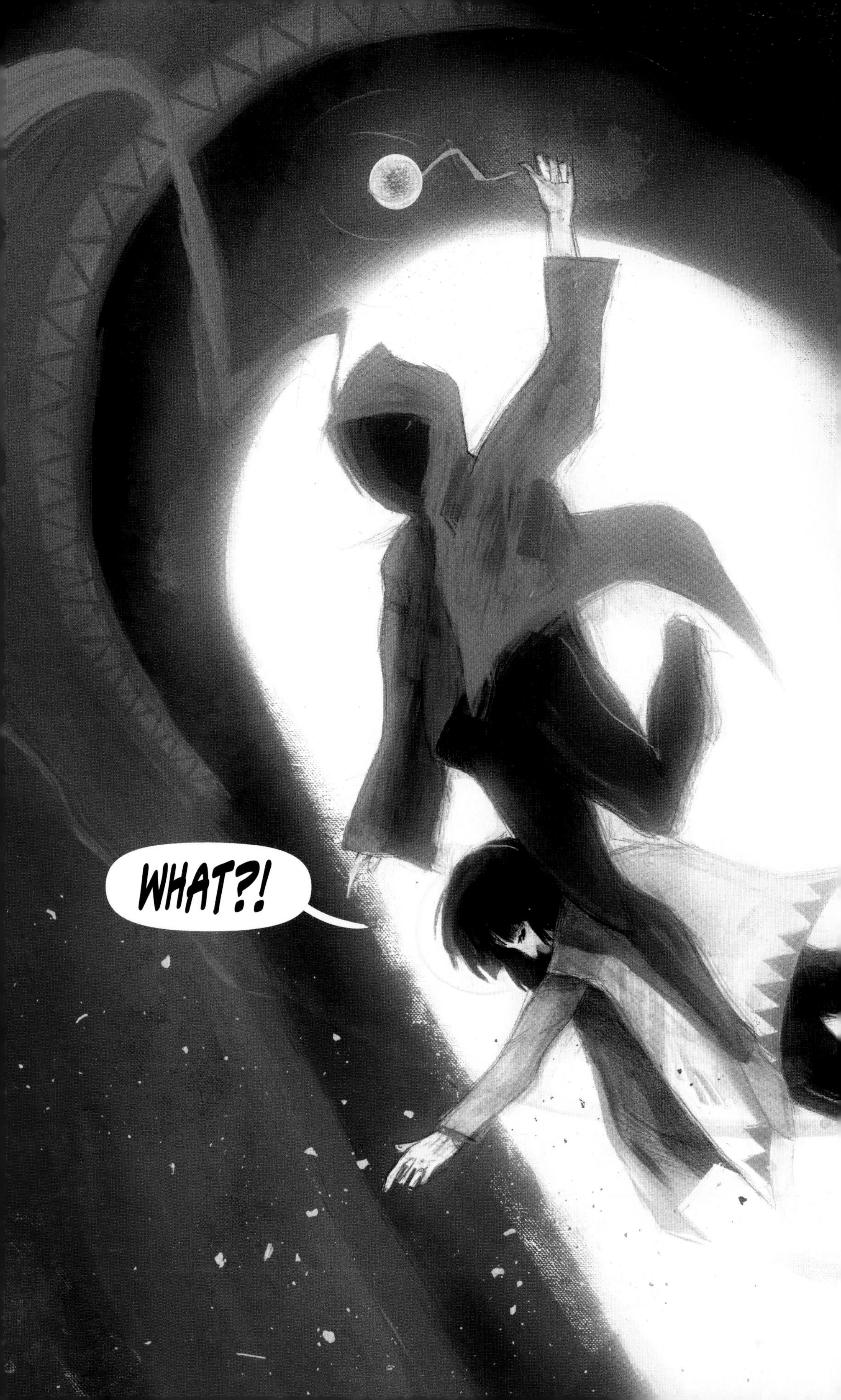
WHAT?!

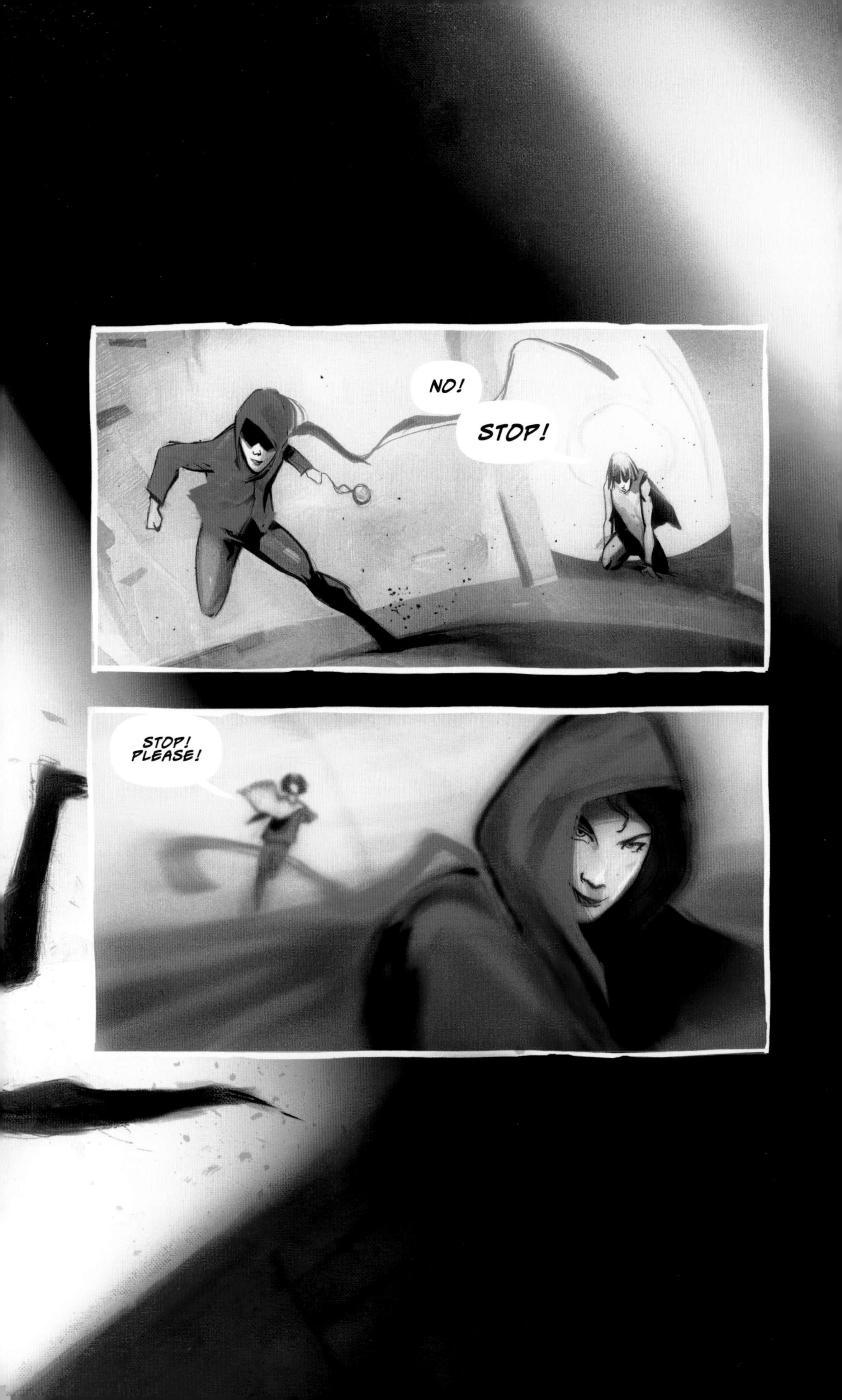
NO!
STOP!
STOP! PLEASE!

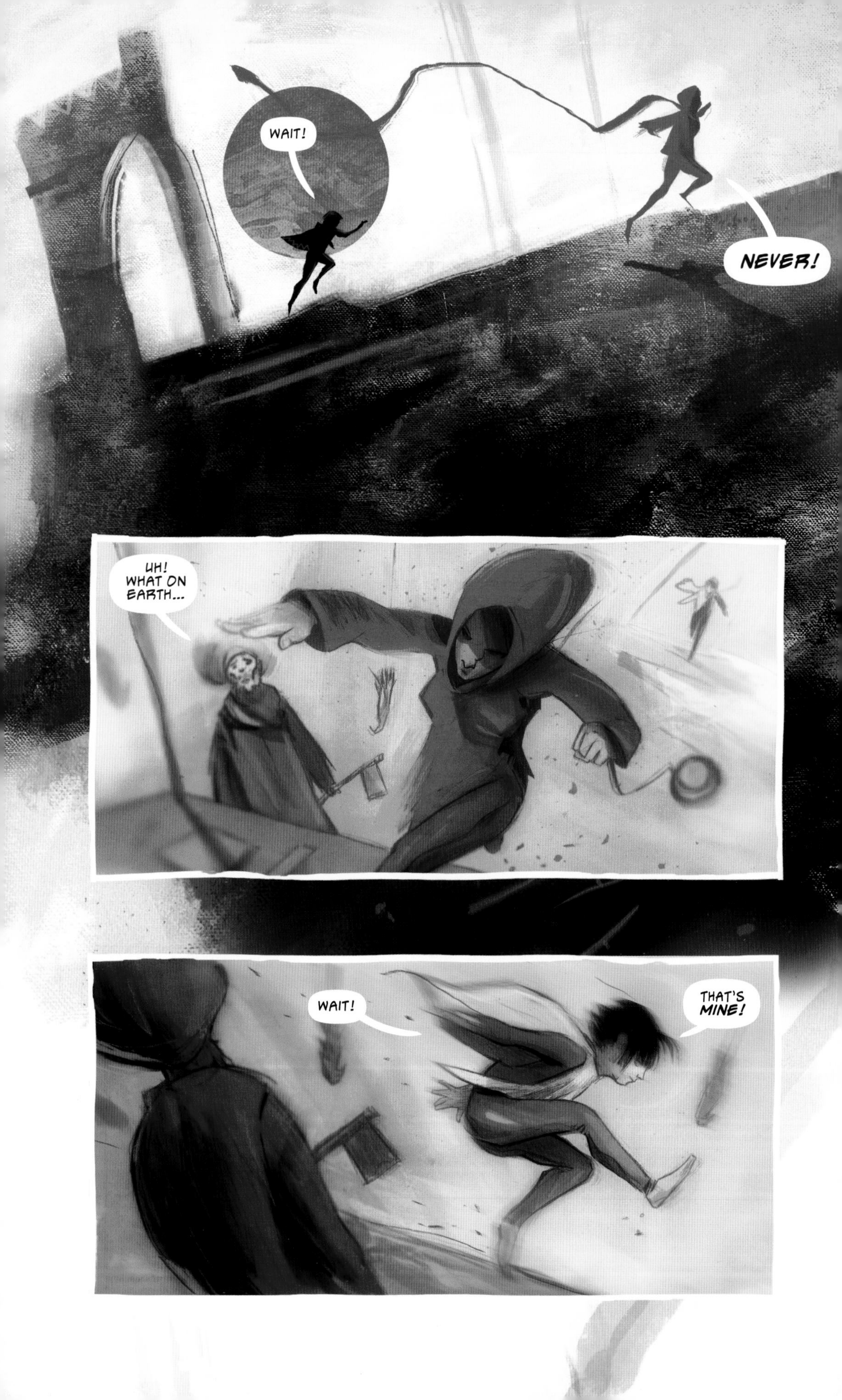
WAIT!
NEVER!
UH! WHAT ON EARTH...
WAIT!
THAT'S MINE!

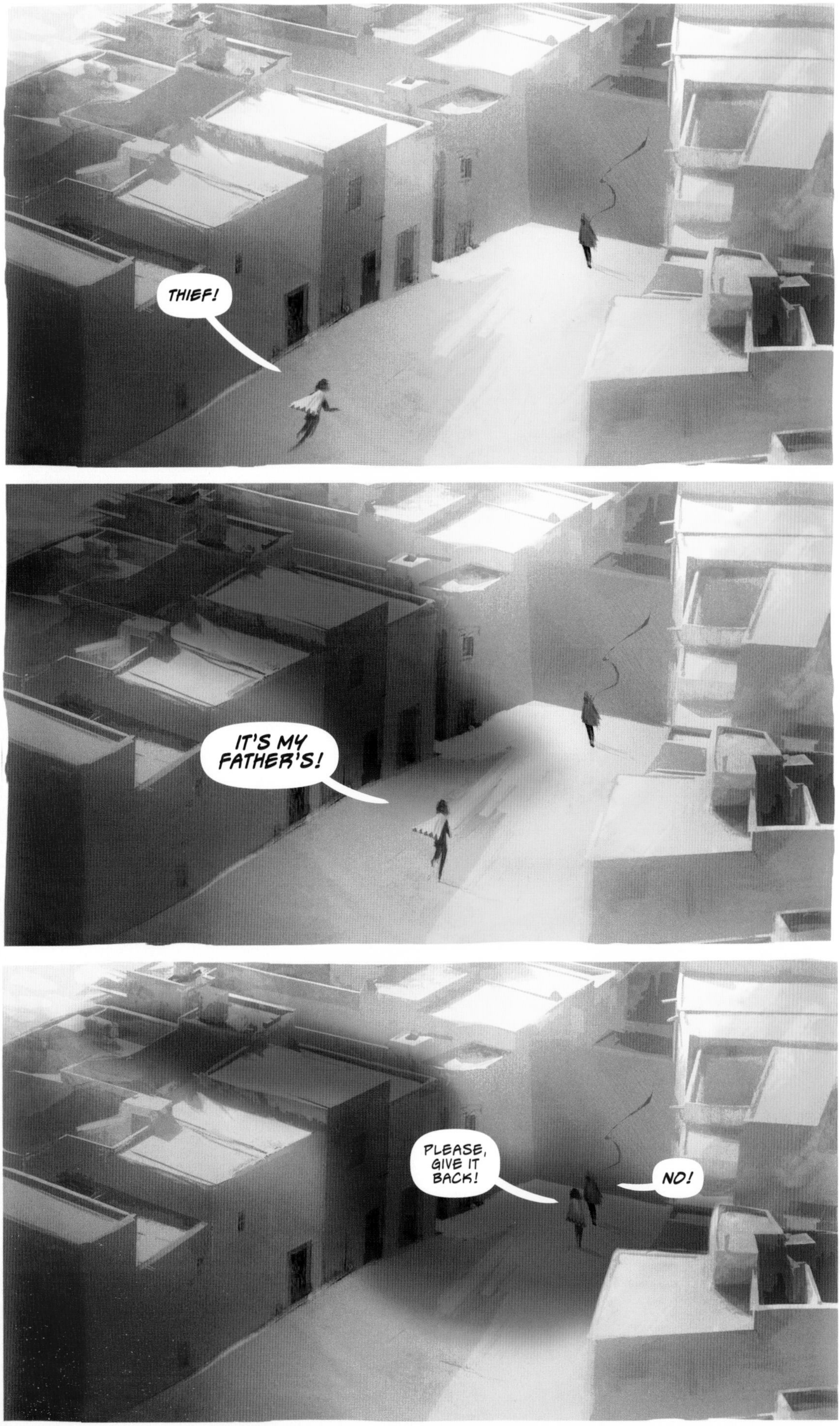
THIEF!
IT'S MY FATHER'S!
PLEASE, GIVE IT BACK!
NO!

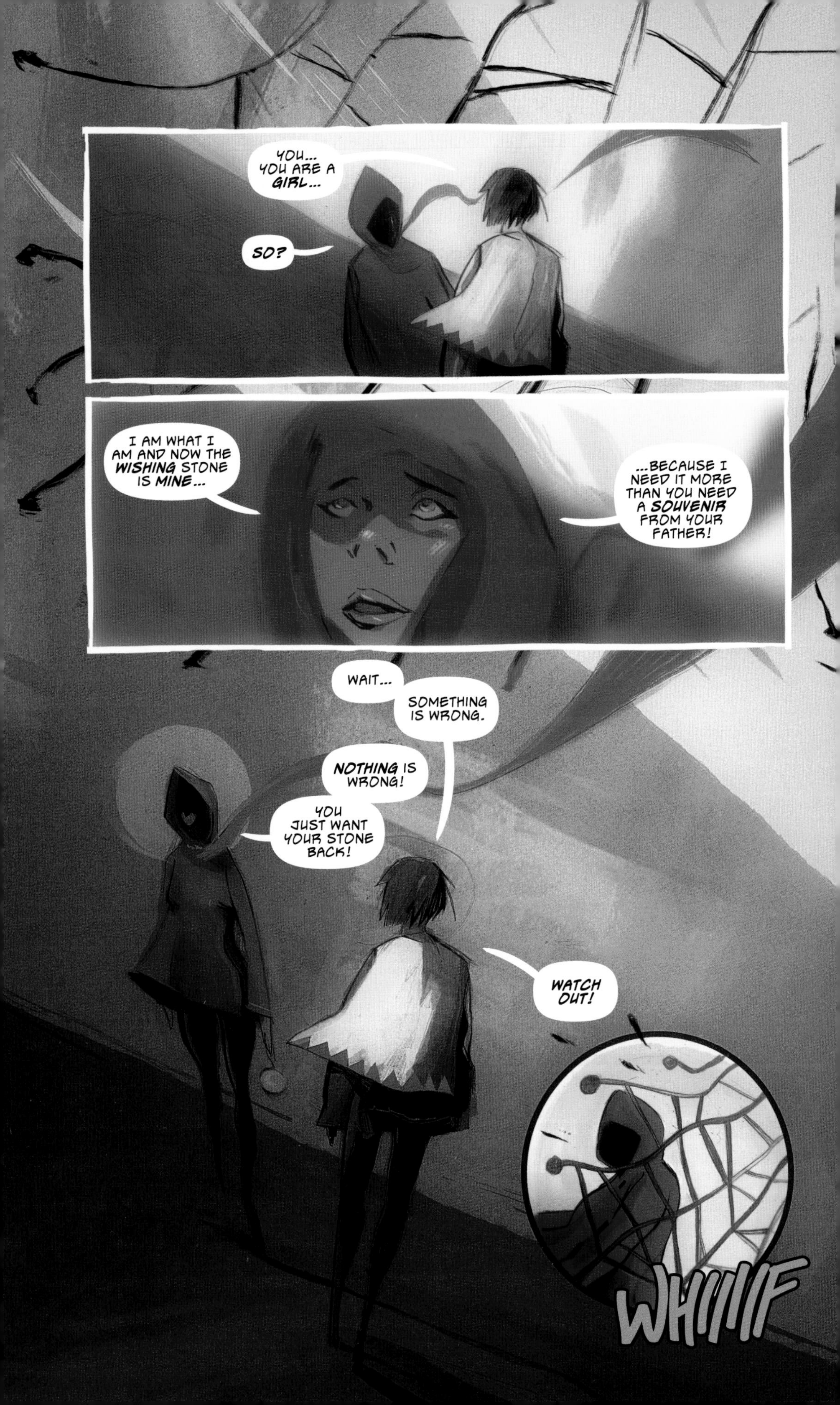
YOU... YOU ARE A GIRL...
SO?
I AM WHAT I AM AND NOW THE WISHING STONE IS MINE...
...BECAUSE I NEED IT MORE THAN YOU NEED A SOUVENIR FROM YOUR FATHER!
WAIT...
SOMETHING IS WRONG.
NOTHING IS WRONG!
YOU JUST WANT YOUR STONE BACK!
WATCH OUT!
WHIIIIF

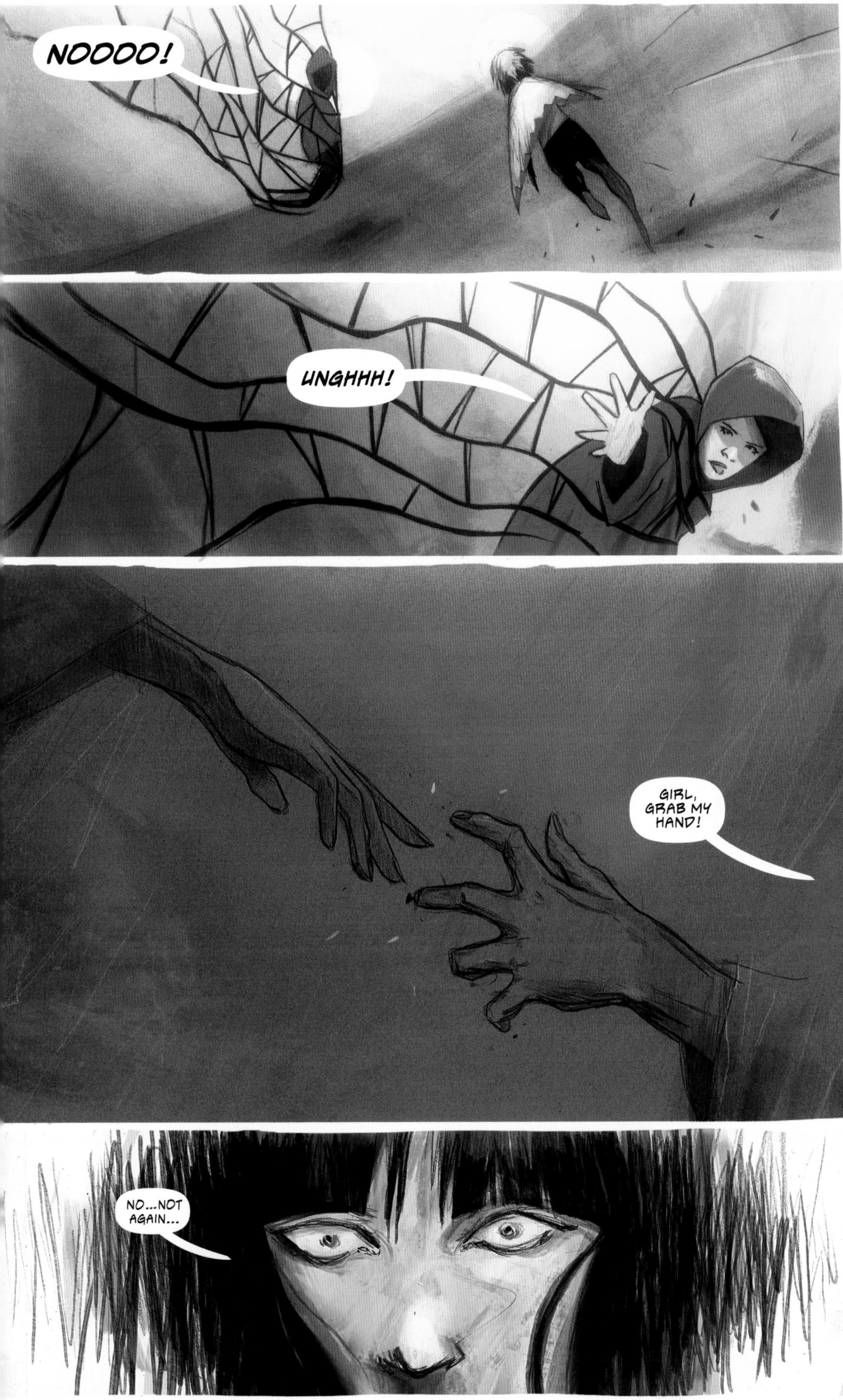
NOOOO!
UNGHHH!
GIRL, GRAB MY HAND!
NO...NOT AGAIN...

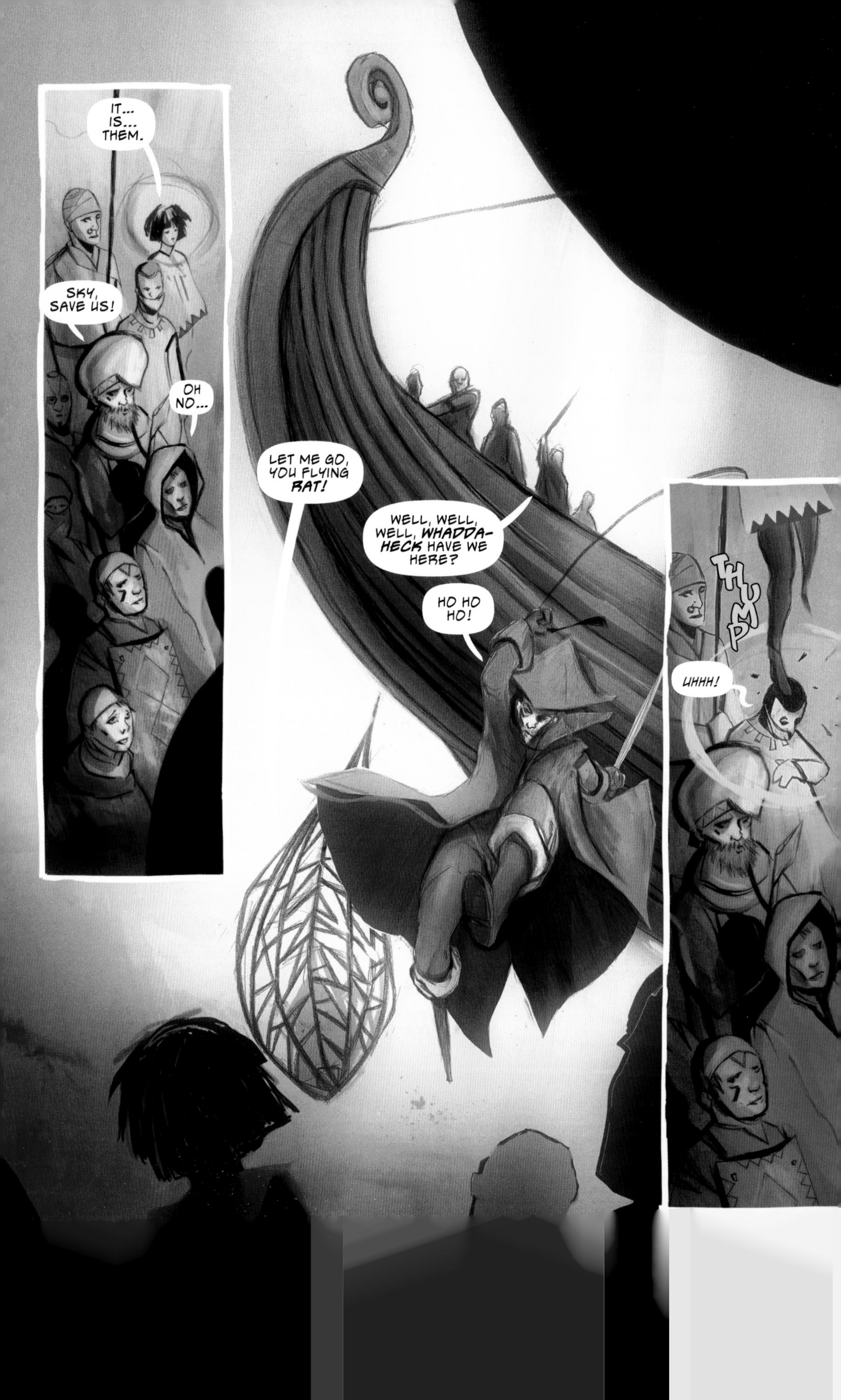
IT... IS... THEM.
SKY, SAVE US!
OH NO...
LET ME GO, YOU FLYING RAT!
WELL, WELL, WELL, WHADDA-HECK HAVE WE HERE?
HO HO HO!
THUMP
UHHH!

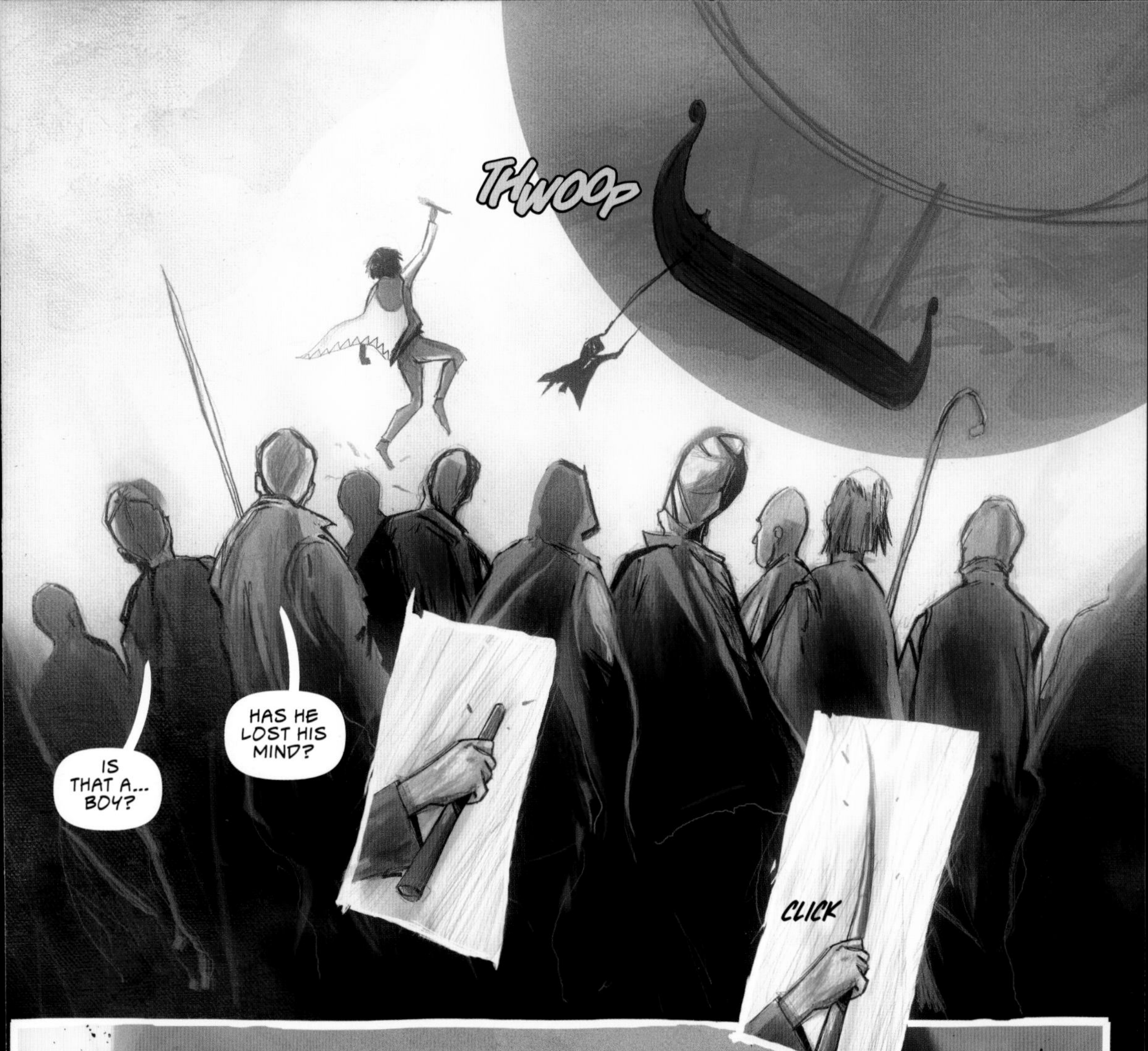
THWOOP
IS THAT A... BOY?
HAS HE LOST HIS MIND?
CLICK

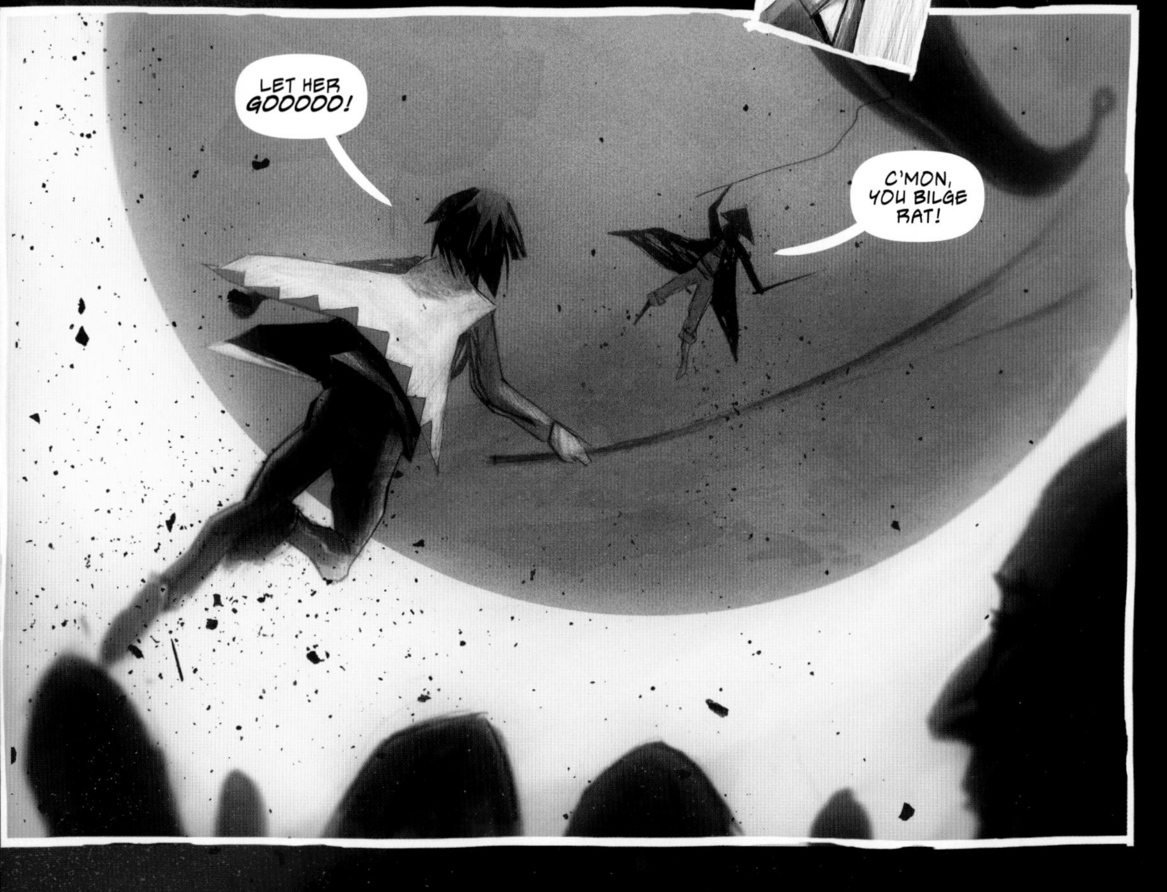
LET HER GOOOOO!
C'MON, YOU BILGE RAT!

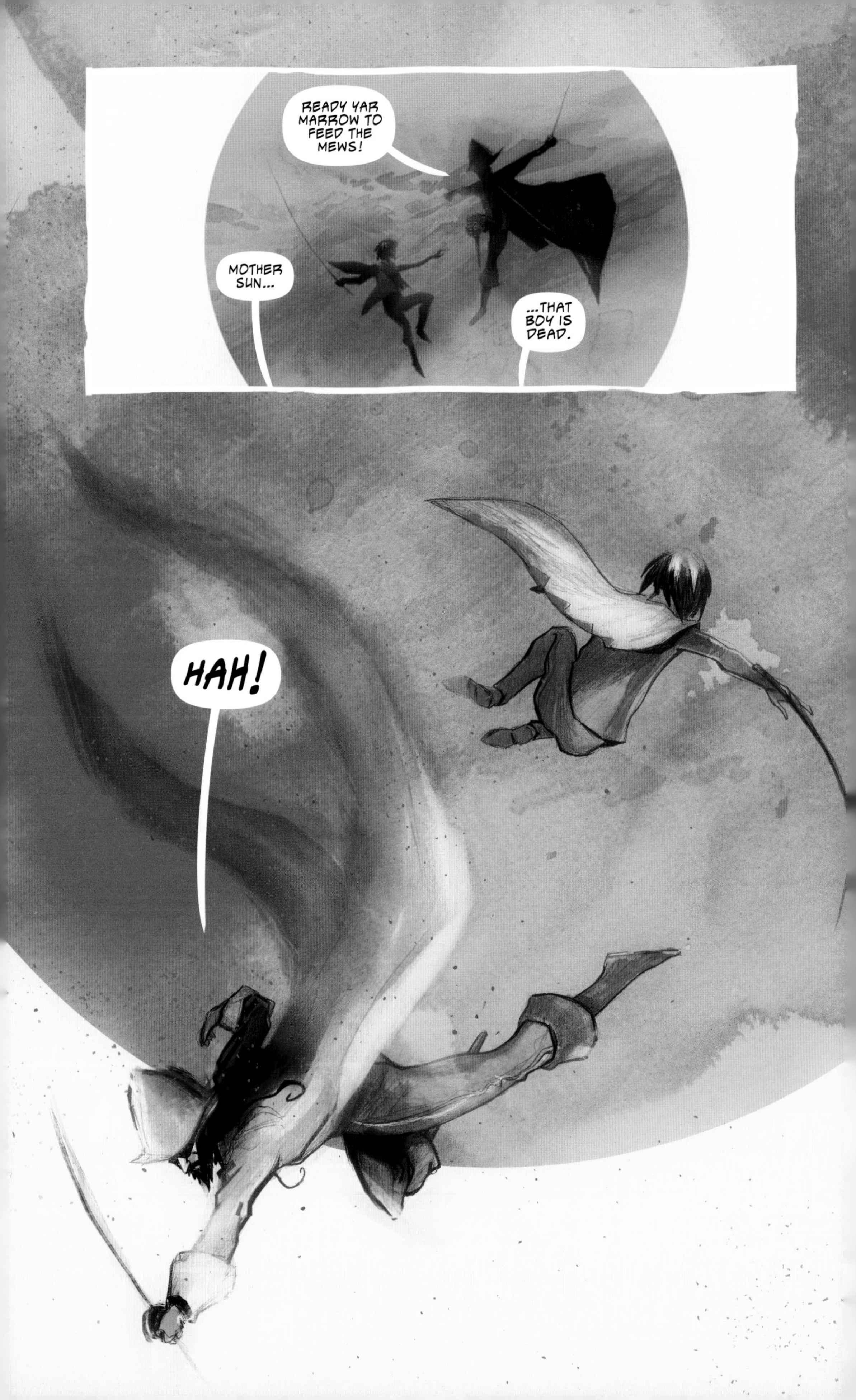
READY YAR MARROW TO FEED THE MEWS!
MOTHER SUN...
...THAT BOY IS DEAD.
HAH!

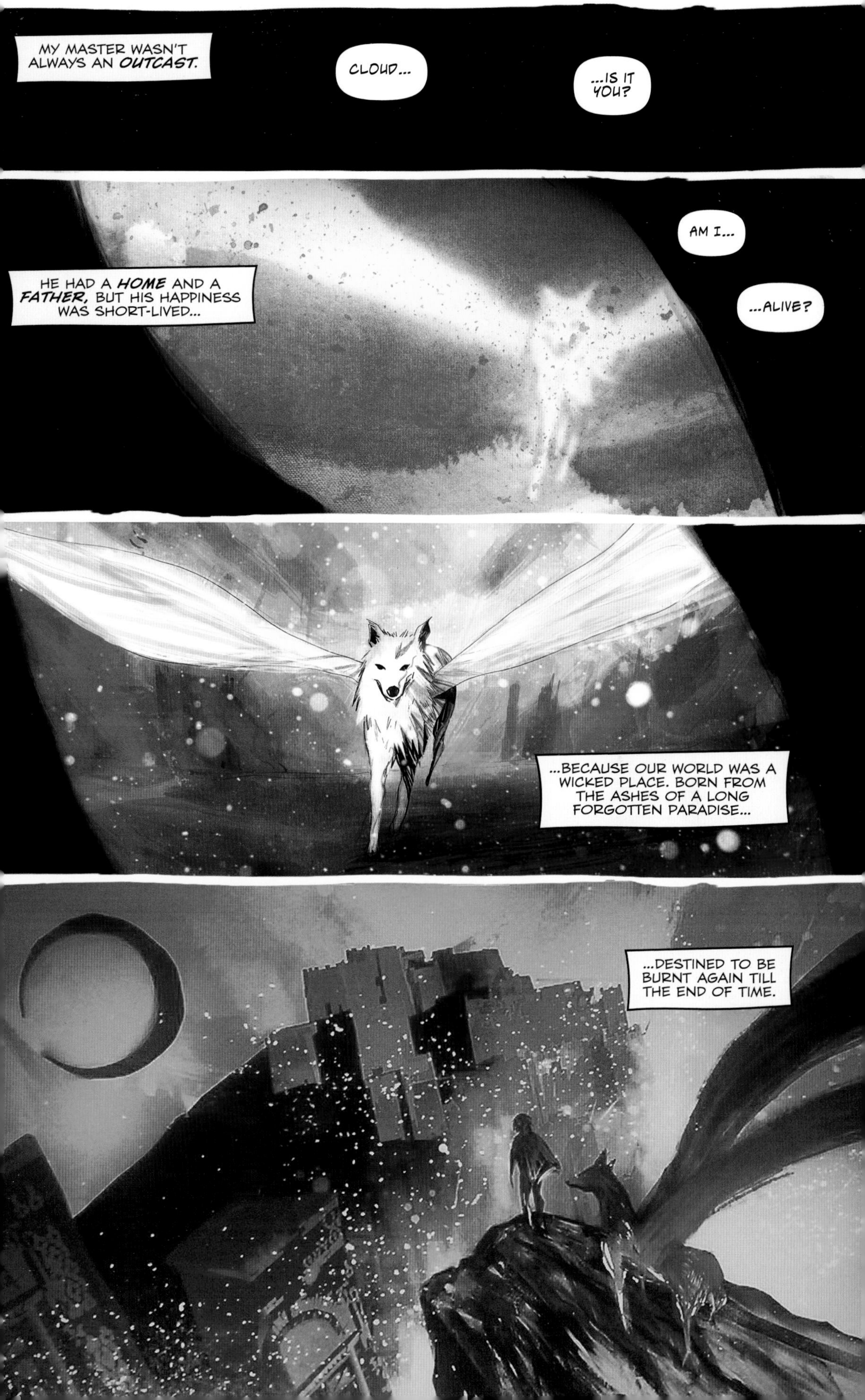
MY MASTER WASN'T ALWAYS AN *OUTCAST.*
CLOUD...
...IS IT YOU?
AM I...
HE HAD A ***HOME*** AND A ***FATHER,*** BUT HIS HAPPINESS WAS SHORT-LIVED...
...ALIVE?
...BECAUSE OUR WORLD WAS A WICKED PLACE. BORN FROM THE ASHES OF A LONG FORGOTTEN PARADISE...
...DESTINED TO BE BURNT AGAIN TILL THE END OF TIME.

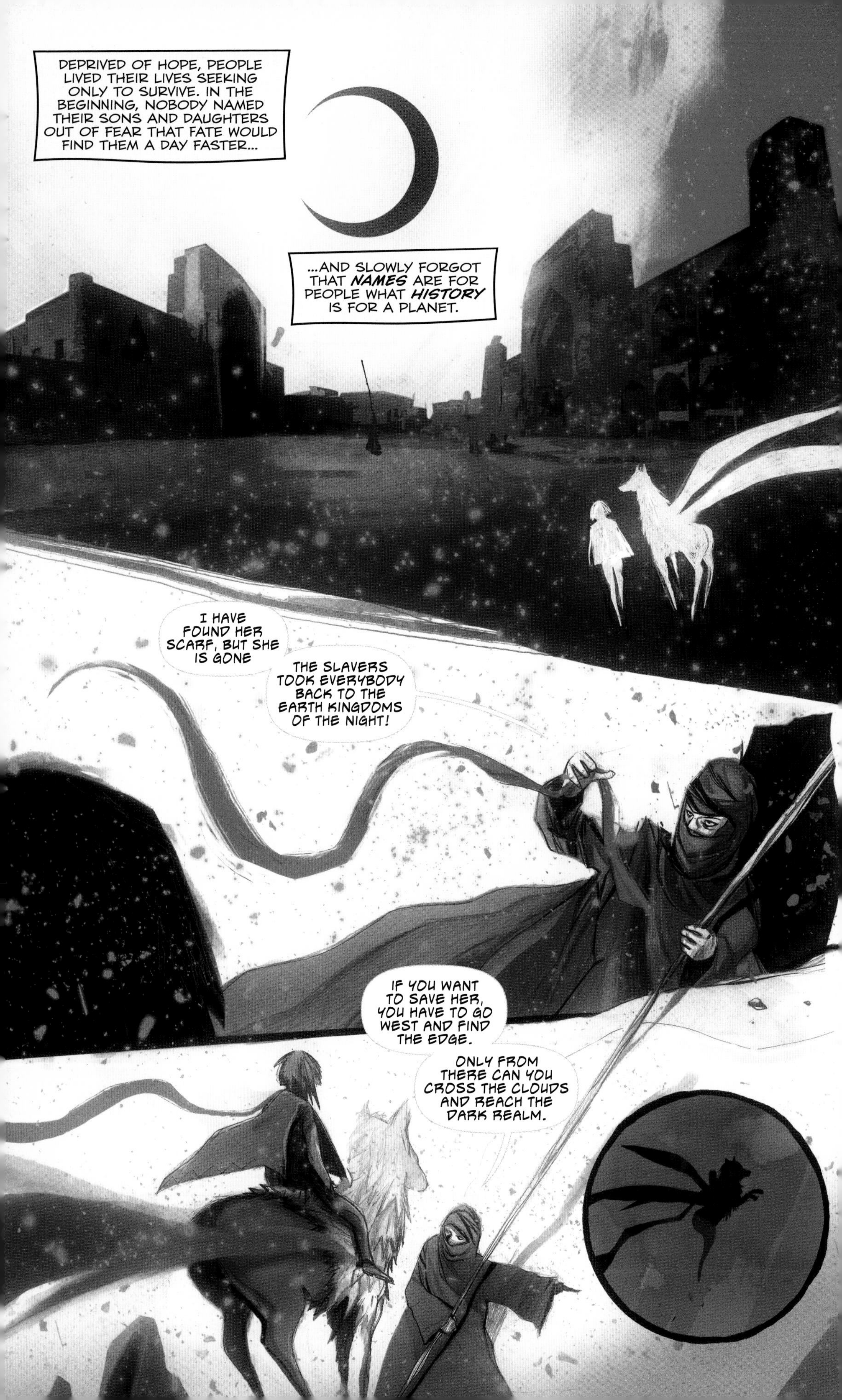
DEPRIVED OF HOPE, PEOPLE LIVED THEIR LIVES SEEKING ONLY TO SURVIVE. IN THE BEGINNING, NOBODY NAMED THEIR SONS AND DAUGHTERS OUT OF FEAR THAT FATE WOULD FIND THEM A DAY FASTER...
...AND SLOWLY FORGOT THAT *NAMES* ARE FOR PEOPLE WHAT *HISTORY* IS FOR A PLANET.
I HAVE FOUND HER SCARF, BUT SHE IS GONE
THE SLAVERS TOOK EVERYBODY BACK TO THE EARTH KINGDOMS OF THE NIGHT!
IF YOU WANT TO SAVE HER, YOU HAVE TO GO WEST AND FIND THE EDGE.
ONLY FROM THERE CAN YOU CROSS THE CLOUDS AND REACH THE DARK REALM.

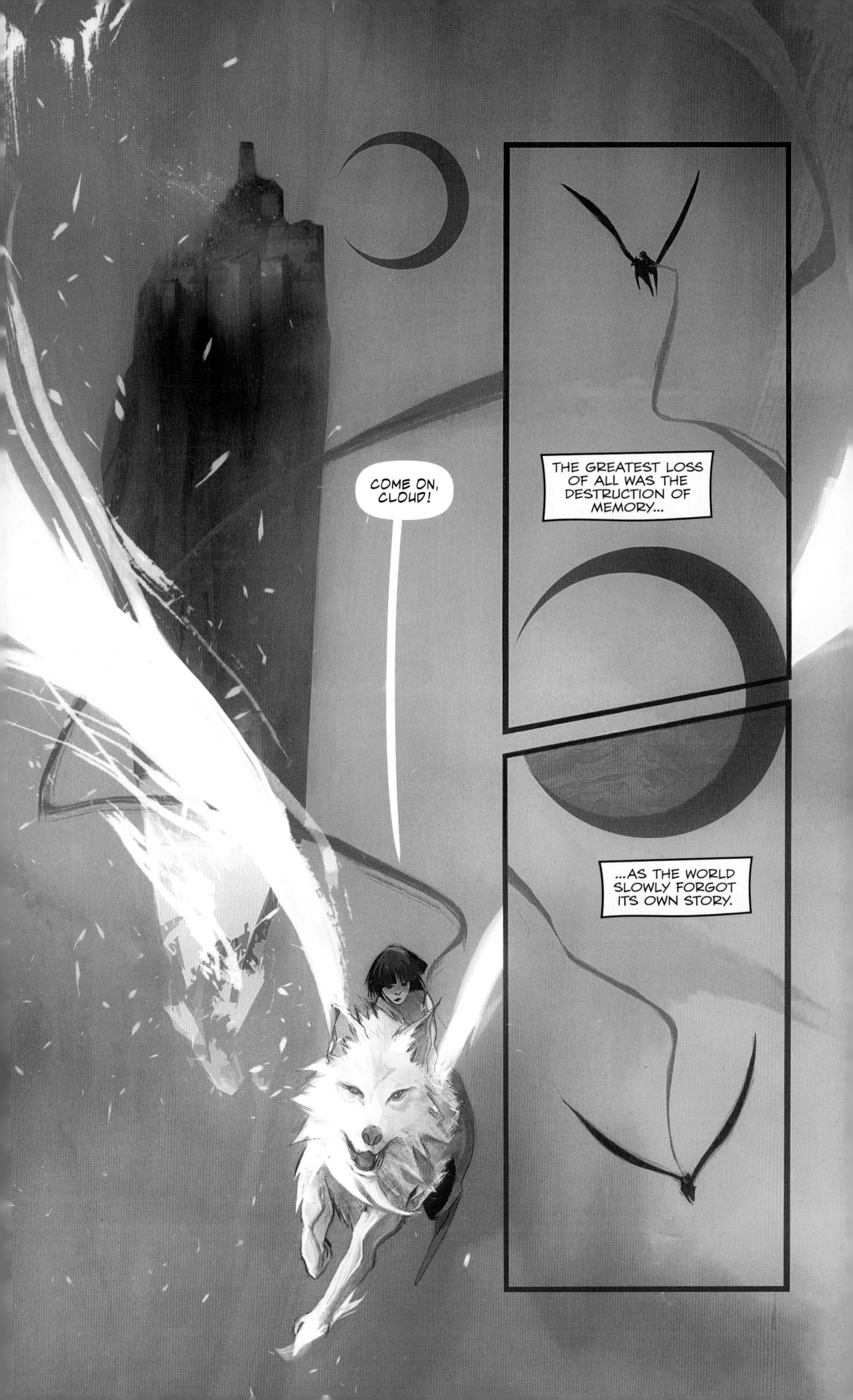
COME ON, CLOUD!
THE GREATEST LOSS OF ALL WAS THE DESTRUCTION OF MEMORY...
...AS THE WORLD SLOWLY FORGOT ITS OWN STORY.

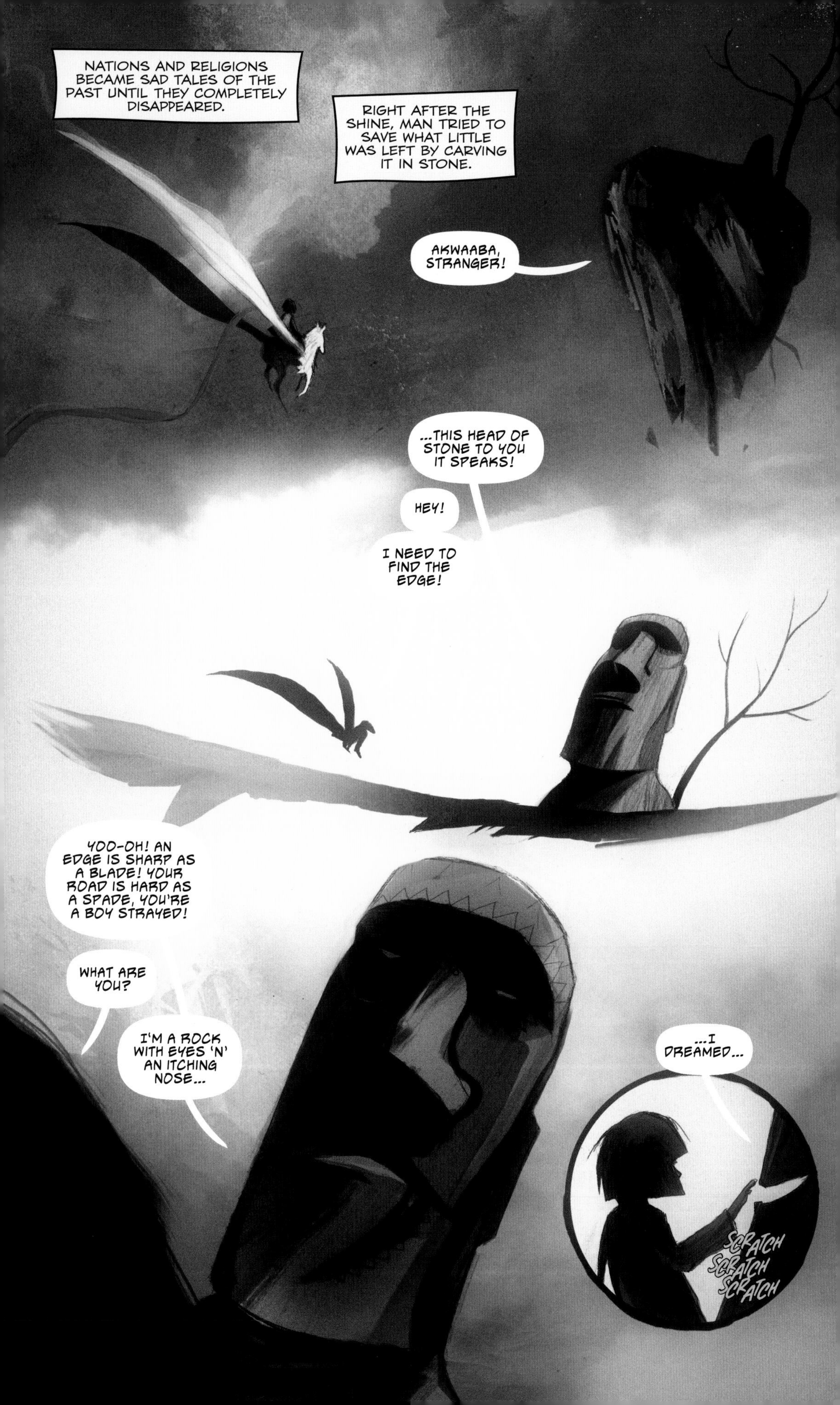
NATIONS AND RELIGIONS BECAME SAD TALES OF THE PAST UNTIL THEY COMPLETELY DISAPPEARED.
RIGHT AFTER THE SHINE, MAN TRIED TO SAVE WHAT LITTLE WAS LEFT BY CARVING IT IN STONE.
AKWAABA, STRANGER!
...THIS HEAD OF STONE TO YOU IT SPEAKS!
HEY!
I NEED TO FIND THE EDGE!
YOO-OH! AN EDGE IS SHARP AS A BLADE! YOUR ROAD IS HARD AS A SPADE, YOU'RE A BOY STRAYED!
WHAT ARE YOU?
I'M A ROCK WITH EYES 'N' AN ITCHING NOSE...
...I DREAMED...
SCRATCH SCRATCH SCRATCH

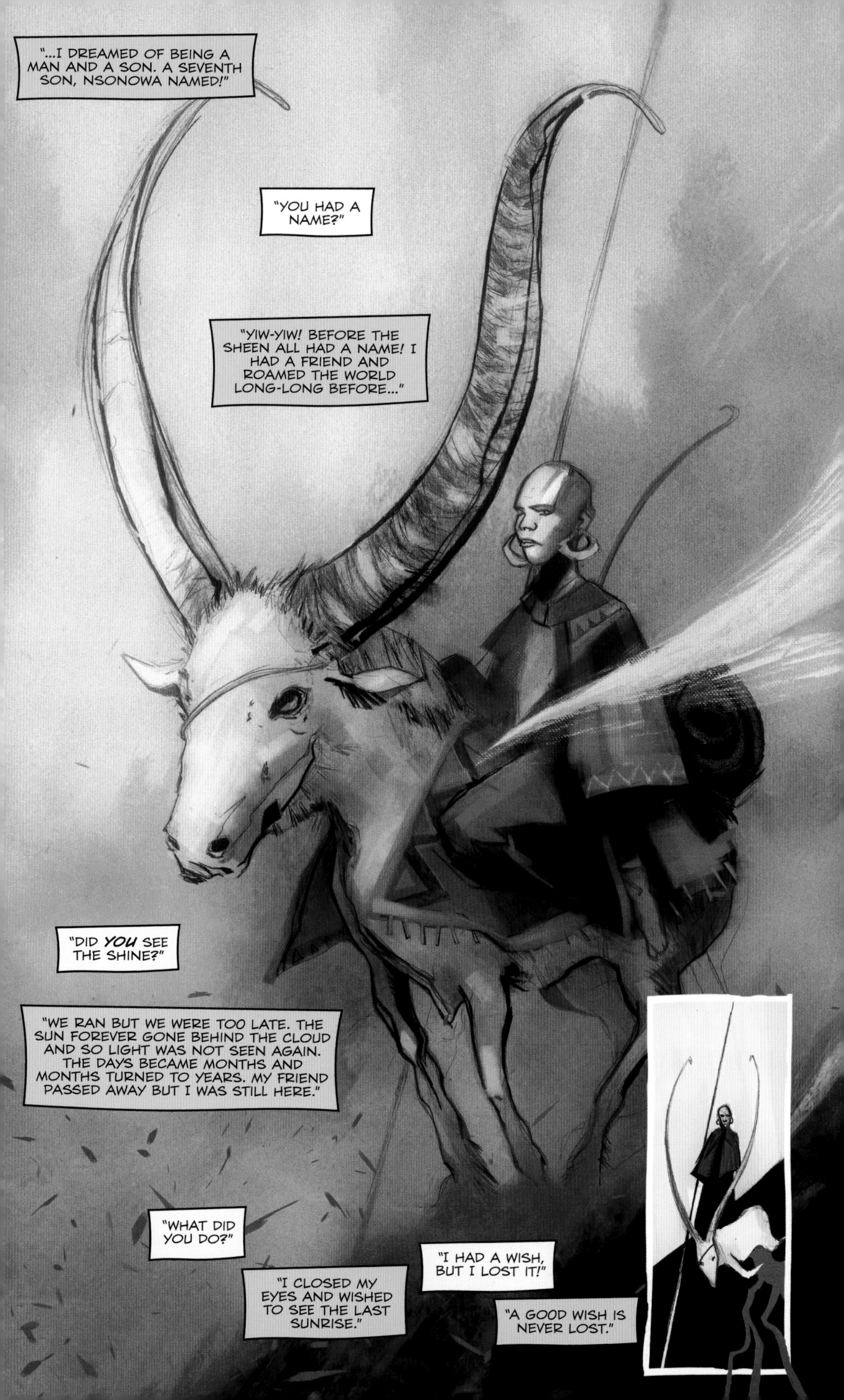
"...I DREAMED OF BEING A MAN AND A SON. A SEVENTH SON, NSONOWA NAMED!"
"YOU HAD A NAME?"
"YIW-YIW! BEFORE THE SHEEN ALL HAD A NAME! I HAD A FRIEND AND ROAMED THE WORLD LONG-LONG BEFORE..."
"DID *YOU* SEE THE SHINE?"
"WE RAN BUT WE WERE TOO LATE. THE SUN FOREVER GONE BEHIND THE CLOUD AND SO LIGHT WAS NOT SEEN AGAIN. THE DAYS BECAME MONTHS AND MONTHS TURNED TO YEARS. MY FRIEND PASSED AWAY BUT I WAS STILL HERE."
"WHAT DID YOU DO?"
"I CLOSED MY EYES AND WISHED TO SEE THE LAST SUNRISE."
"I HAD A WISH, BUT I LOST IT!"
"A GOOD WISH IS NEVER LOST."

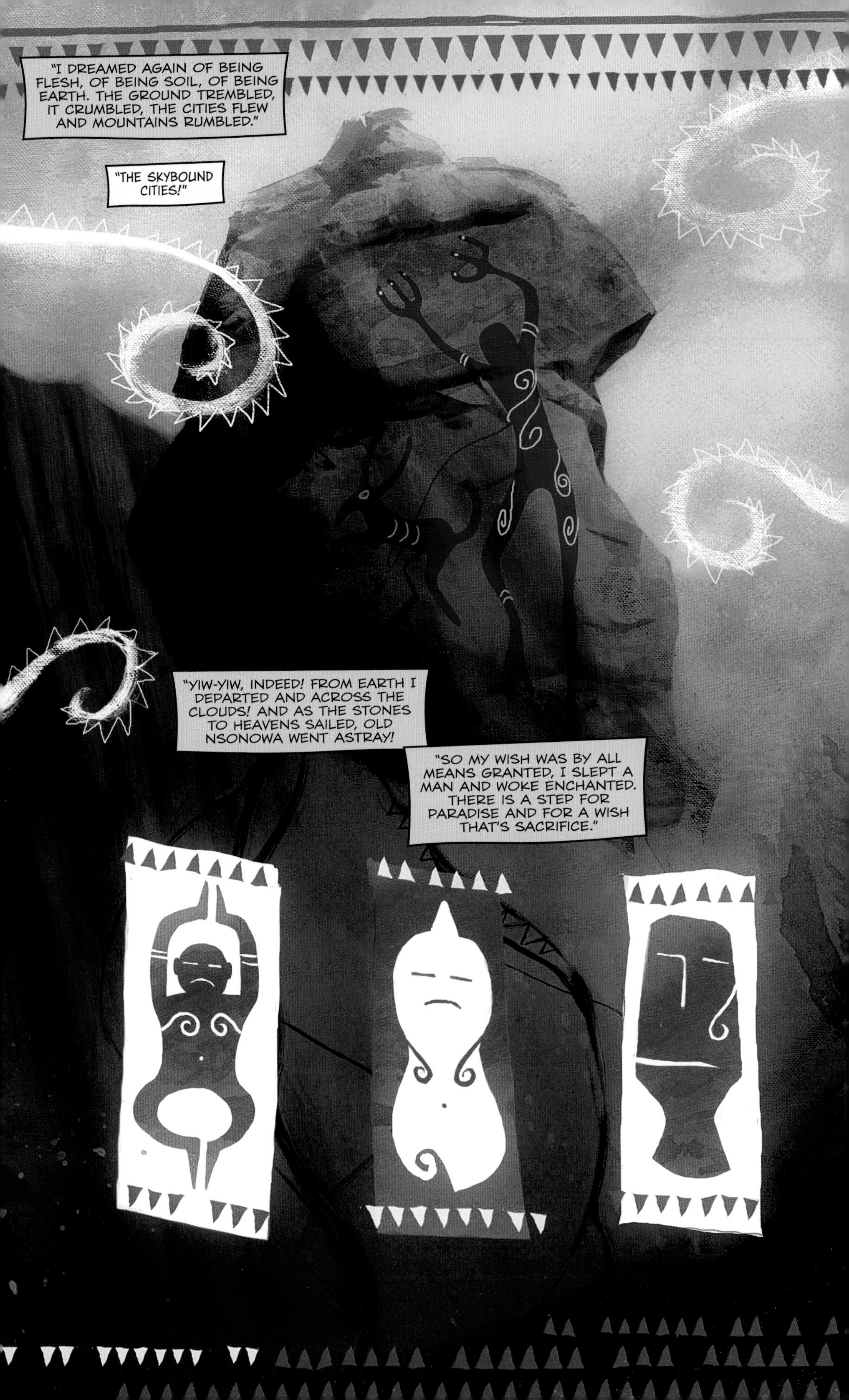
"I DREAMED AGAIN OF BEING FLESH, OF BEING SOIL, OF BEING EARTH. THE GROUND TREMBLED, IT CRUMBLED, THE CITIES FLEW AND MOUNTAINS RUMBLED."
"THE SKYBOUND CITIES!"
"YIW-YIW, INDEED! FROM EARTH I DEPARTED AND ACROSS THE CLOUDS! AND AS THE STONES TO HEAVENS SAILED, OLD NSONOWA WENT ASTRAY!
"SO MY WISH WAS BY ALL MEANS GRANTED, I SLEPT A MAN AND WOKE ENCHANTED. THERE IS A STEP FOR PARADISE AND FOR A WISH THAT'S SACRIFICE."

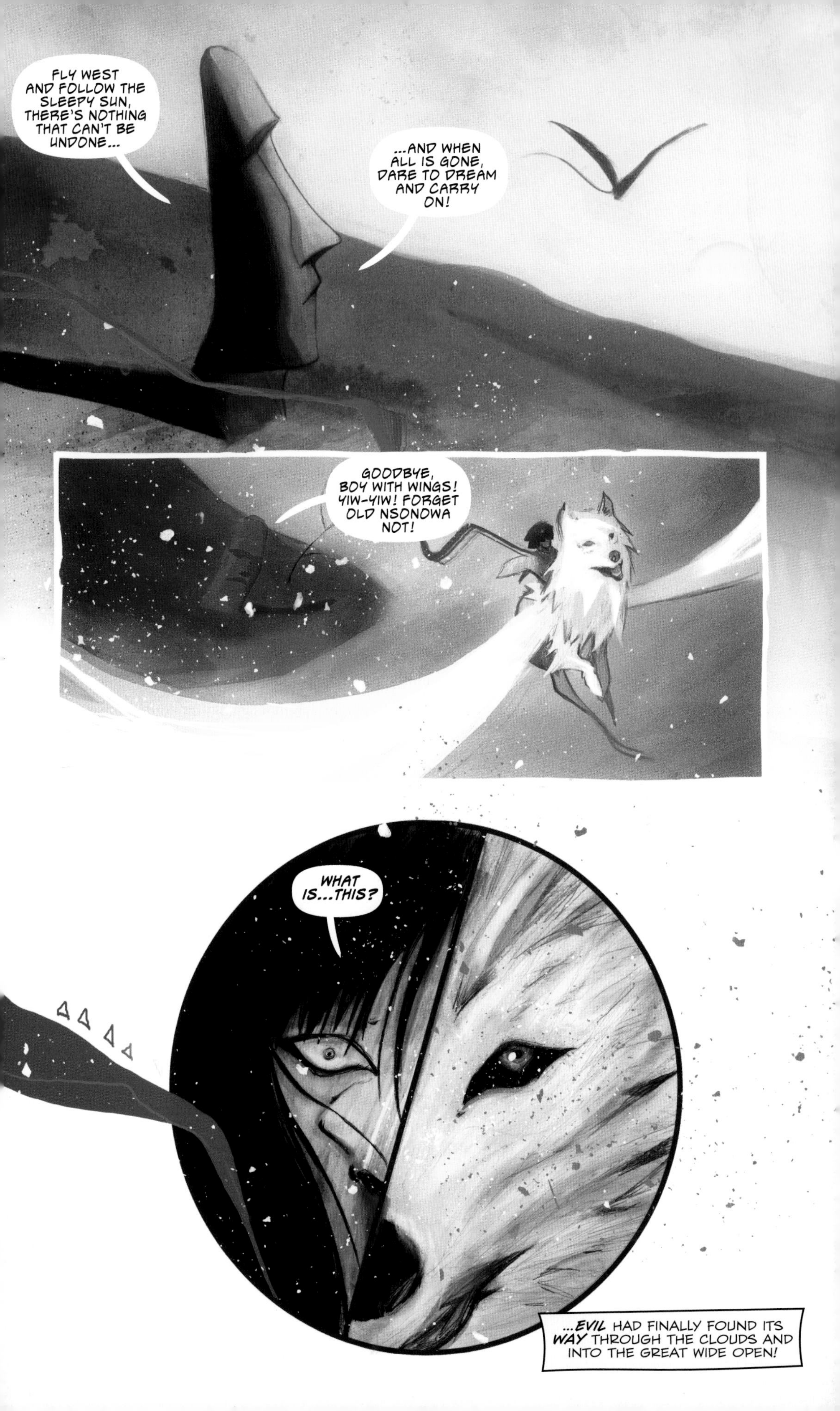

FLY WEST AND FOLLOW THE SLEEPY SUN, THERE'S NOTHING THAT CAN'T BE UNDONE...
...AND WHEN ALL IS GONE, DARE TO DREAM AND CARRY ON!
GOODBYE, BOY WITH WINGS! YIW-YIW! FORGET OLD NSONOWA NOT!
WHAT IS...THIS?
...EVIL HAD FINALLY FOUND ITS WAY THROUGH THE CLOUDS AND INTO THE GREAT WIDE OPEN!

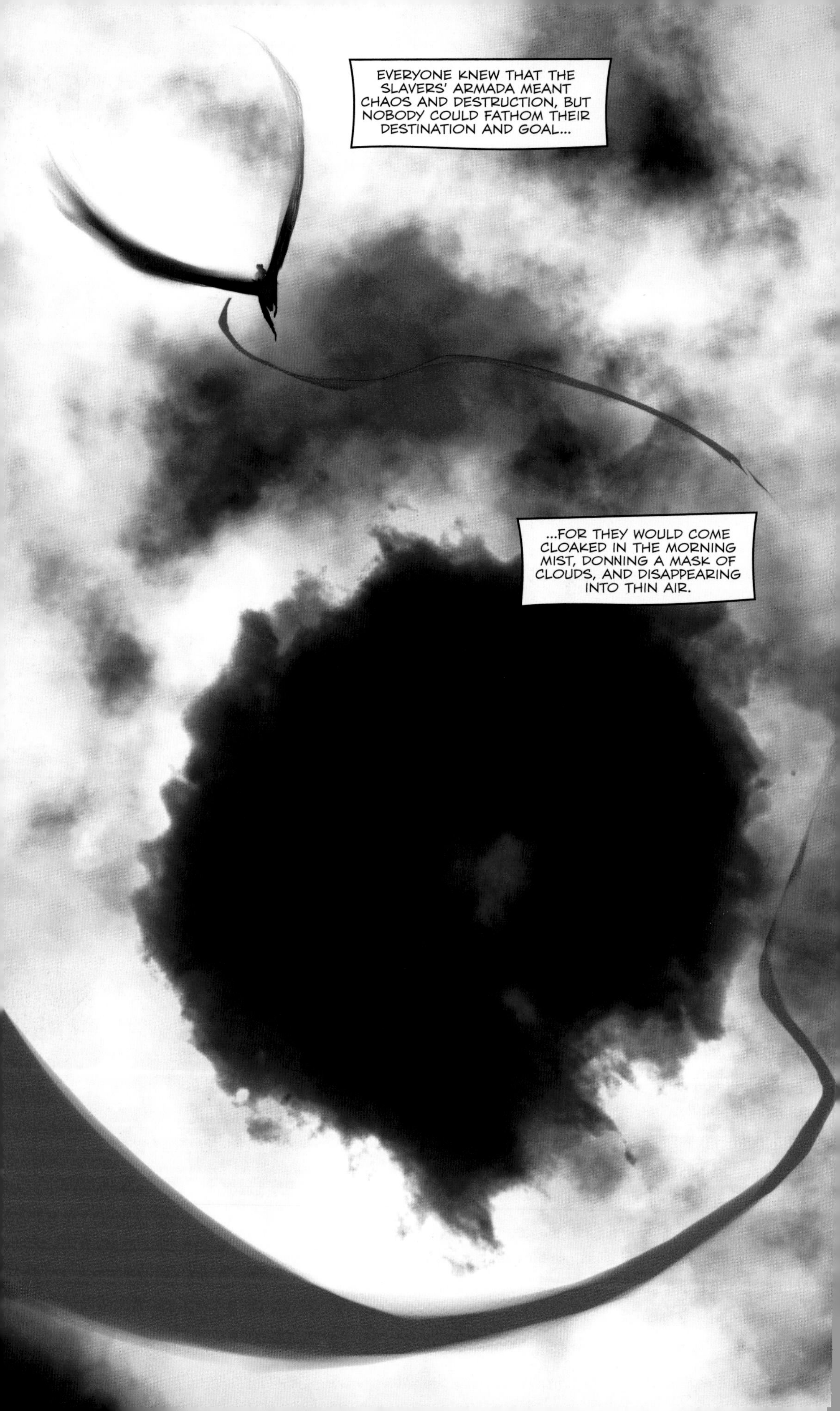
EVERYONE KNEW THAT THE SLAVERS' ARMADA MEANT CHAOS AND DESTRUCTION, BUT NOBODY COULD FATHOM THEIR DESTINATION AND GOAL...
...FOR THEY WOULD COME CLOAKED IN THE MORNING MIST, DONNING A MASK OF CLOUDS, AND DISAPPEARING INTO THIN AIR.

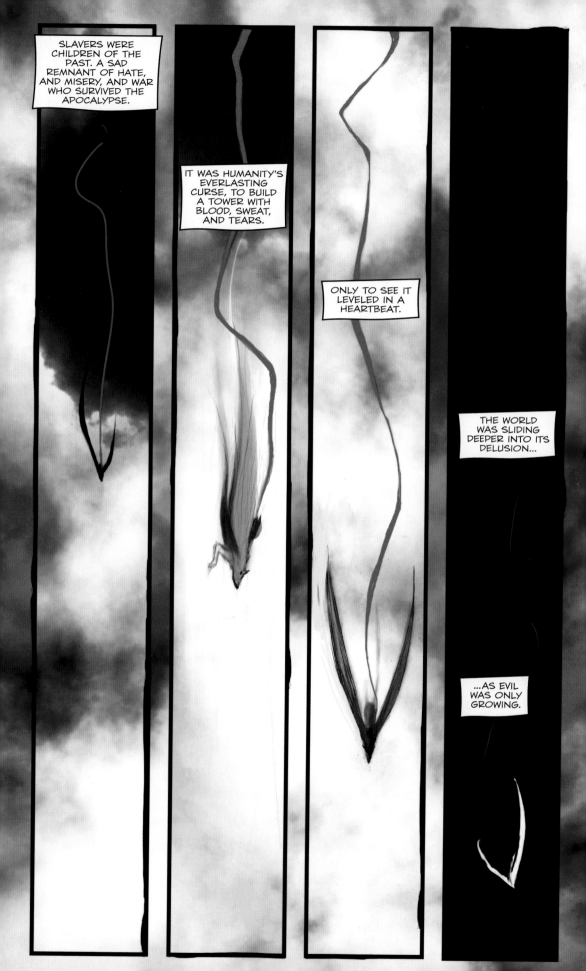

SLAVERS WERE CHILDREN OF THE PAST. A SAD REMNANT OF HATE, AND MISERY, AND WAR WHO SURVIVED THE APOCALYPSE.

IT WAS HUMANITY'S EVERLASTING CURSE, TO BUILD A TOWER WITH BLOOD, SWEAT, AND TEARS.

ONLY TO SEE IT LEVELED IN A HEARTBEAT.

THE WORLD WAS SLIDING DEEPER INTO ITS DELUSION...

...AS EVIL WAS ONLY GROWING.

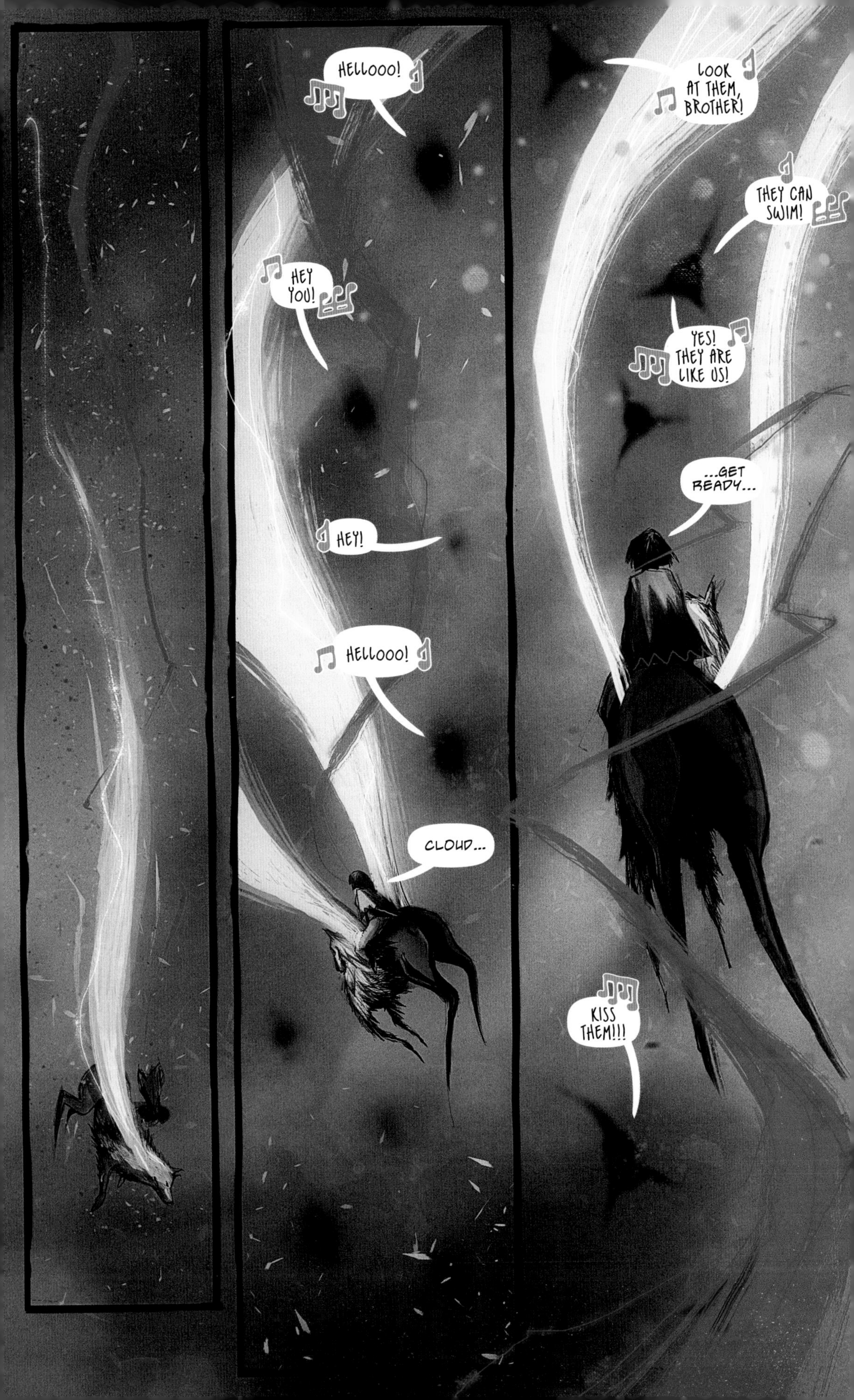
HELLOOO!
HEY YOU!
HEY!
HELLOOO!
CLOUD...
LOOK AT THEM, BROTHER!
THEY CAN SWIM!
YES! THEY ARE LIKE US!
...GET READY...
KISS THEM!!!

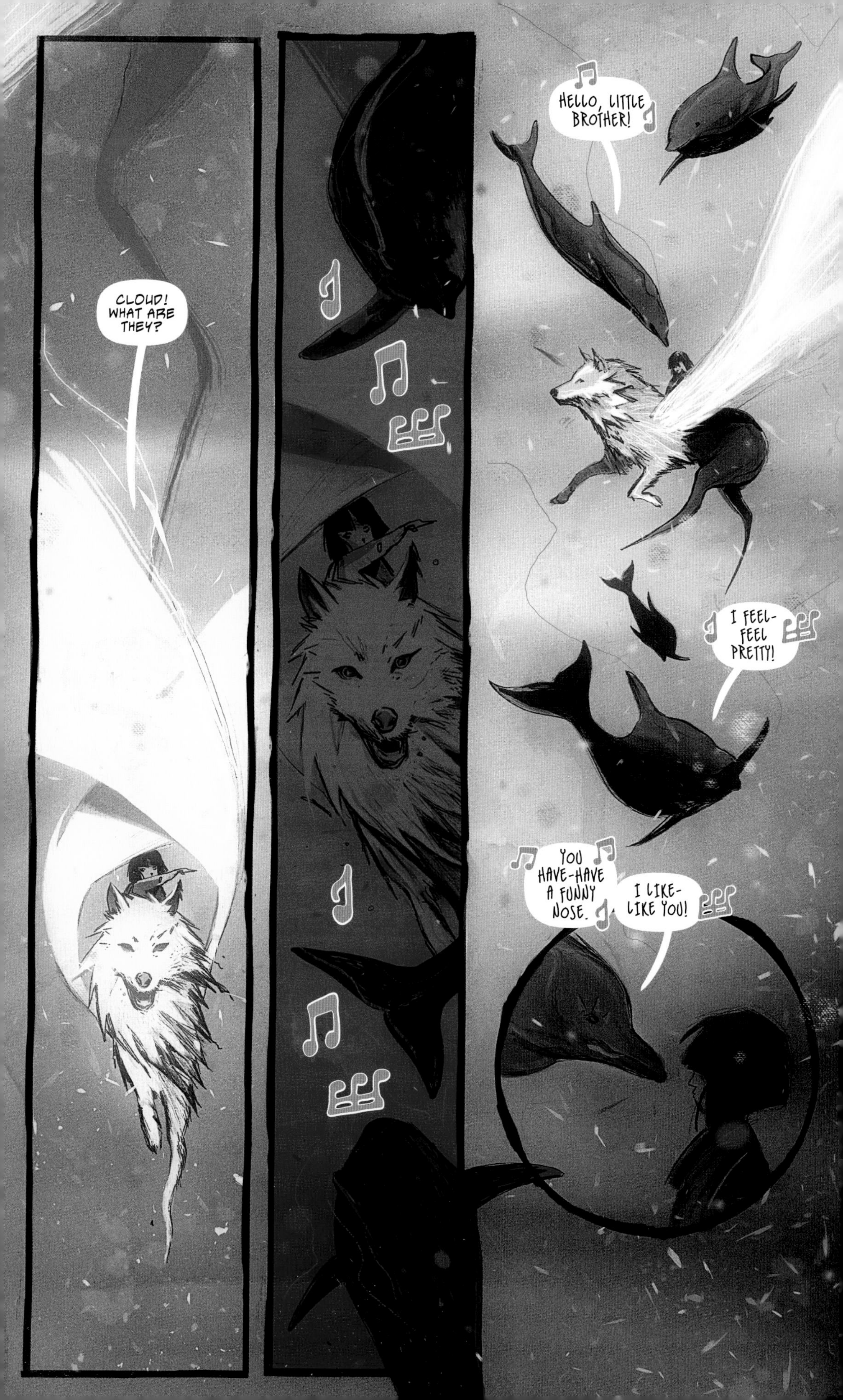
CLOUD! WHAT ARE THEY?
HELLO, LITTLE BROTHER!
I FEEL-FEEL PRETTY!
YOU HAVE-HAVE A FUNNY NOSE.
I LIKE-LIKE YOU!

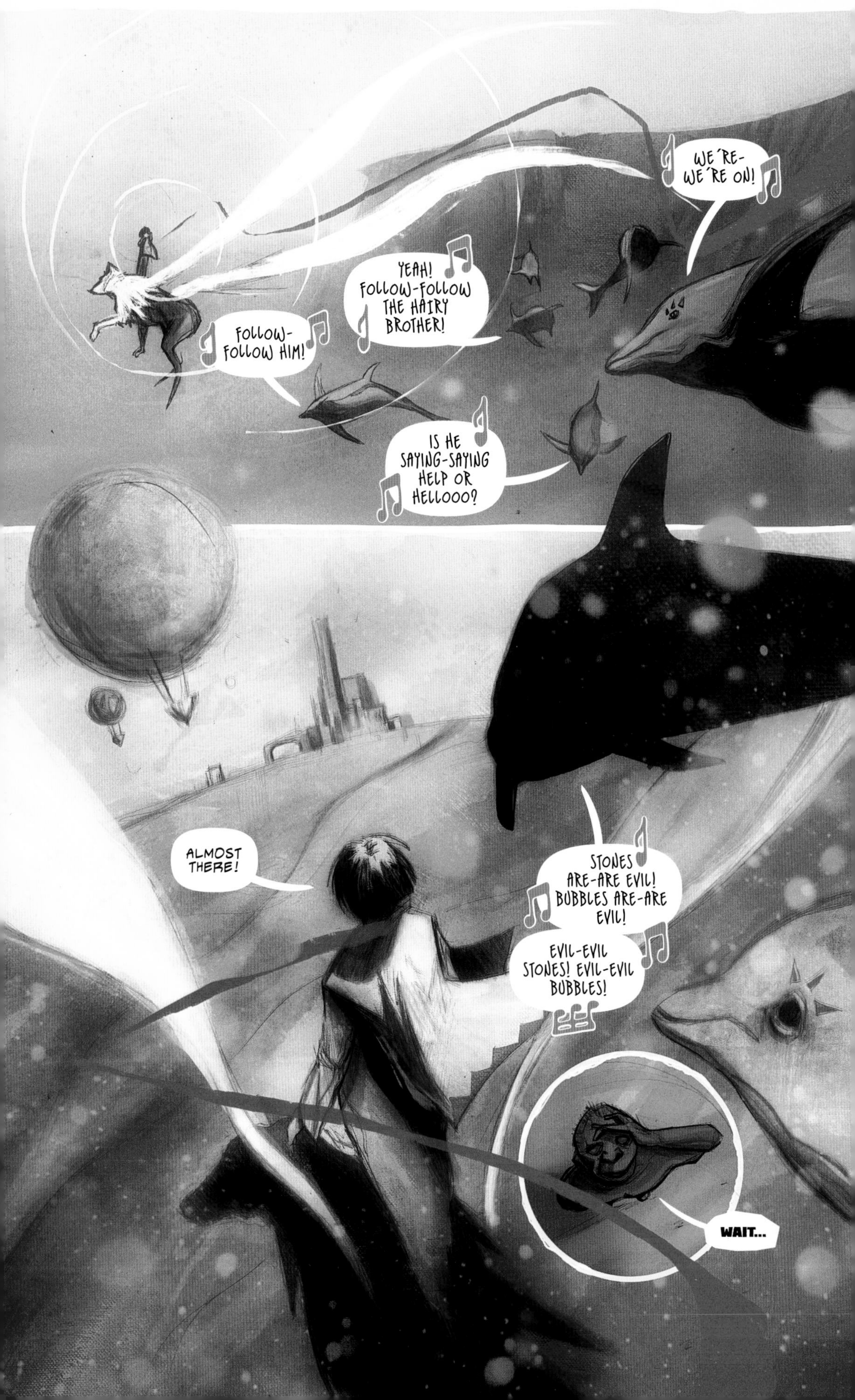
WE´RE-WE´RE ON!
YEAH! FOLLOW-FOLLOW THE HAIRY BROTHER!
FOLLOW-FOLLOW HIM!
IS HE SAYING-SAYING HELP OR HELLOOO?
ALMOST THERE!
STONES ARE-ARE EVIL! BUBBLES ARE-ARE EVIL!
EVIL-EVIL STONES! EVIL-EVIL BUBBLES!
WAIT...

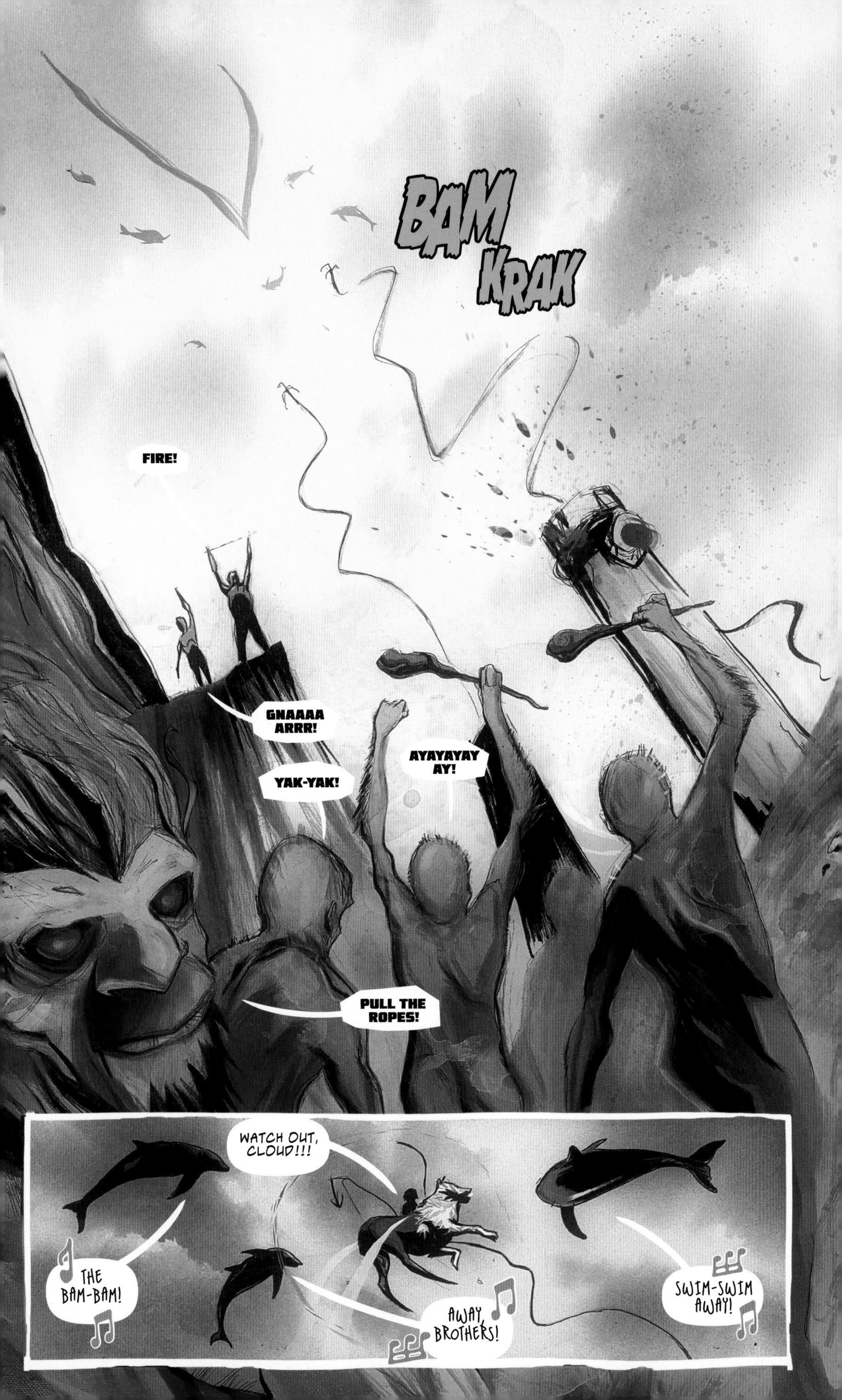
BAM
KRAK
FIRE!
GNAAAA ARRR!
YAK-YAK!
AYAYAYAY AY!
PULL THE ROPES!
WATCH OUT, CLOUD!!!
THE BAM-BAM!
AWAY, BROTHERS!
SWIM-SWIM AWAY!

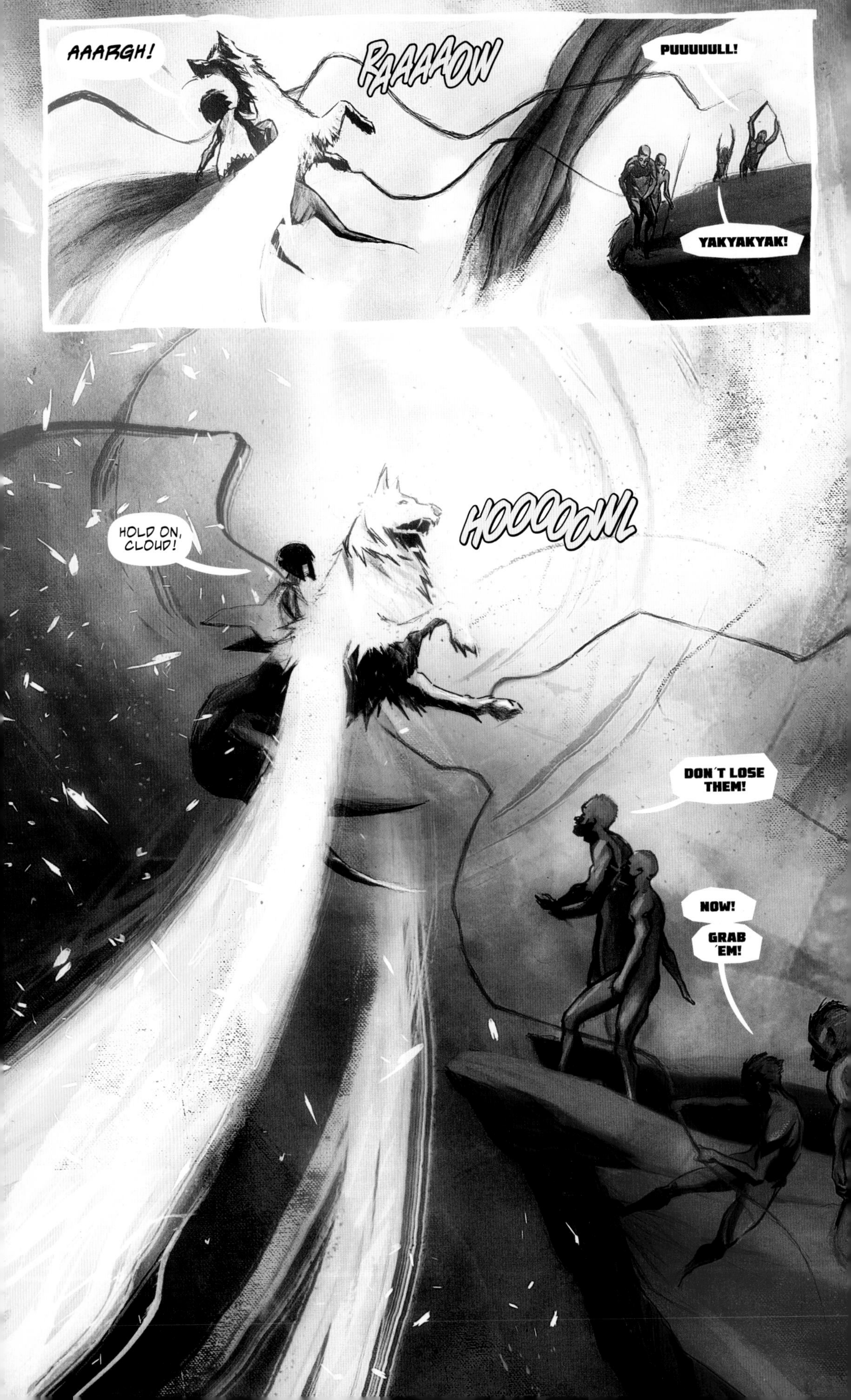
AAARGH!
RAAAAOW
PUUUUULL!
YAKYAKYAK!
HOOOOOWL
HOLD ON, CLOUD!
DON´T LOSE THEM!
NOW!
GRAB ´EM!

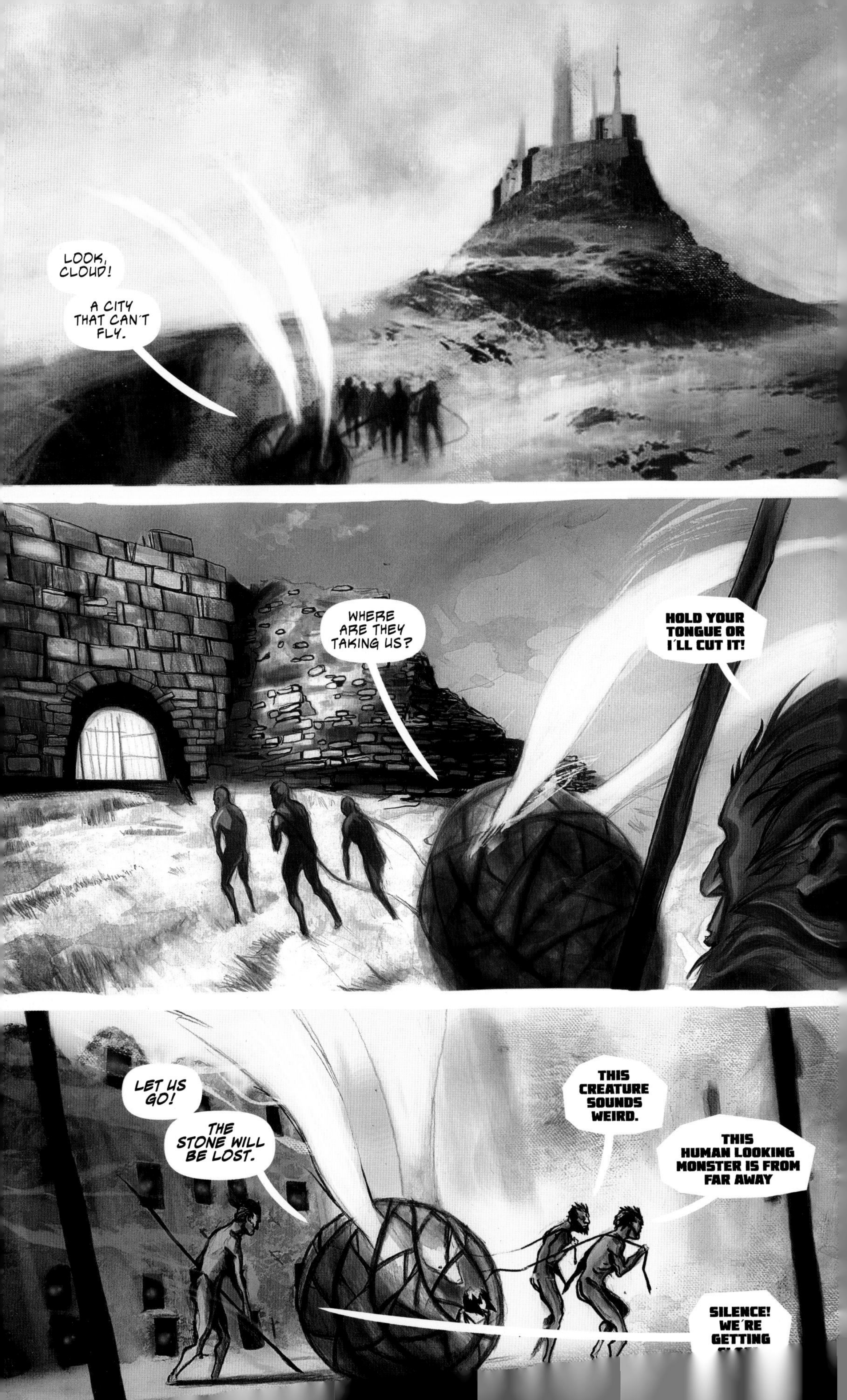
LOOK, CLOUD!
A CITY THAT CAN'T FLY.
WHERE ARE THEY TAKING US?
HOLD YOUR TONGUE OR I'LL CUT IT!
LET US GO!
THE STONE WILL BE LOST.
THIS CREATURE SOUNDS WEIRD.
THIS HUMAN LOOKING MONSTER IS FROM FAR AWAY
SILENCE! WE'RE GETTING

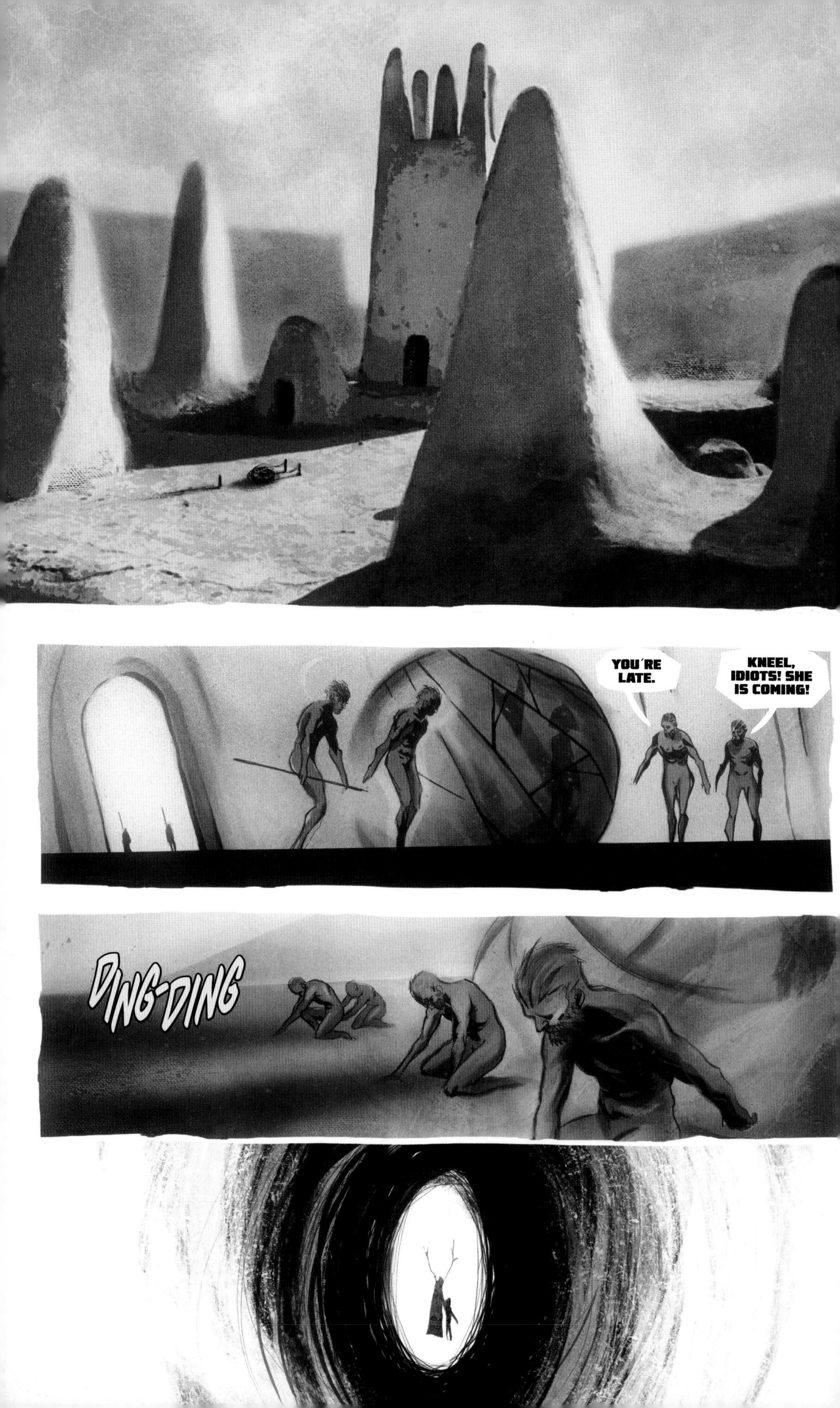
YOU´RE LATE.
KNEEL, IDIOTS! SHE IS COMING!
DING-DING

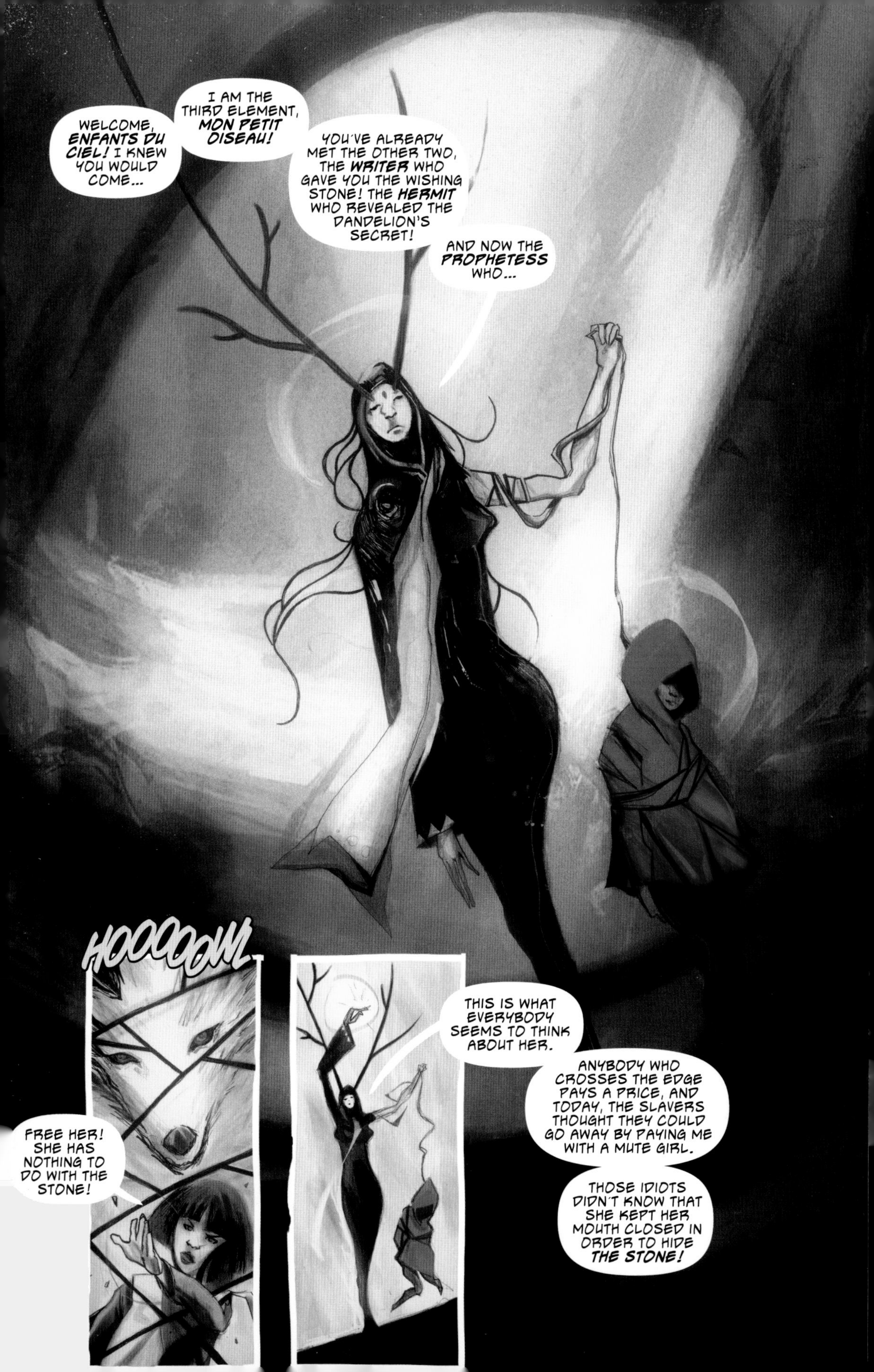
WELCOME, ENFANTS DU CIEL! I KNEW YOU WOULD COME...
I AM THE THIRD ELEMENT, MON PETIT OISEAU!
YOU'VE ALREADY MET THE OTHER TWO, THE WRITER WHO GAVE YOU THE WISHING STONE! THE HERMIT WHO REVEALED THE DANDELION'S SECRET!
AND NOW THE PROPHETESS WHO...
HOOOOOWL
FREE HER! SHE HAS NOTHING TO DO WITH THE STONE!
THIS IS WHAT EVERYBODY SEEMS TO THINK ABOUT HER.
ANYBODY WHO CROSSES THE EDGE PAYS A PRICE, AND TODAY, THE SLAVERS THOUGHT THEY COULD GO AWAY BY PAYING ME WITH A MUTE GIRL.
THOSE IDIOTS DIDN'T KNOW THAT SHE KEPT HER MOUTH CLOSED IN ORDER TO HIDE THE STONE!

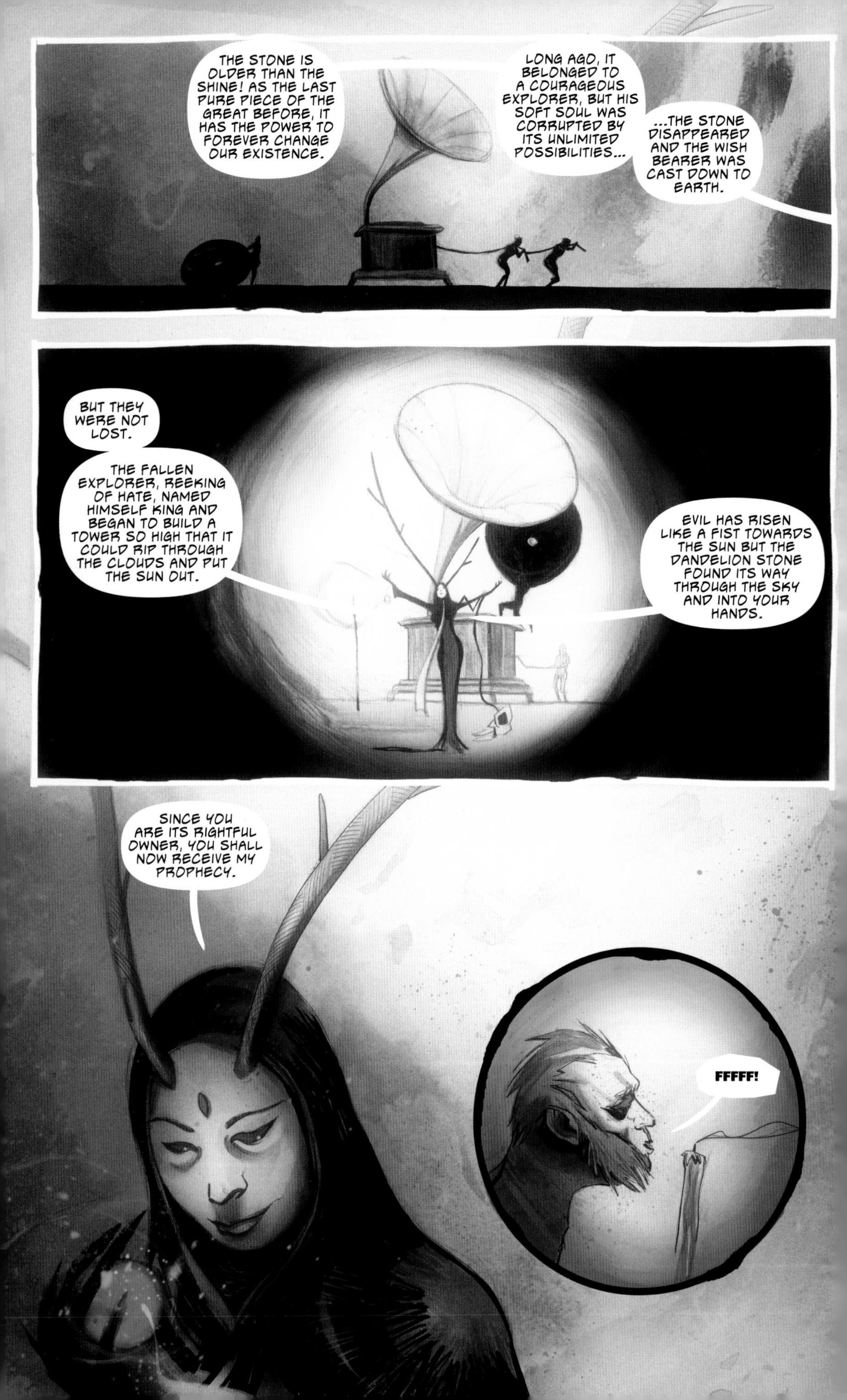
THE STONE IS OLDER THAN THE SHINE! AS THE LAST PURE PIECE OF THE GREAT BEFORE, IT HAS THE POWER TO FOREVER CHANGE OUR EXISTENCE.
LONG AGO, IT BELONGED TO A COURAGEOUS EXPLORER, BUT HIS SOFT SOUL WAS CORRUPTED BY ITS UNLIMITED POSSIBILITIES...
...THE STONE DISAPPEARED AND THE WISH BEARER WAS CAST DOWN TO EARTH.
BUT THEY WERE NOT LOST.
THE FALLEN EXPLORER, REEKING OF HATE, NAMED HIMSELF KING AND BEGAN TO BUILD A TOWER SO HIGH THAT IT COULD RIP THROUGH THE CLOUDS AND PUT THE SUN OUT.
EVIL HAS RISEN LIKE A FIST TOWARDS THE SUN BUT THE DANDELION STONE FOUND ITS WAY THROUGH THE SKY AND INTO YOUR HANDS.
SINCE YOU ARE ITS RIGHTFUL OWNER, YOU SHALL NOW RECEIVE MY PROPHECY.
FFFFF!

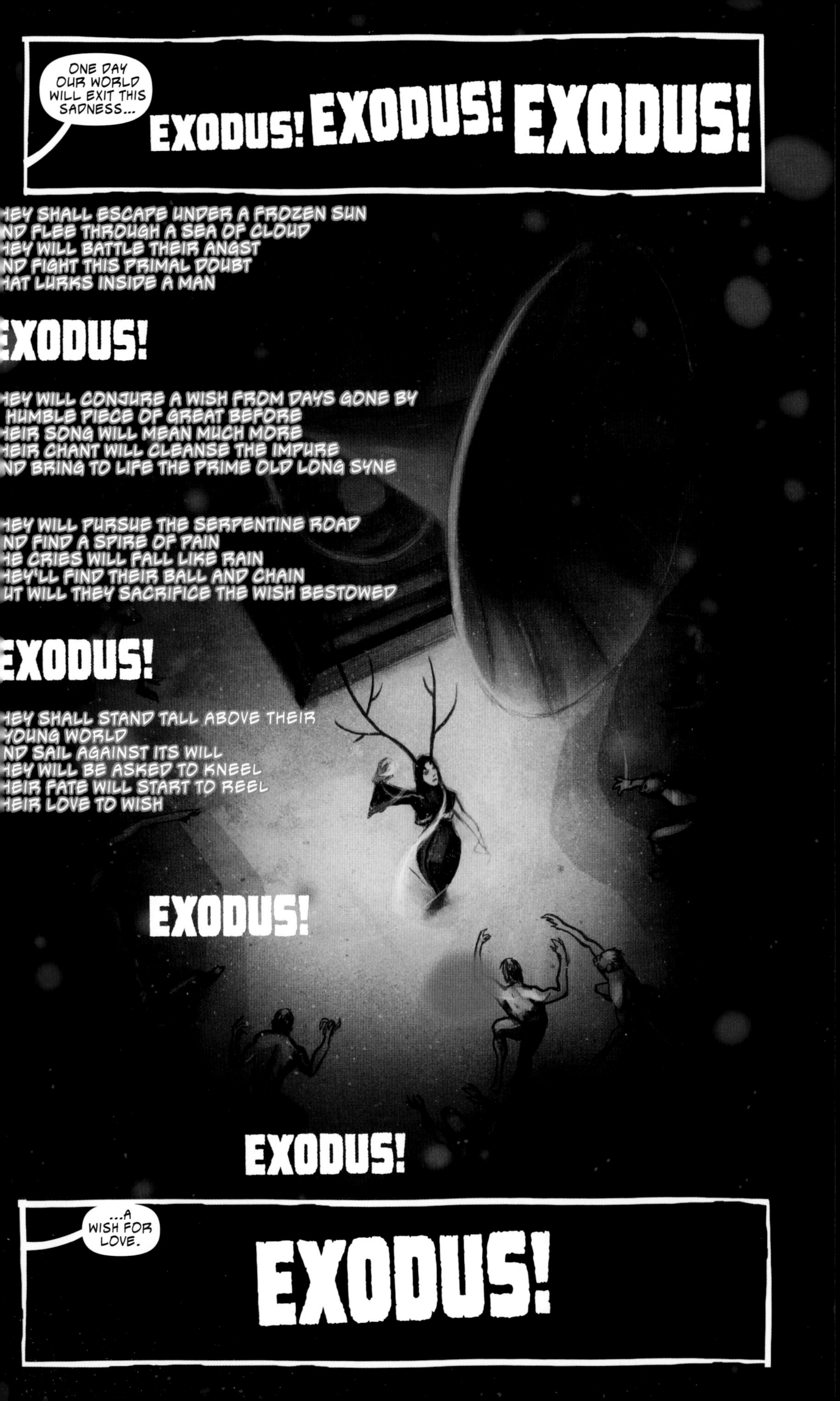
ONE DAY OUR WORLD WILL EXIT THIS SADNESS...
EXODUS! EXODUS! EXODUS!
HEY SHALL ESCAPE UNDER A FROZEN SUN
ND FLEE THROUGH A SEA OF CLOUD
HEY WILL BATTLE THEIR ANGST
ND FIGHT THIS PRIMAL DOUBT
HAT LURKS INSIDE A MAN
EXODUS!
HEY WILL CONJURE A WISH FROM DAYS GONE BY
HUMBLE PIECE OF GREAT BEFORE
HEIR SONG WILL MEAN MUCH MORE
HEIR CHANT WILL CLEANSE THE IMPURE
ND BRING TO LIFE THE PRIME OLD LONG SYNE
HEY WILL PURSUE THE SERPENTINE ROAD
ND FIND A SPIRE OF PAIN
HE CRIES WILL FALL LIKE RAIN
HEY'LL FIND THEIR BALL AND CHAIN
UT WILL THEY SACRIFICE THE WISH BESTOWED
EXODUS!
HEY SHALL STAND TALL ABOVE THEIR YOUNG WORLD
ND SAIL AGAINST ITS WILL
HEY WILL BE ASKED TO KNEEL
HEIR FATE WILL START TO REEL
HEIR LOVE TO WISH
EXODUS!
EXODUS!
...A WISH FOR LOVE.
EXODUS!

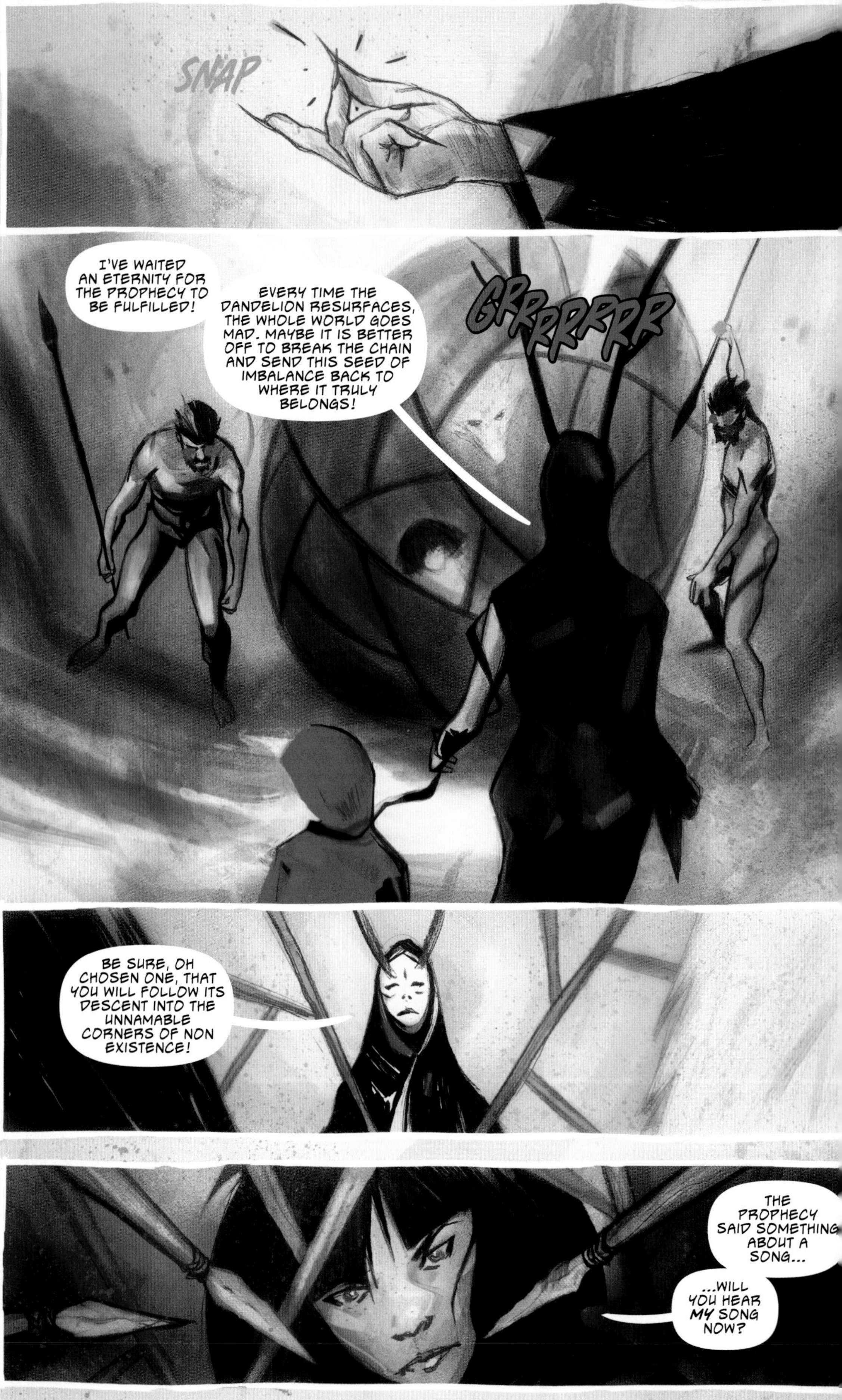
SNAP
I'VE WAITED AN ETERNITY FOR THE PROPHECY TO BE FULFILLED!
EVERY TIME THE DANDELION RESURFACES, THE WHOLE WORLD GOES MAD. MAYBE IT IS BETTER OFF TO BREAK THE CHAIN AND SEND THIS SEED OF IMBALANCE BACK TO WHERE IT TRULY BELONGS!
GRRRRRRR
BE SURE, OH CHOSEN ONE, THAT YOU WILL FOLLOW ITS DESCENT INTO THE UNNAMABLE CORNERS OF NON EXISTENCE!
THE PROPHECY SAID SOMETHING ABOUT A SONG...
...WILL YOU HEAR MY SONG NOW?

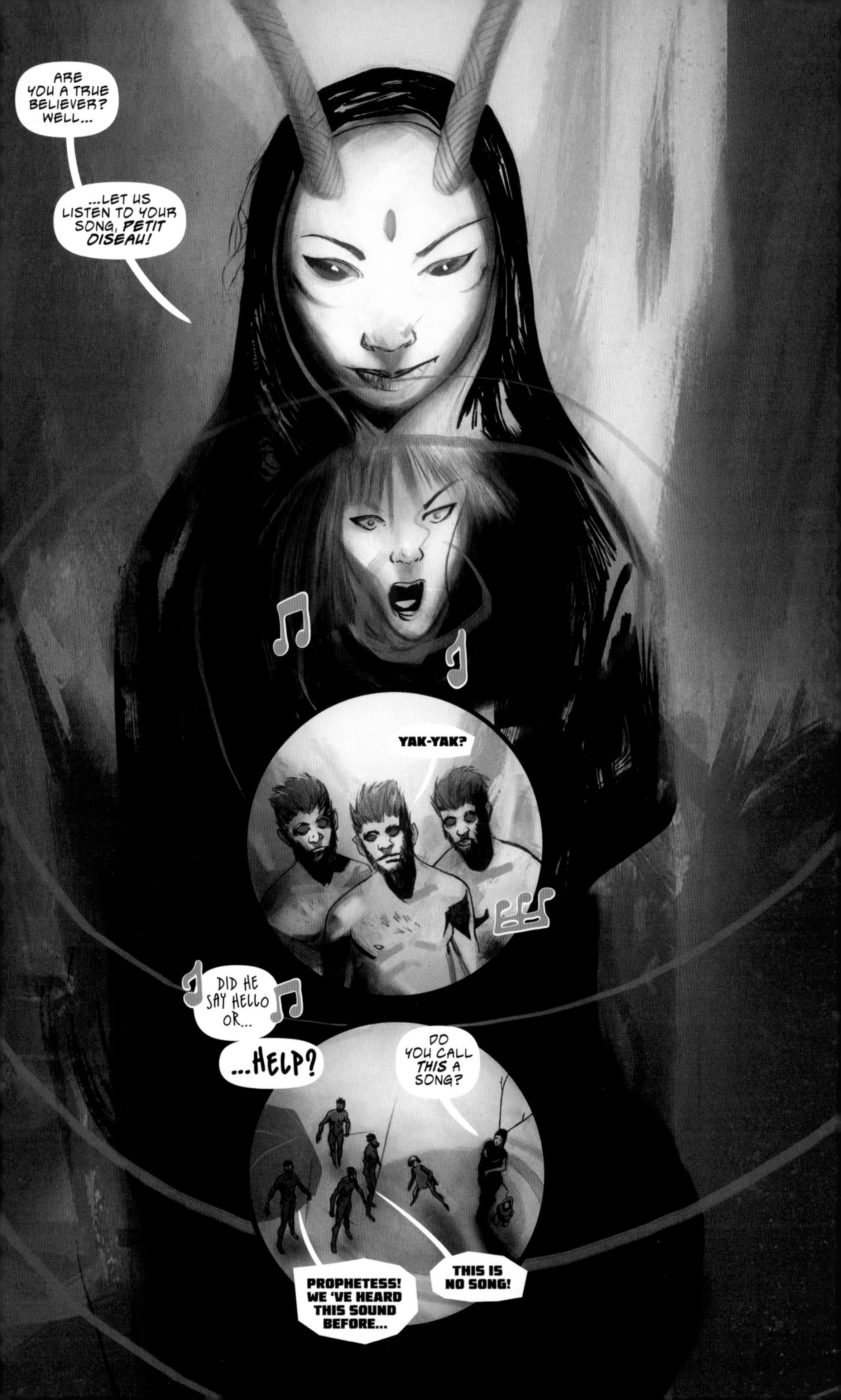
ARE YOU A TRUE BELIEVER? WELL...
...LET US LISTEN TO YOUR SONG, PETIT OISEAU!
YAK-YAK?
DID HE SAY HELLO OR...
...HELP?
DO YOU CALL THIS A SONG?
PROPHETESS! WE 'VE HEARD THIS SOUND BEFORE...
THIS IS NO SONG!

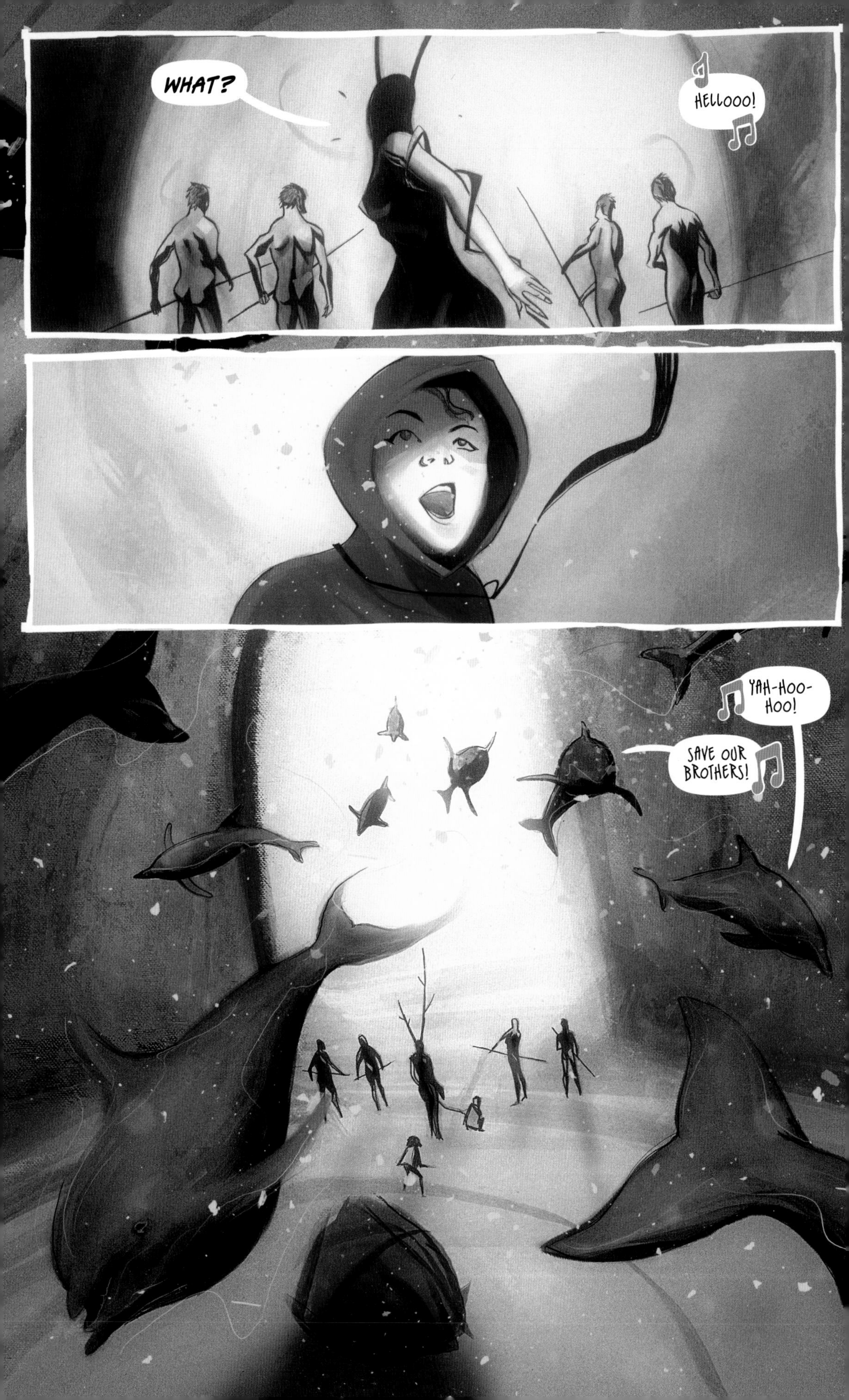
WHAT?
HELLOOO!
YAH-HOO-HOO!
SAVE OUR BROTHERS!

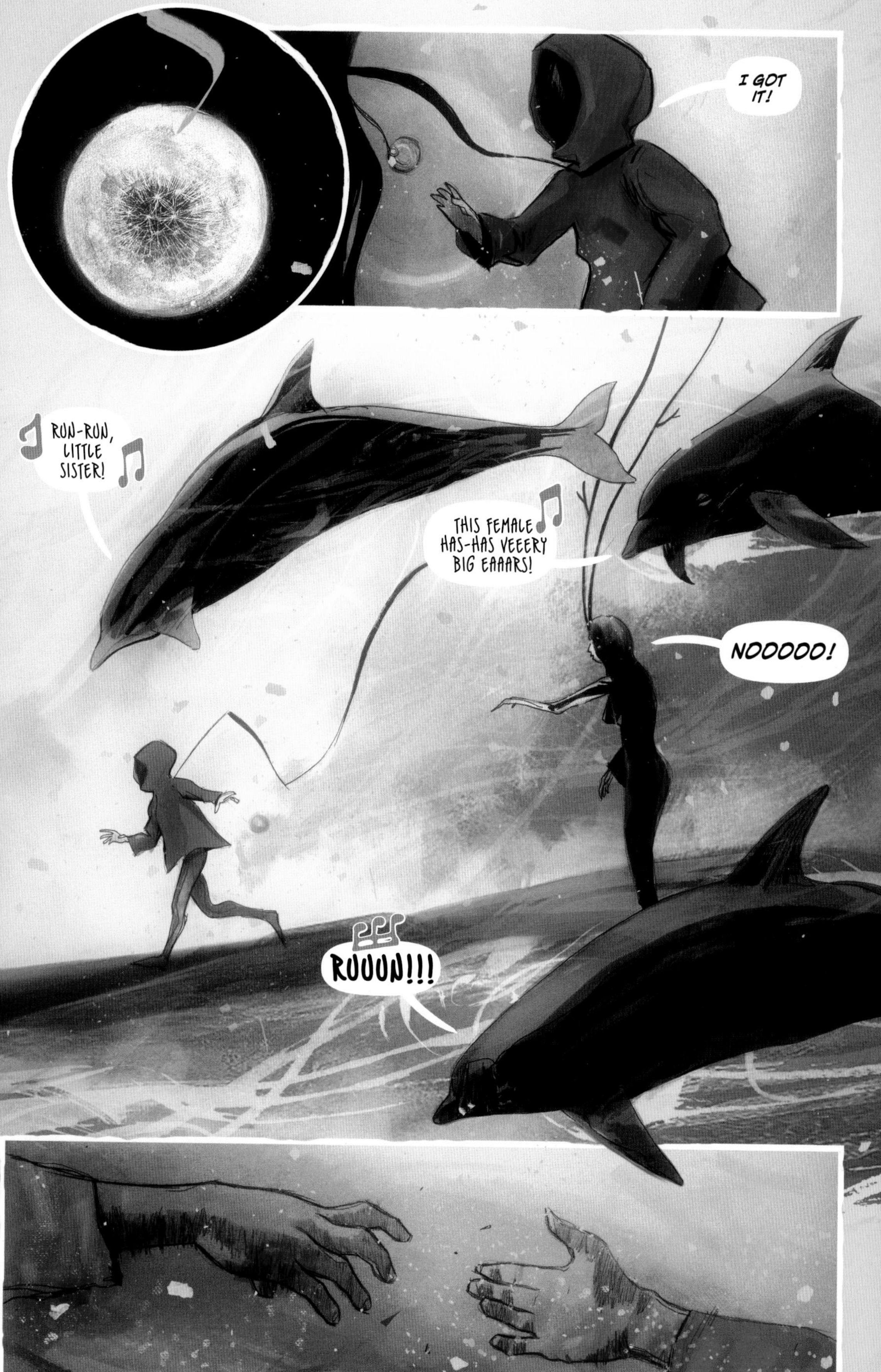
I GOT IT!
RUN-RUN, LITTLE SISTER!
THIS FEMALE HAS-HAS VEEERY BIG EAAARS!
NOOOOO!
RUUUN!!!

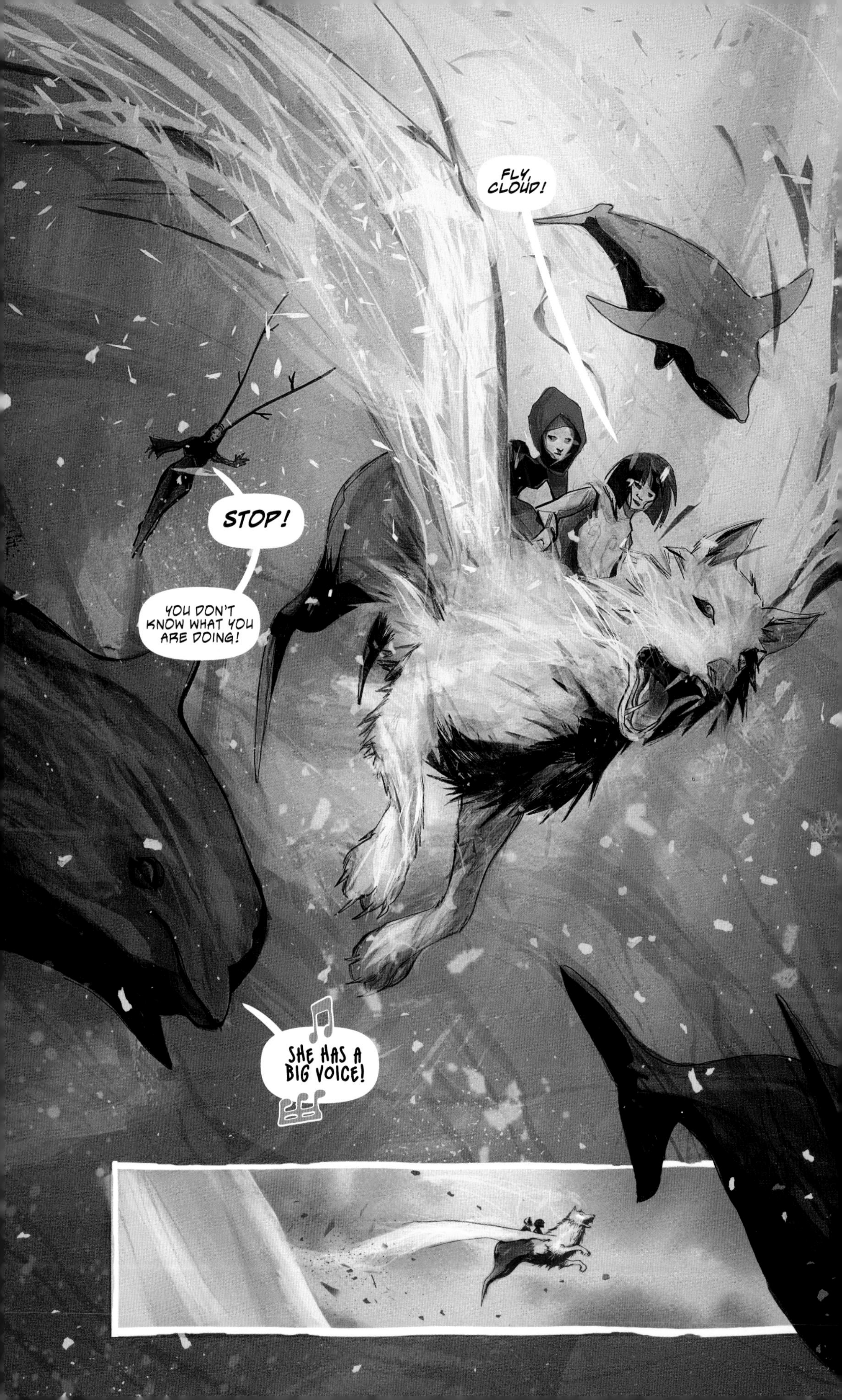
FLY, CLOUD!
STOP!
YOU DON'T KNOW WHAT YOU ARE DOING!
SHE HAS A BIG VOICE!

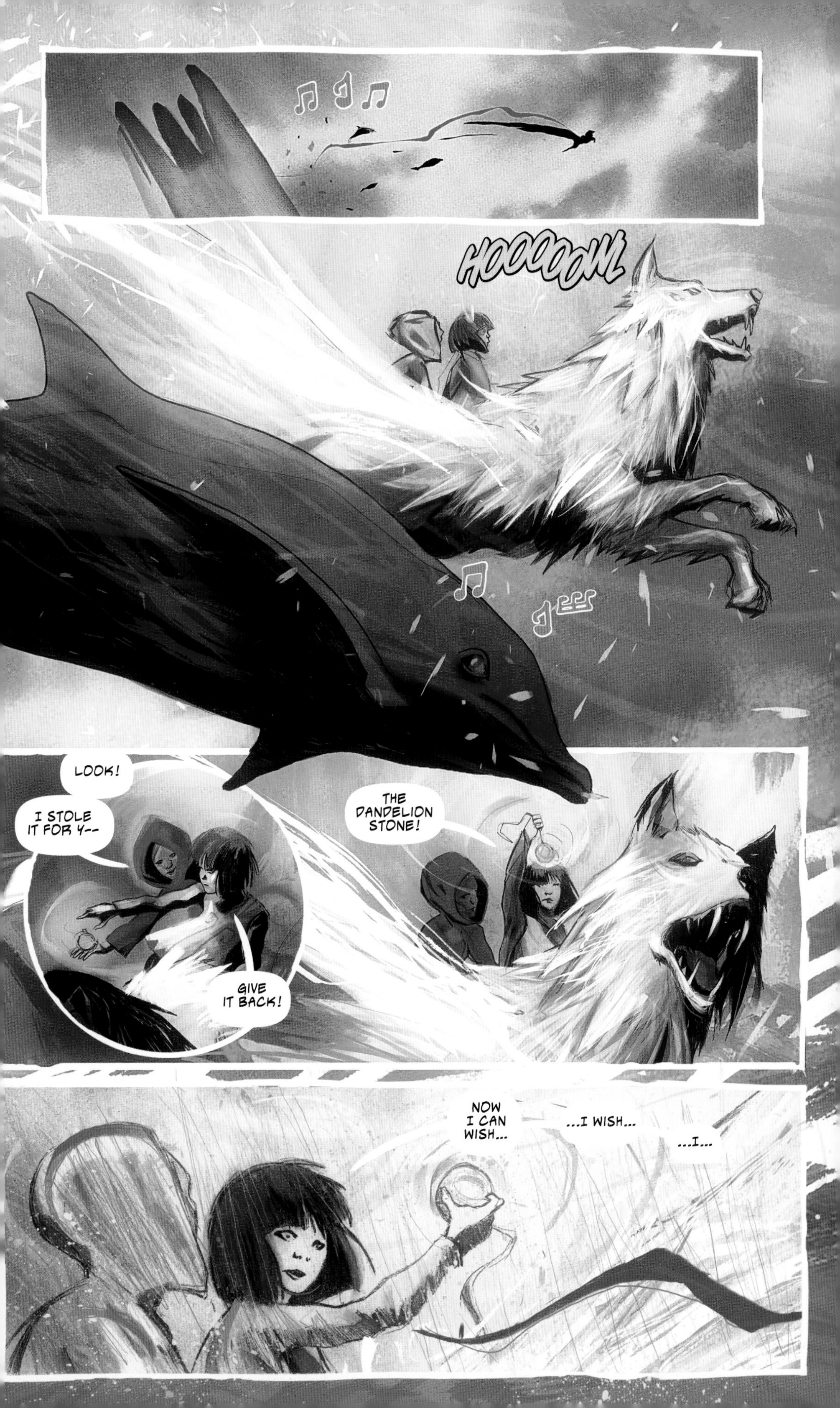
HOOOOOWL
LOOK!
I STOLE IT FOR Y--
GIVE IT BACK!
THE DANDELION STONE!
NOW I CAN WISH...
...I WISH...
...I...

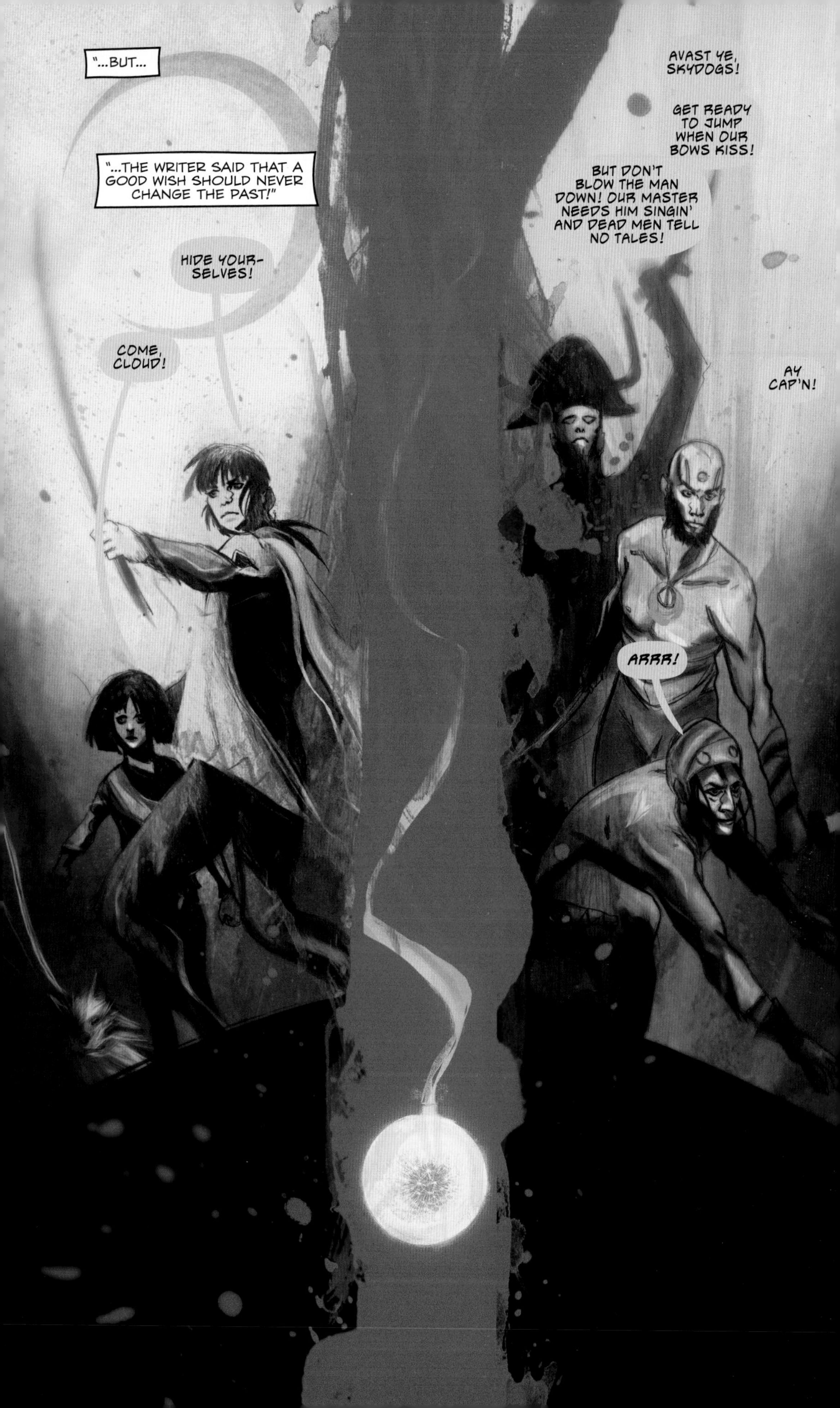
"...BUT...
"...THE WRITER SAID THAT A GOOD WISH SHOULD NEVER CHANGE THE PAST!"
HIDE YOURSELVES!
COME, CLOUD!
AVAST YE, SKYDOGS!
GET READY TO JUMP WHEN OUR BOWS KISS!
BUT DON'T BLOW THE MAN DOWN! OUR MASTER NEEDS HIM SINGIN' AND DEAD MEN TELL NO TALES!
AY CAP'N!
ARRR!

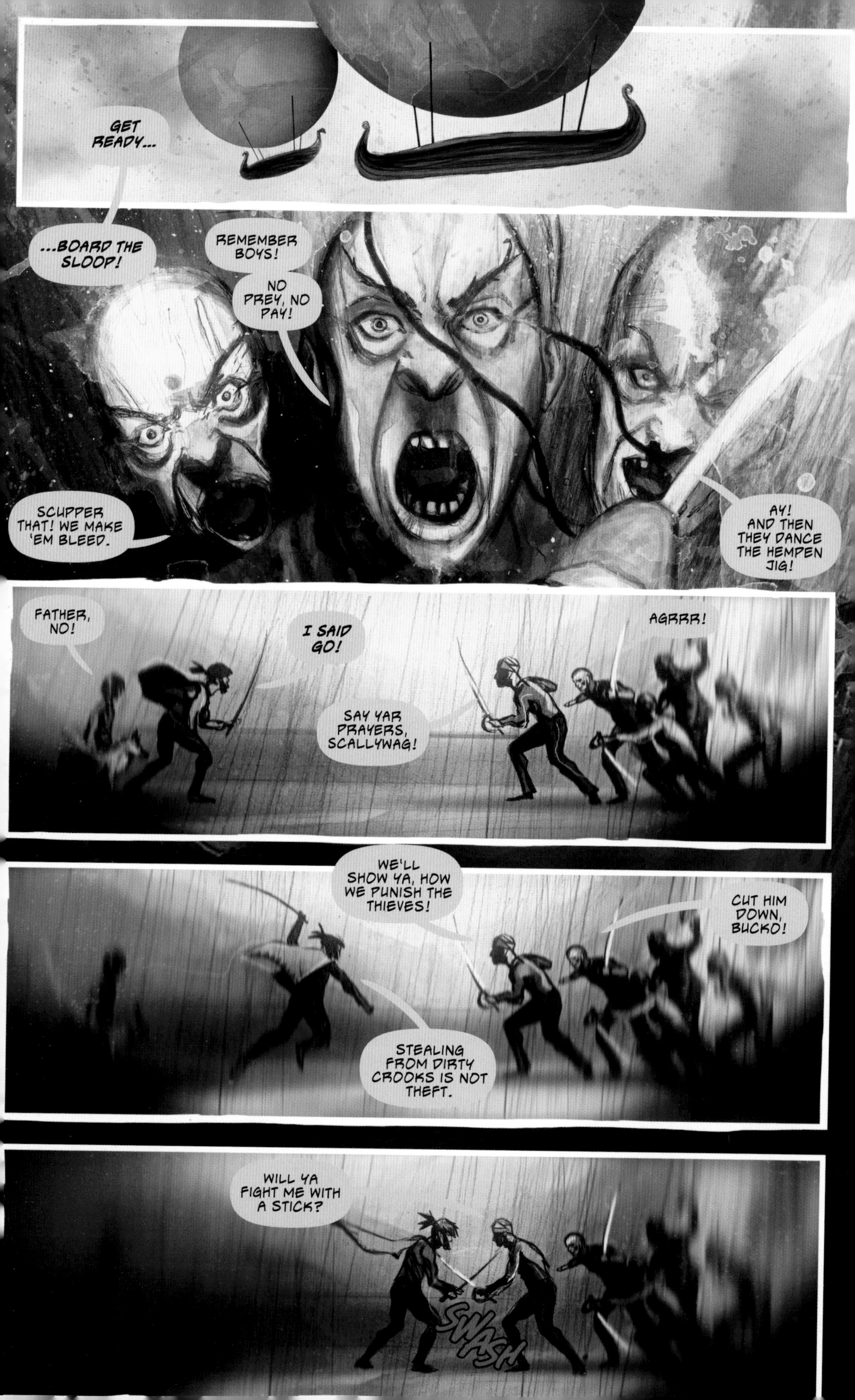
GET READY...
...BOARD THE SLOOP!
REMEMBER BOYS!
NO PREY, NO PAY!
SCUPPER THAT! WE MAKE 'EM BLEED.
AY! AND THEN THEY DANCE THE HEMPEN JIG!
FATHER, NO!
I SAID GO!
AGRRR!
SAY YAR PRAYERS, SCALLYWAG!
WE'LL SHOW YA, HOW WE PUNISH THE THIEVES!
CUT HIM DOWN, BUCKO!
STEALING FROM DIRTY CROOKS IS NOT THEFT.
WILL YA FIGHT ME WITH A STICK?
SWASH

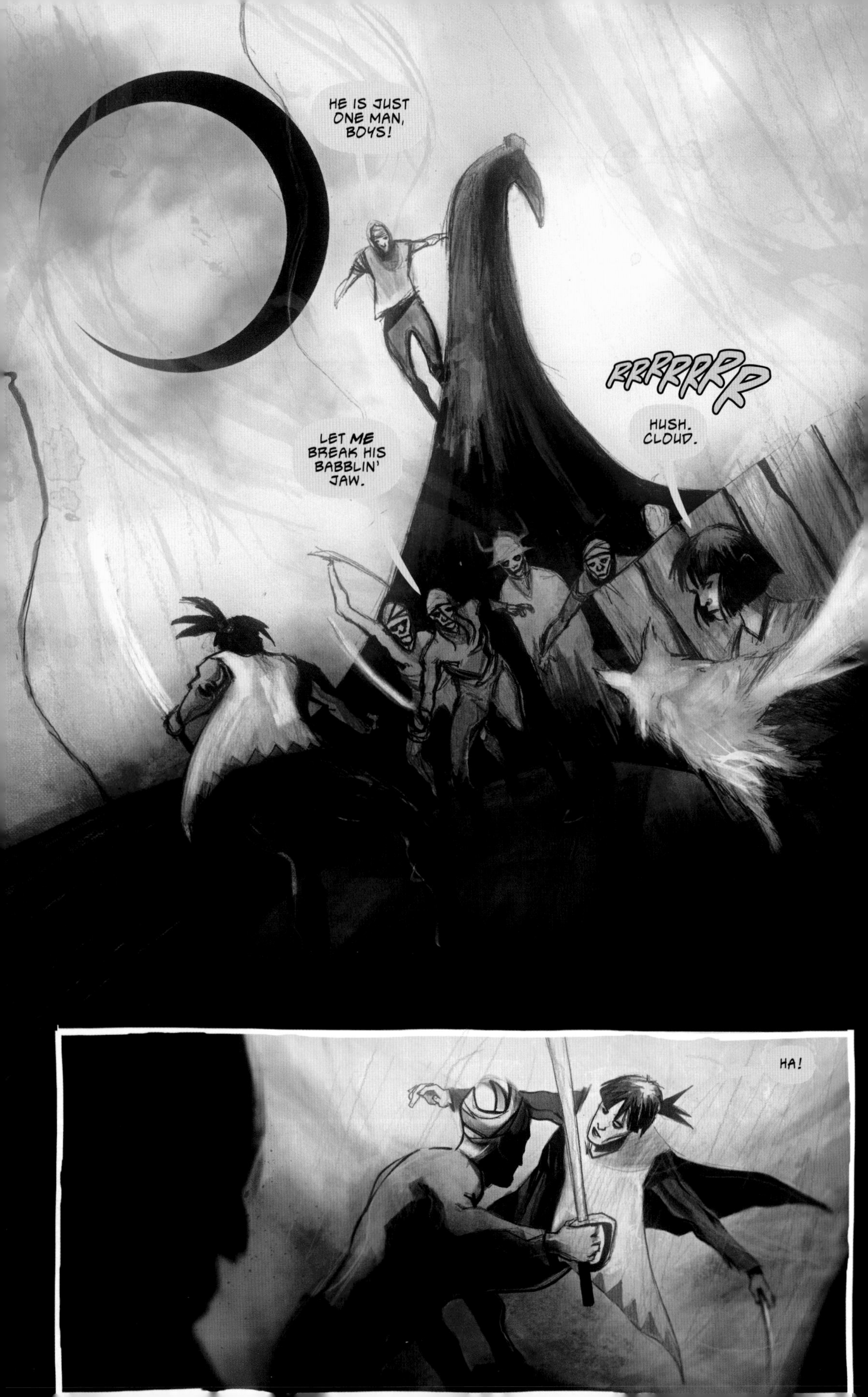
HE IS JUST ONE MAN, BOYS!
RRRRRRR
LET ME BREAK HIS BABBLIN' JAW.
HUSH. CLOUD.
HA!

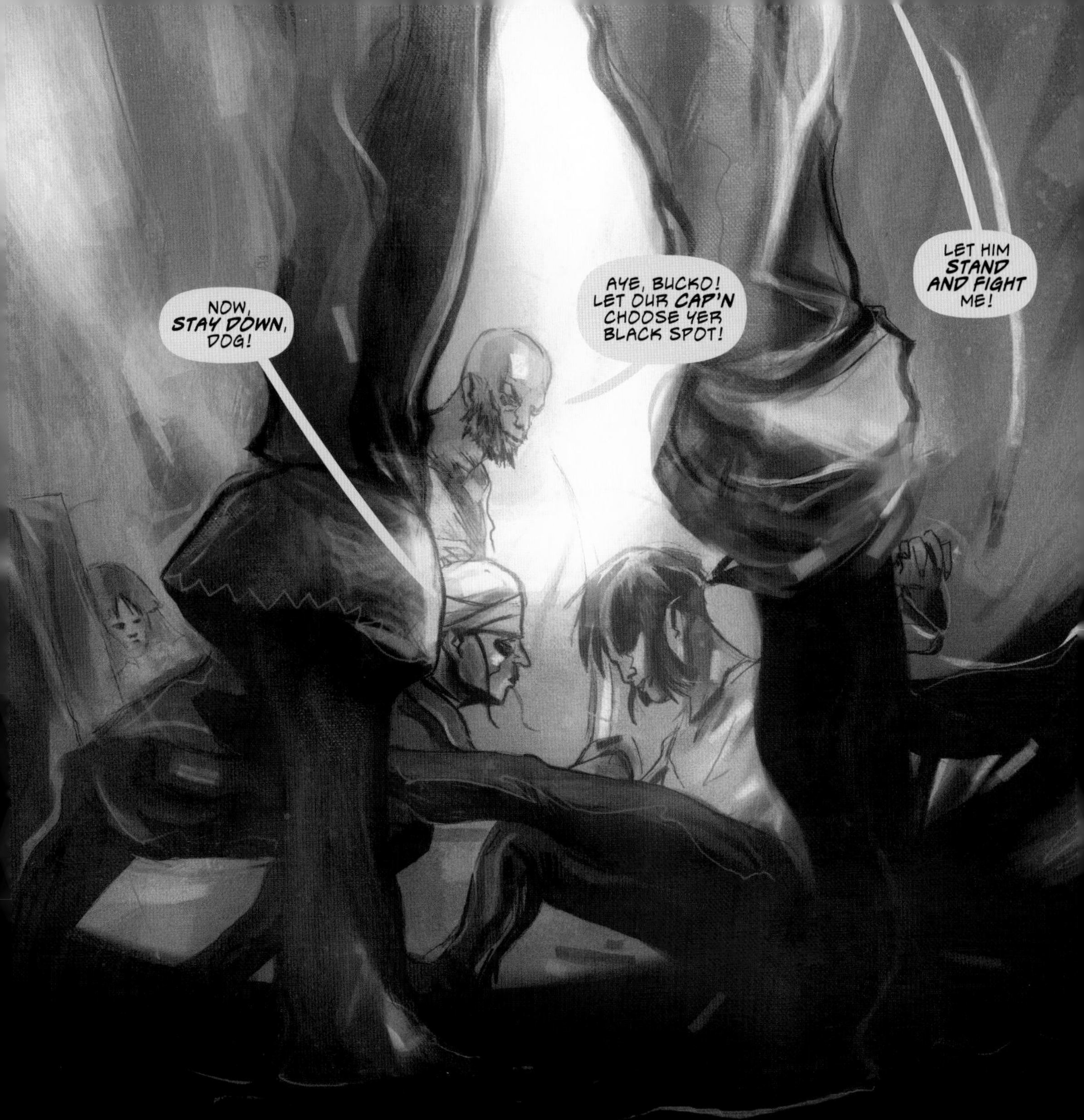
NOW, STAY DOWN, DOG!
AYE, BUCKO! LET OUR CAP'N CHOOSE YER BLACK SPOT!
LET HIM STAND AND FIGHT ME!

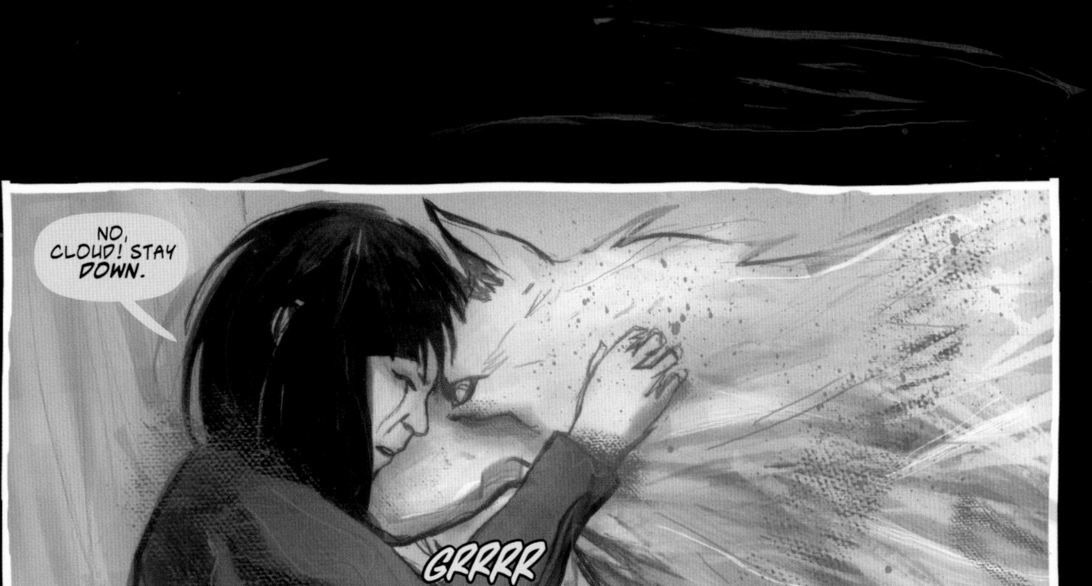
NO, CLOUD! STAY DOWN.
GRRRR

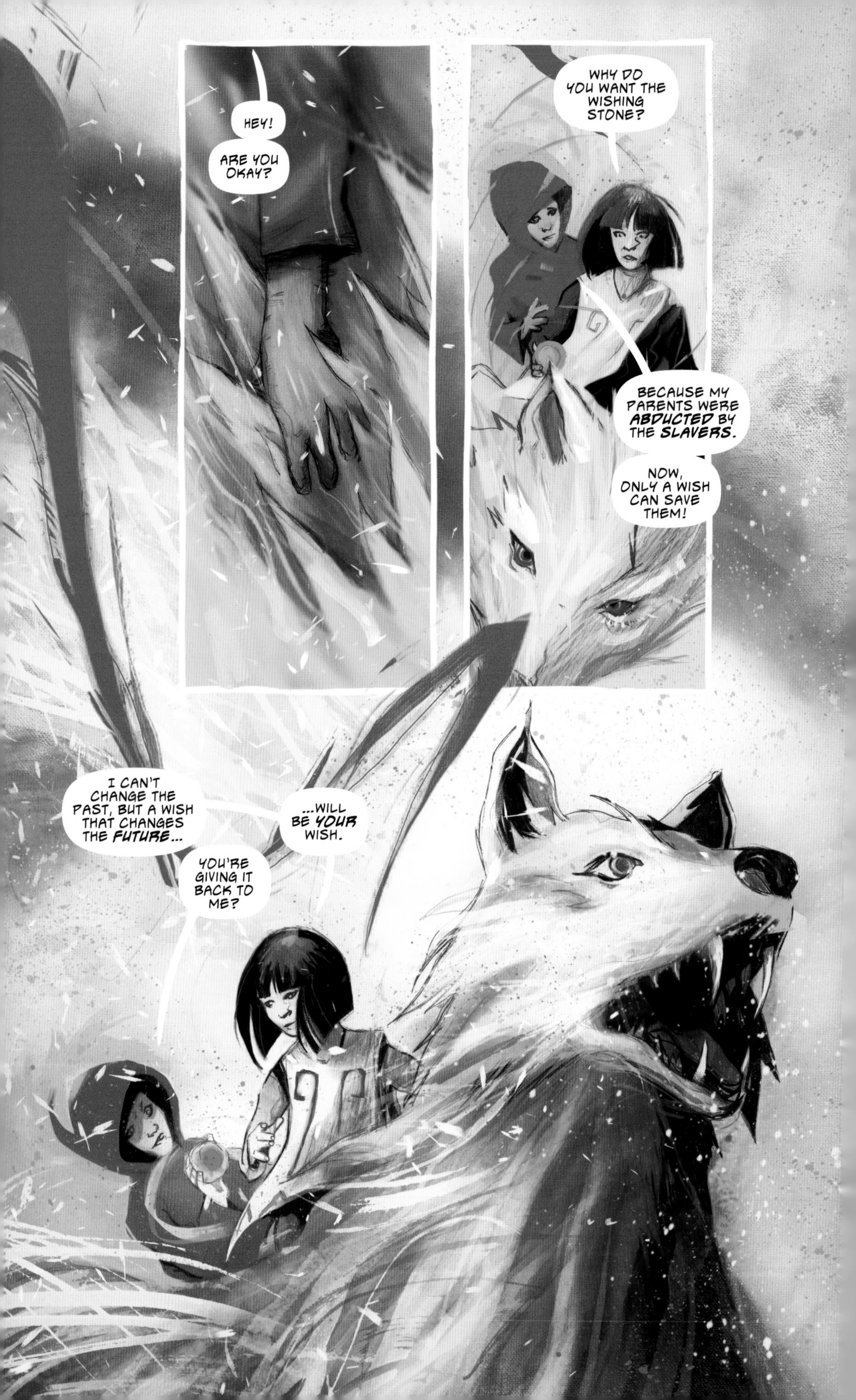
HEY!
ARE YOU OKAY?
WHY DO YOU WANT THE WISHING STONE?
BECAUSE MY PARENTS WERE ABDUCTED BY THE SLAVERS.
NOW, ONLY A WISH CAN SAVE THEM!
I CAN'T CHANGE THE PAST, BUT A WISH THAT CHANGES THE FUTURE...
...WILL BE YOUR WISH.
YOU'RE GIVING IT BACK TO ME?

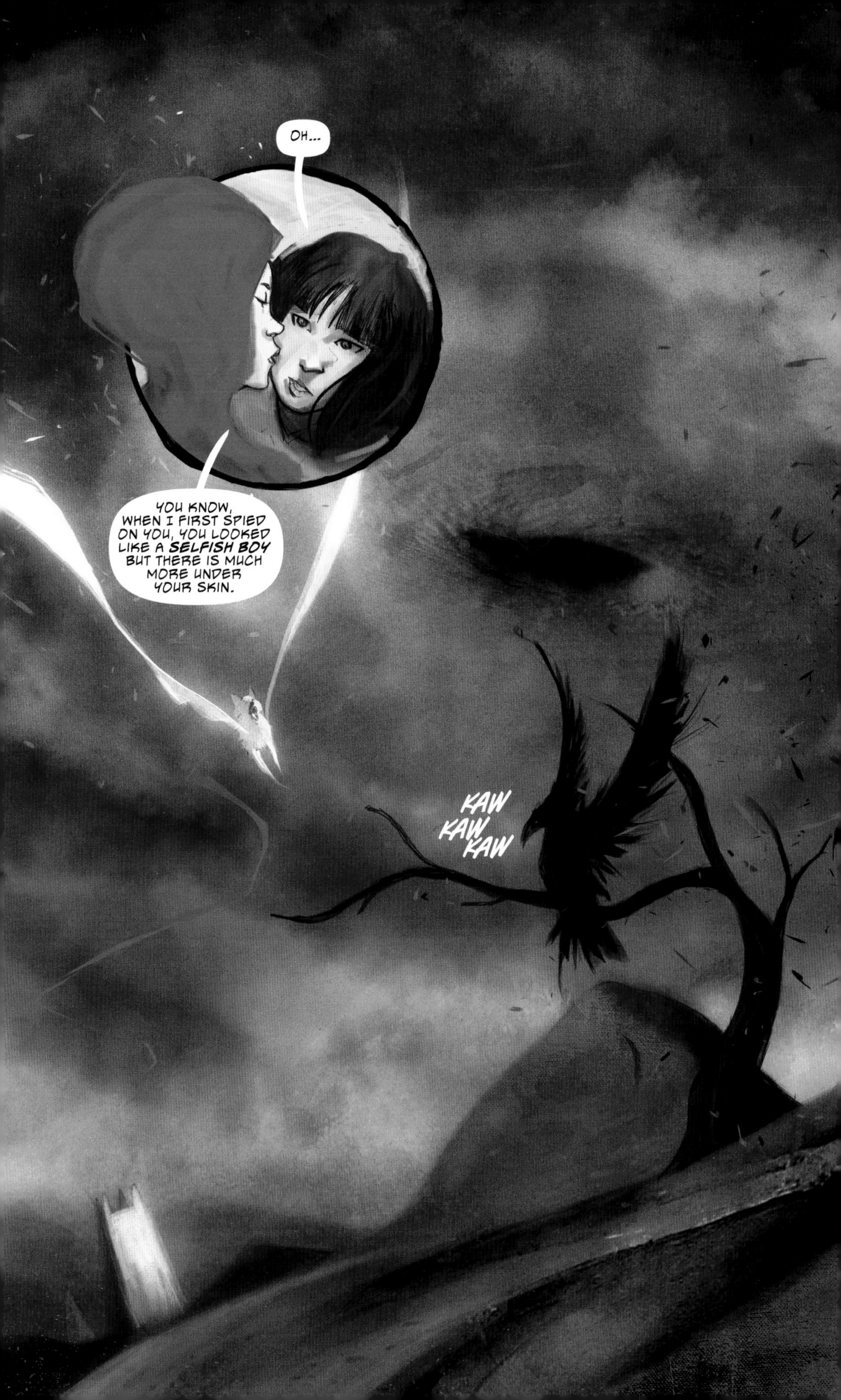
OH...
YOU KNOW, WHEN I FIRST SPIED ON YOU, YOU LOOKED LIKE A **SELFISH BOY** BUT THERE IS MUCH MORE UNDER YOUR SKIN.
KAW KAW KAW

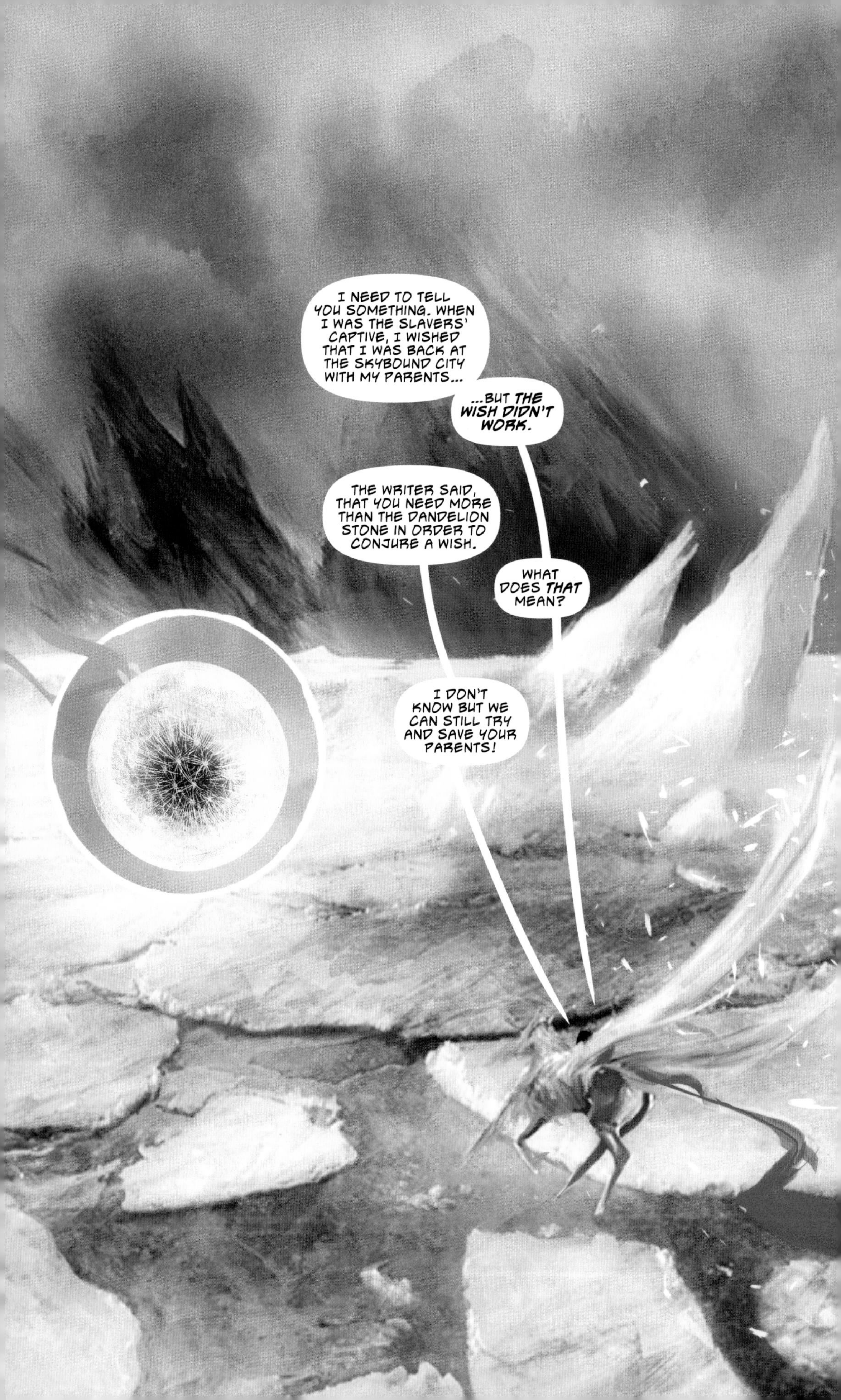
I NEED TO TELL YOU SOMETHING. WHEN I WAS THE SLAVERS' CAPTIVE, I WISHED THAT I WAS BACK AT THE SKYBOUND CITY WITH MY PARENTS...
...BUT THE WISH DIDN'T WORK.
THE WRITER SAID, THAT YOU NEED MORE THAN THE DANDELION STONE IN ORDER TO CONJURE A WISH.
WHAT DOES THAT MEAN?
I DON'T KNOW BUT WE CAN STILL TRY AND SAVE YOUR PARENTS!

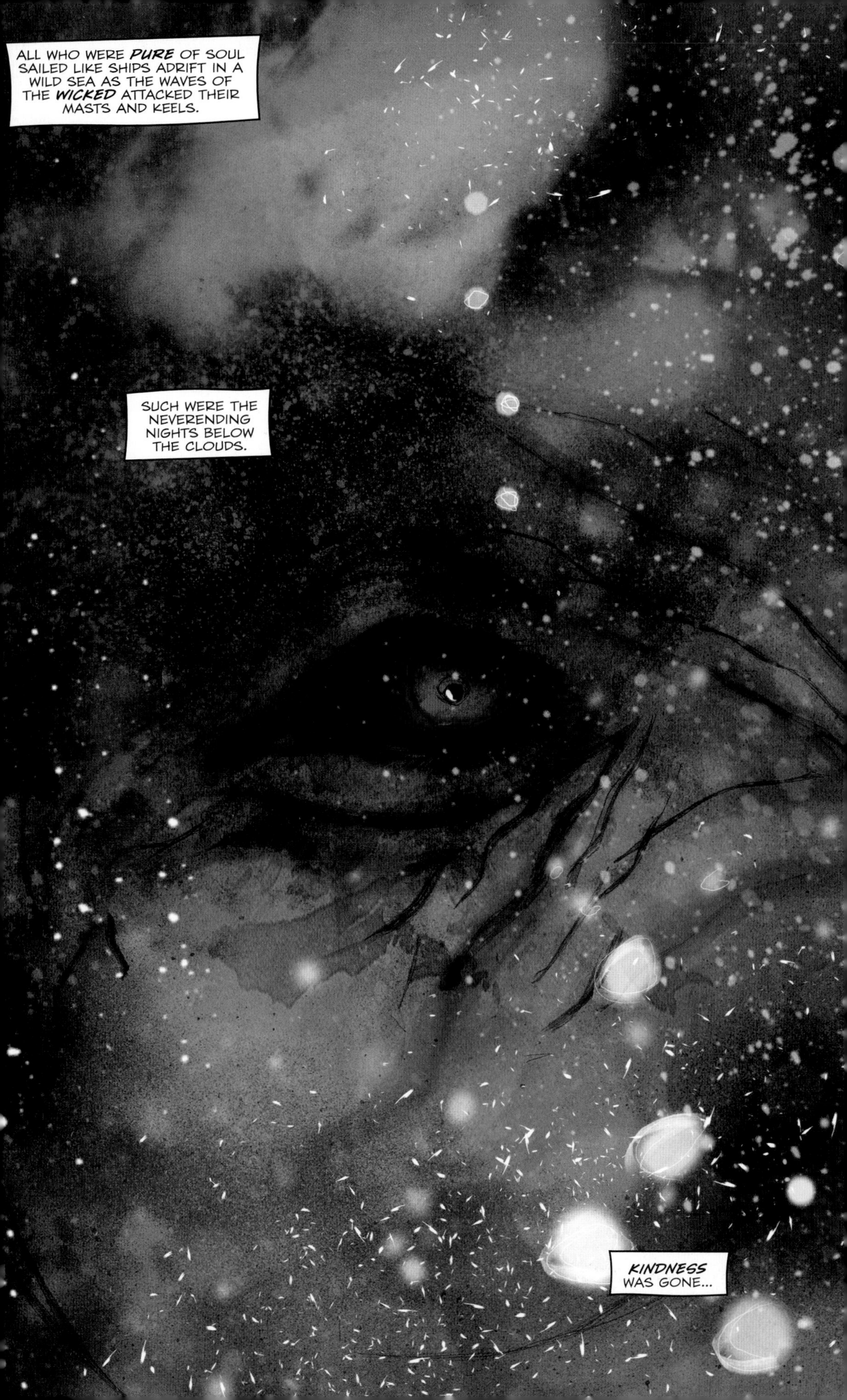
ALL WHO WERE PURE OF SOUL SAILED LIKE SHIPS ADRIFT IN A WILD SEA AS THE WAVES OF THE WICKED ATTACKED THEIR MASTS AND KEELS.
SUCH WERE THE NEVERENDING NIGHTS BELOW THE CLOUDS.
KINDNESS WAS GONE...

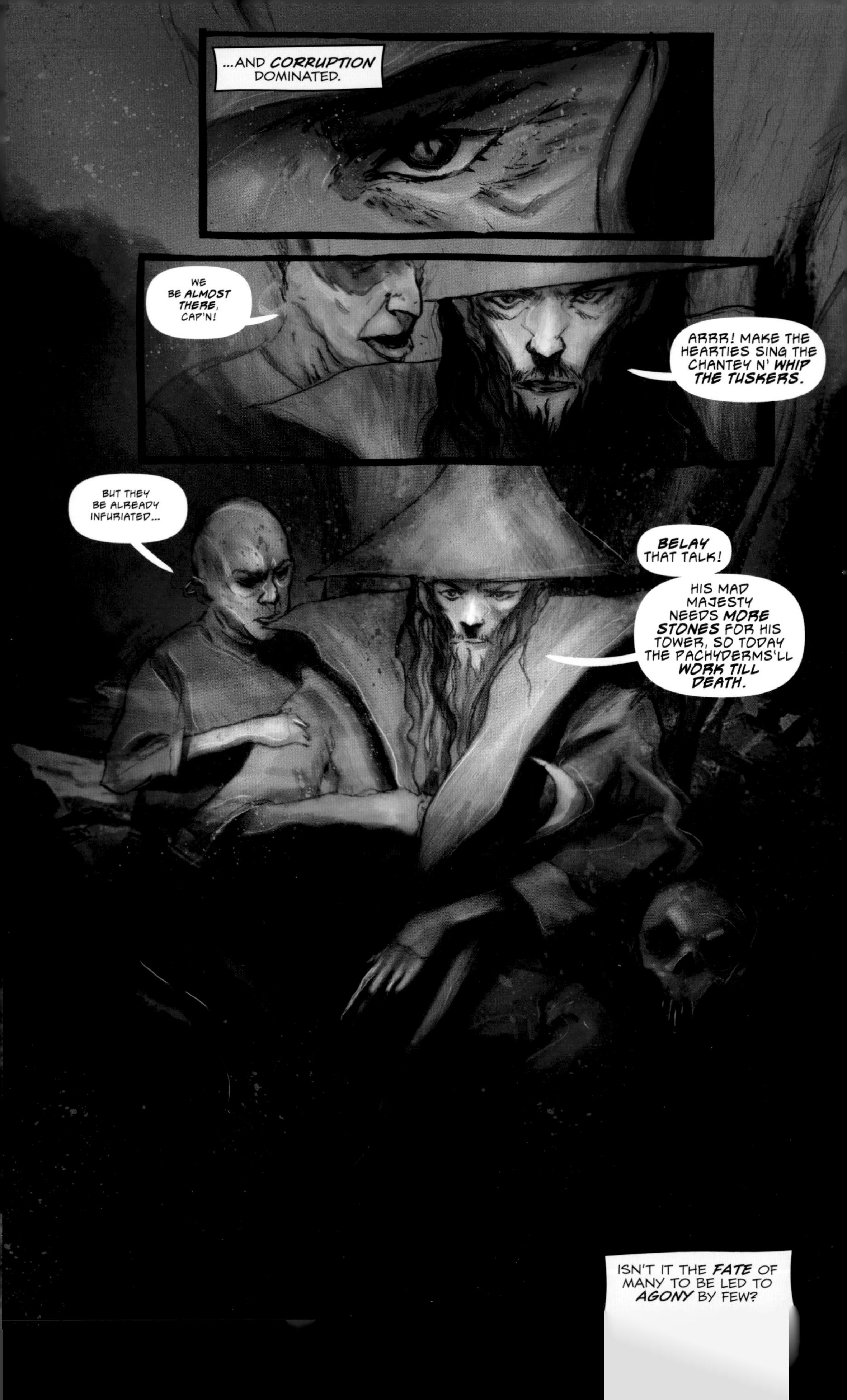

...AND CORRUPTION DOMINATED.
WE BE ALMOST THERE, CAP'N!
ARRR! MAKE THE HEARTIES SING THE CHANTEY N' WHIP THE TUSKERS.
BUT THEY BE ALREADY INFURIATED...
BELAY THAT TALK!
HIS MAD MAJESTY NEEDS MORE STONES FOR HIS TOWER, SO TODAY THE PACHYDERMS'LL WORK TILL DEATH.
ISN'T IT THE FATE OF MANY TO BE LED TO AGONY BY FEW?

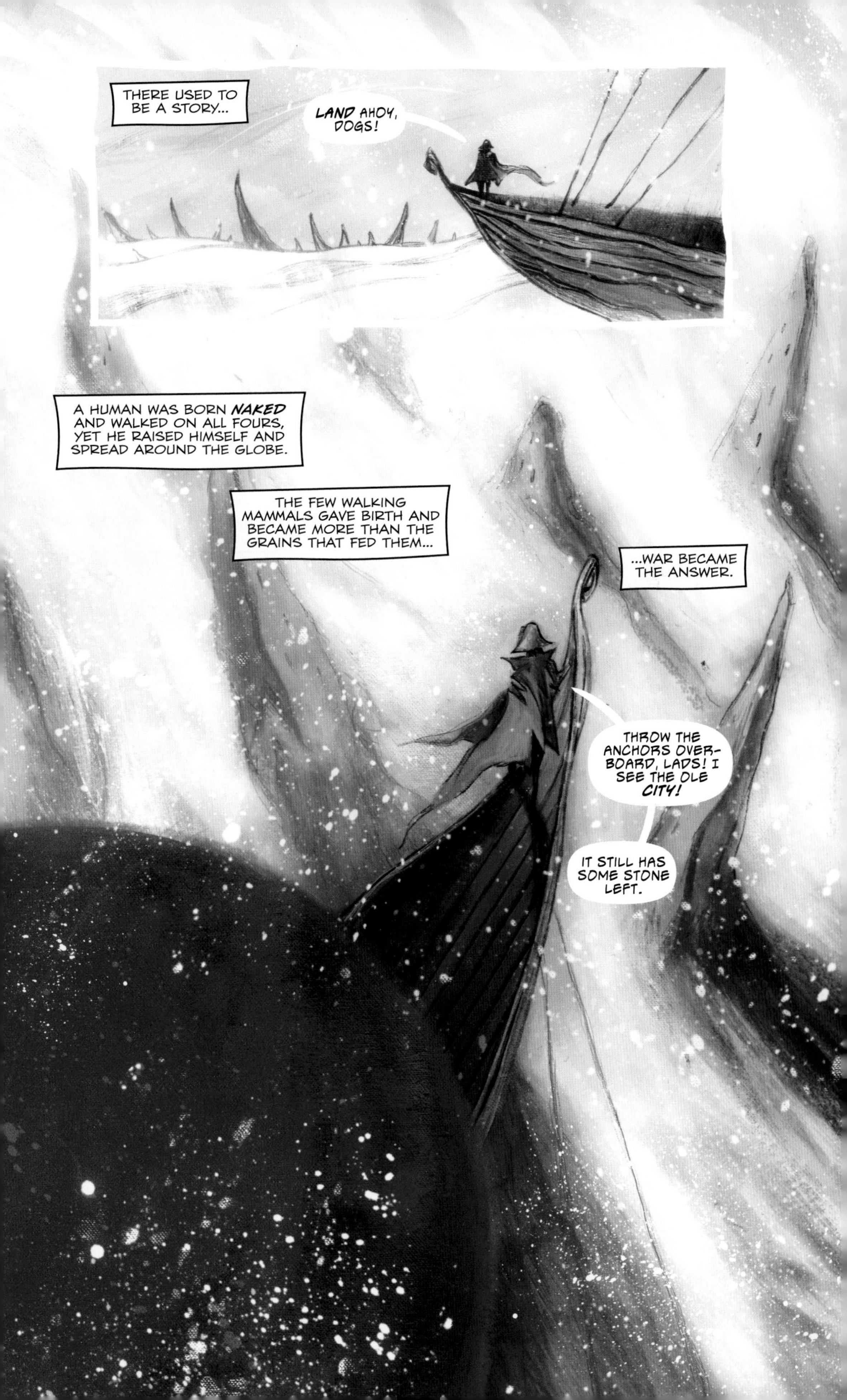
THERE USED TO BE A STORY...
LAND AHOY, DOGS!
A HUMAN WAS BORN NAKED AND WALKED ON ALL FOURS, YET HE RAISED HIMSELF AND SPREAD AROUND THE GLOBE.
THE FEW WALKING MAMMALS GAVE BIRTH AND BECAME MORE THAN THE GRAINS THAT FED THEM...
...WAR BECAME THE ANSWER.
THROW THE ANCHORS OVER-BOARD, LADS! I SEE THE OLE CITY!
IT STILL HAS SOME STONE LEFT.

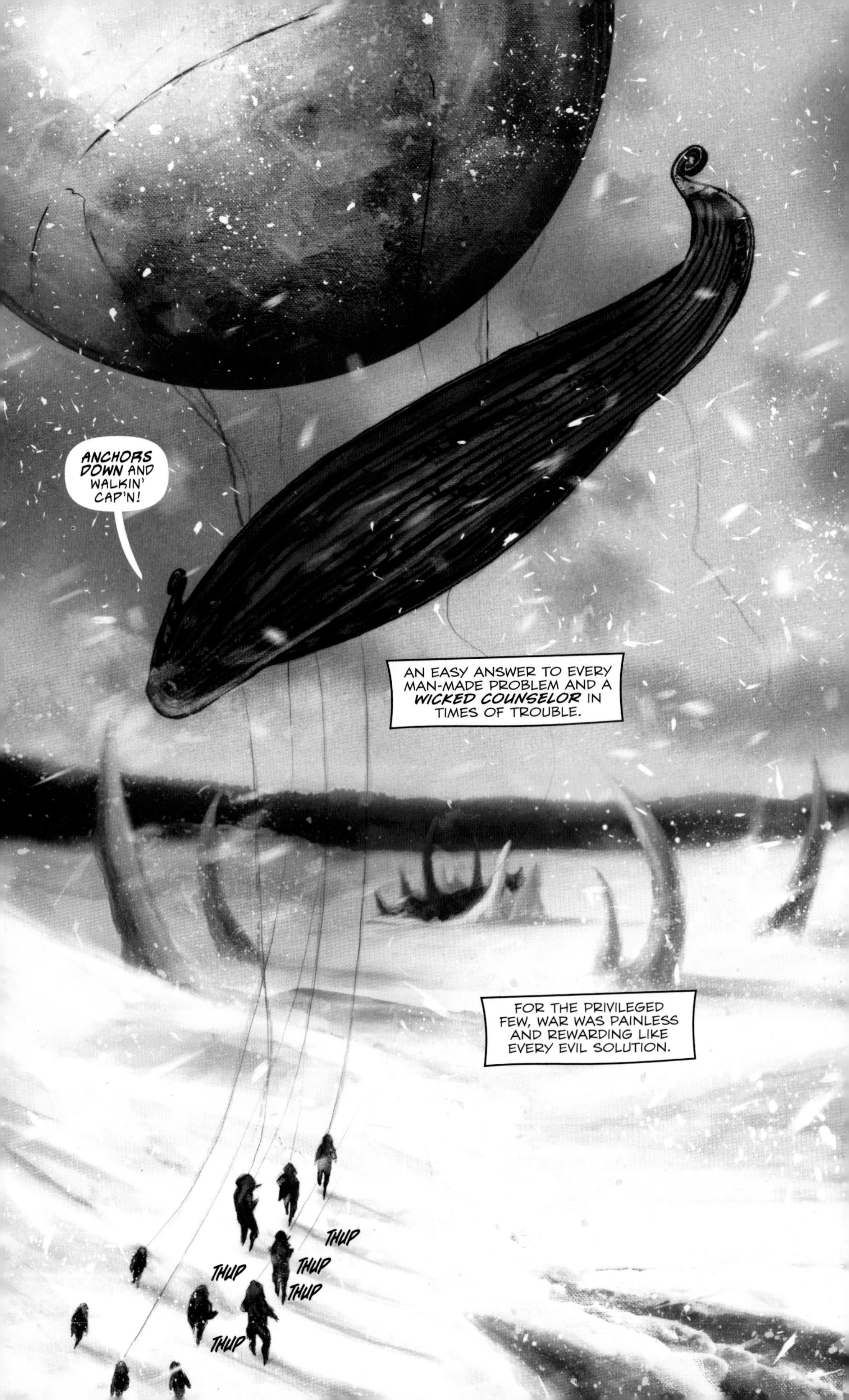
ANCHORS DOWN AND WALKIN' CAP'N!
AN EASY ANSWER TO EVERY MAN-MADE PROBLEM AND A WICKED COUNSELOR IN TIMES OF TROUBLE.
FOR THE PRIVILEGED FEW, WAR WAS PAINLESS AND REWARDING LIKE EVERY EVIL SOLUTION.
THUP
THUP
THUP
THUP
THUP
THUP

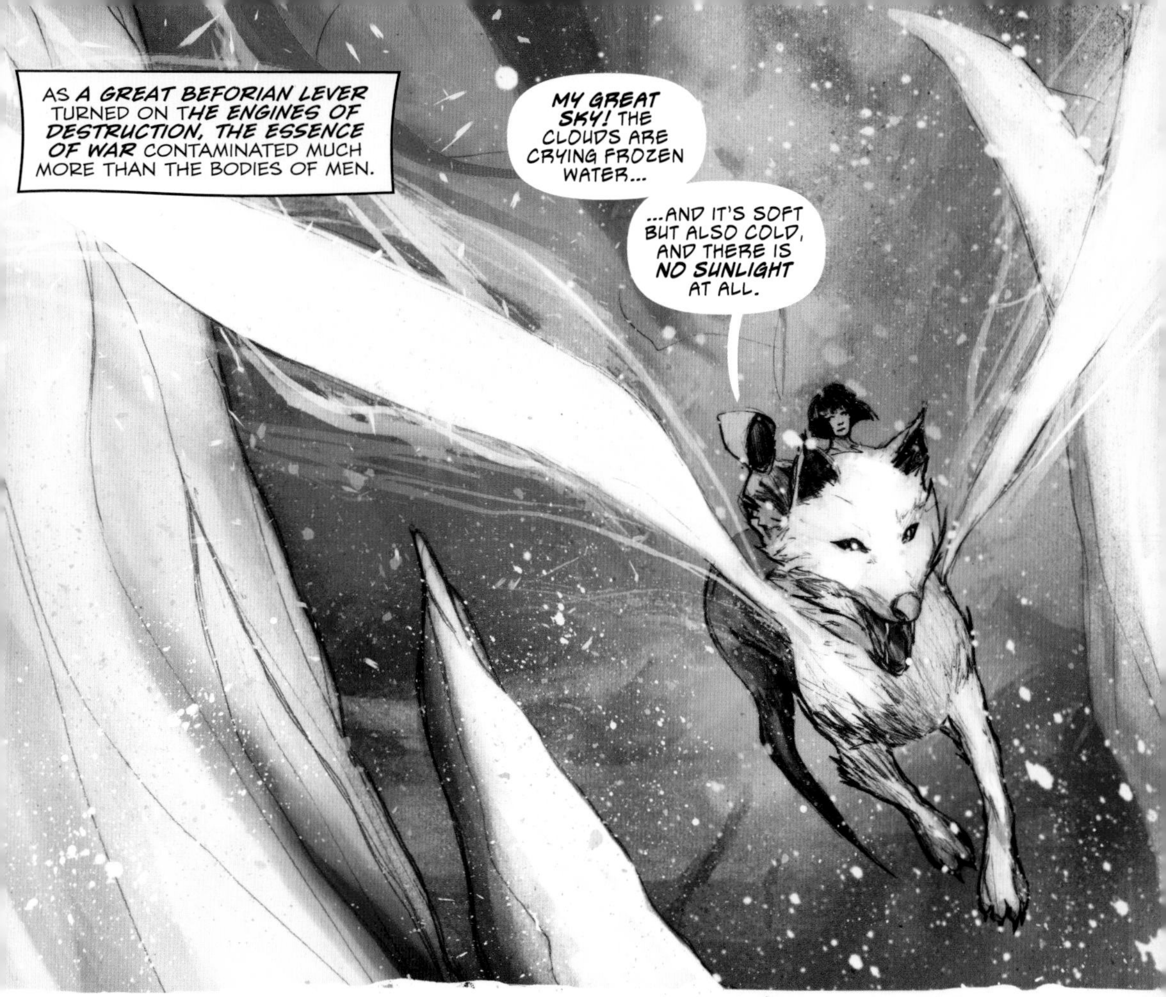
AS A GREAT BEFORIAN LEVER TURNED ON THE ENGINES OF DESTRUCTION, THE ESSENCE OF WAR CONTAMINATED MUCH MORE THAN THE BODIES OF MEN.
MY GREAT SKY! THE CLOUDS ARE CRYING FROZEN WATER...
...AND IT'S SOFT BUT ALSO COLD, AND THERE IS NO SUNLIGHT AT ALL.

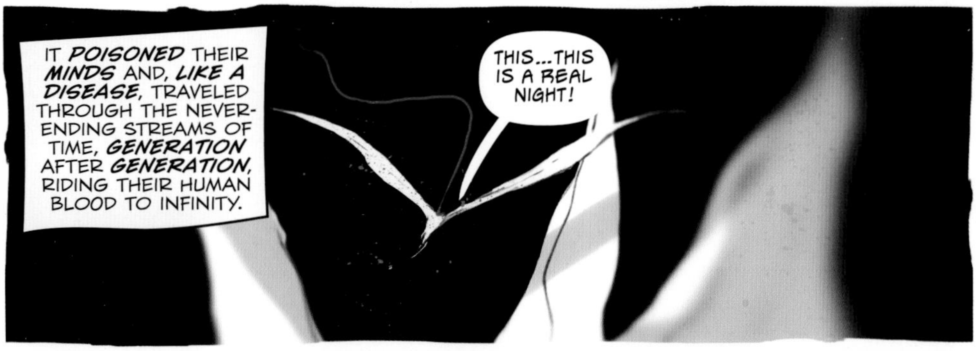
IT POISONED THEIR MINDS AND, LIKE A DISEASE, TRAVELED THROUGH THE NEVER-ENDING STREAMS OF TIME, GENERATION AFTER GENERATION, RIDING THEIR HUMAN BLOOD TO INFINITY.
THIS...THIS IS A REAL NIGHT!

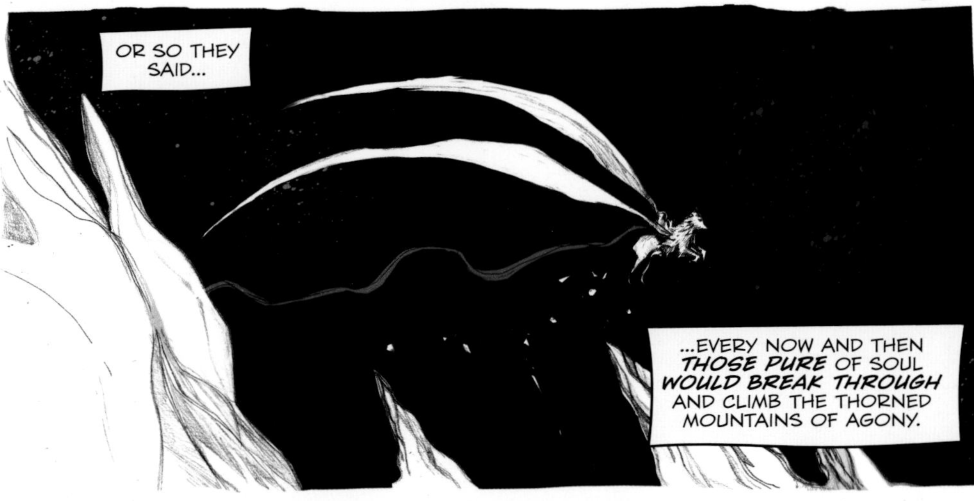
OR SO THEY SAID...
...EVERY NOW AND THEN THOSE PURE OF SOUL WOULD BREAK THROUGH AND CLIMB THE THORNED MOUNTAINS OF AGONY.

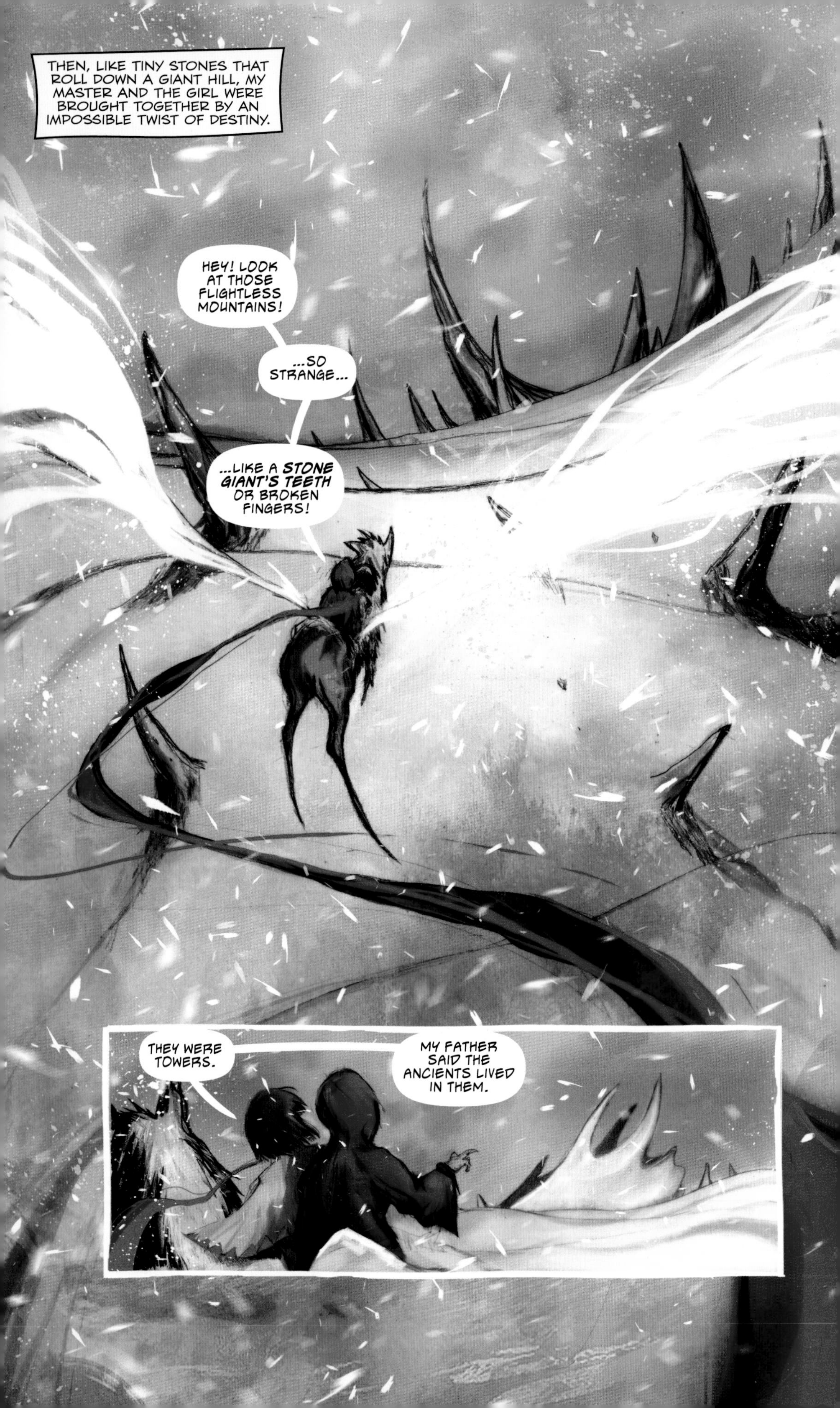
THEN, LIKE TINY STONES THAT ROLL DOWN A GIANT HILL, MY MASTER AND THE GIRL WERE BROUGHT TOGETHER BY AN IMPOSSIBLE TWIST OF DESTINY.
HEY! LOOK AT THOSE FLIGHTLESS MOUNTAINS!
...SO STRANGE...
...LIKE A **STONE GIANT'S TEETH** OR BROKEN FINGERS!
THEY WERE TOWERS.
MY FATHER SAID THE ANCIENTS LIVED IN THEM.

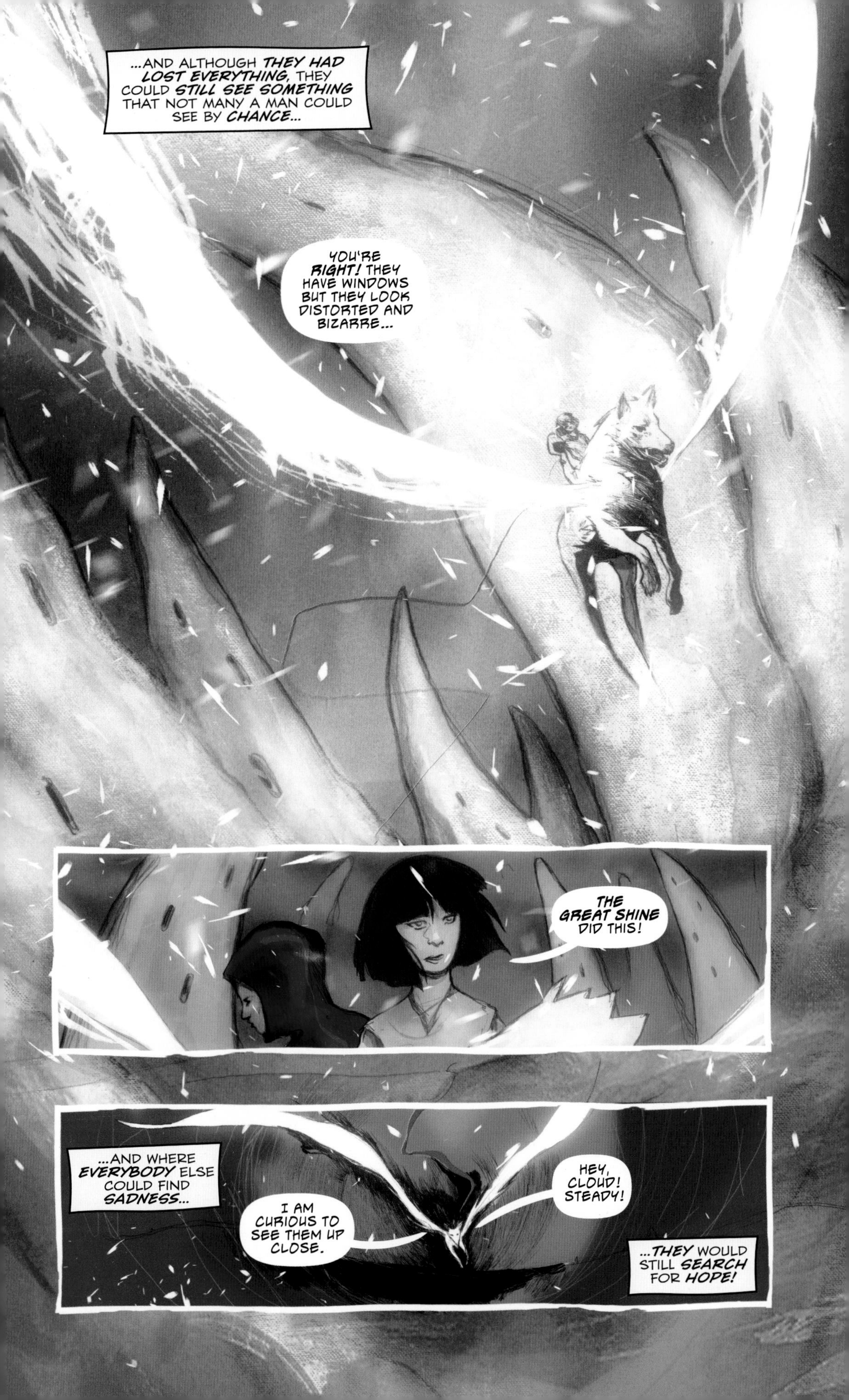
...AND ALTHOUGH THEY HAD LOST EVERYTHING, THEY COULD STILL SEE SOMETHING THAT NOT MANY A MAN COULD SEE BY CHANCE...
YOU'RE RIGHT! THEY HAVE WINDOWS BUT THEY LOOK DISTORTED AND BIZARRE...
THE GREAT SHINE DID THIS!
...AND WHERE EVERYBODY ELSE COULD FIND SADNESS...
HEY, CLOUD! STEADY!
I AM CURIOUS TO SEE THEM UP CLOSE.
...THEY WOULD STILL SEARCH FOR HOPE!

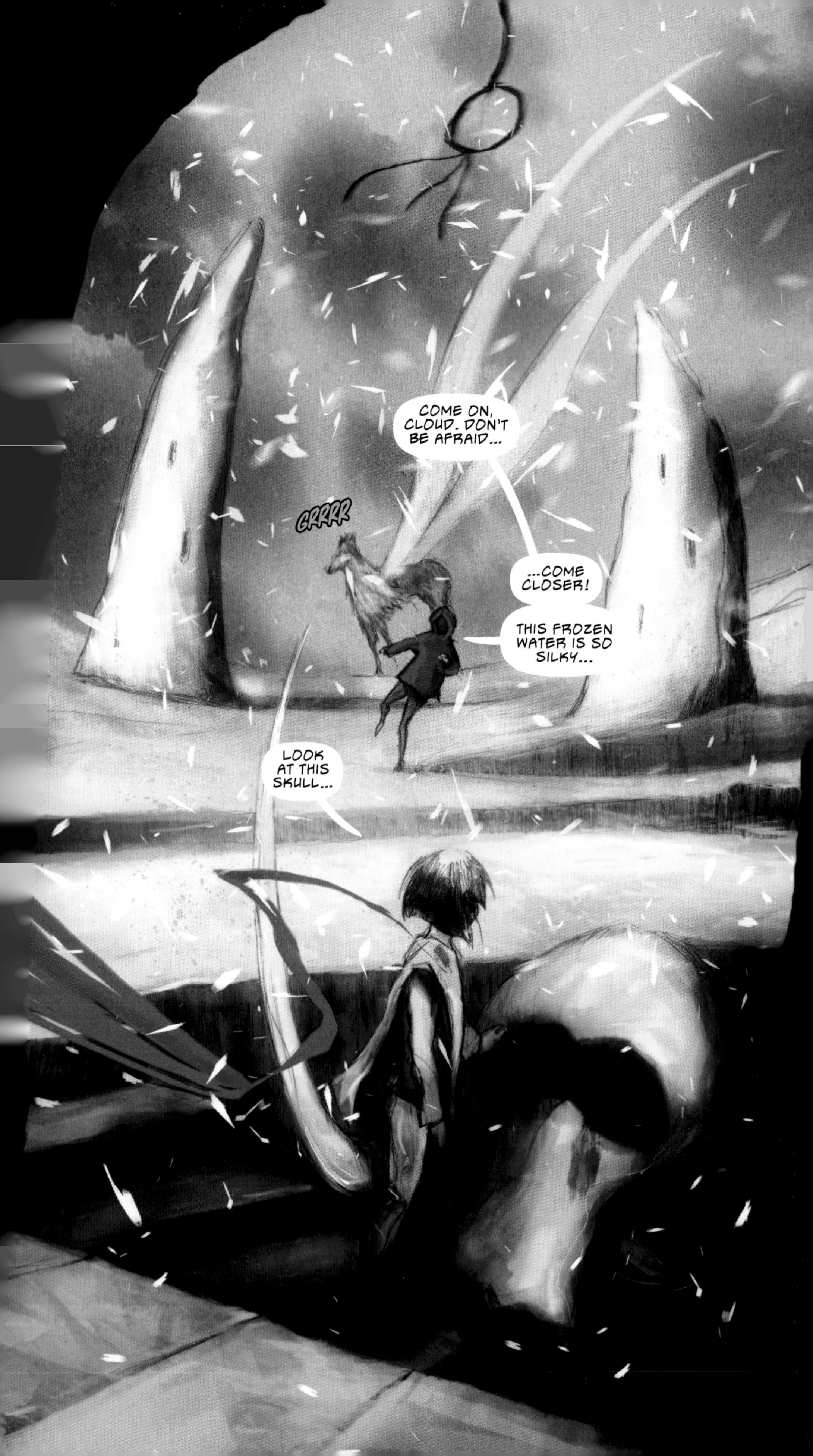
COME ON, CLOUD. DON'T BE AFRAID...
GRRRR
...COME CLOSER!
THIS FROZEN WATER IS SO SILKY...
LOOK AT THIS SKULL...

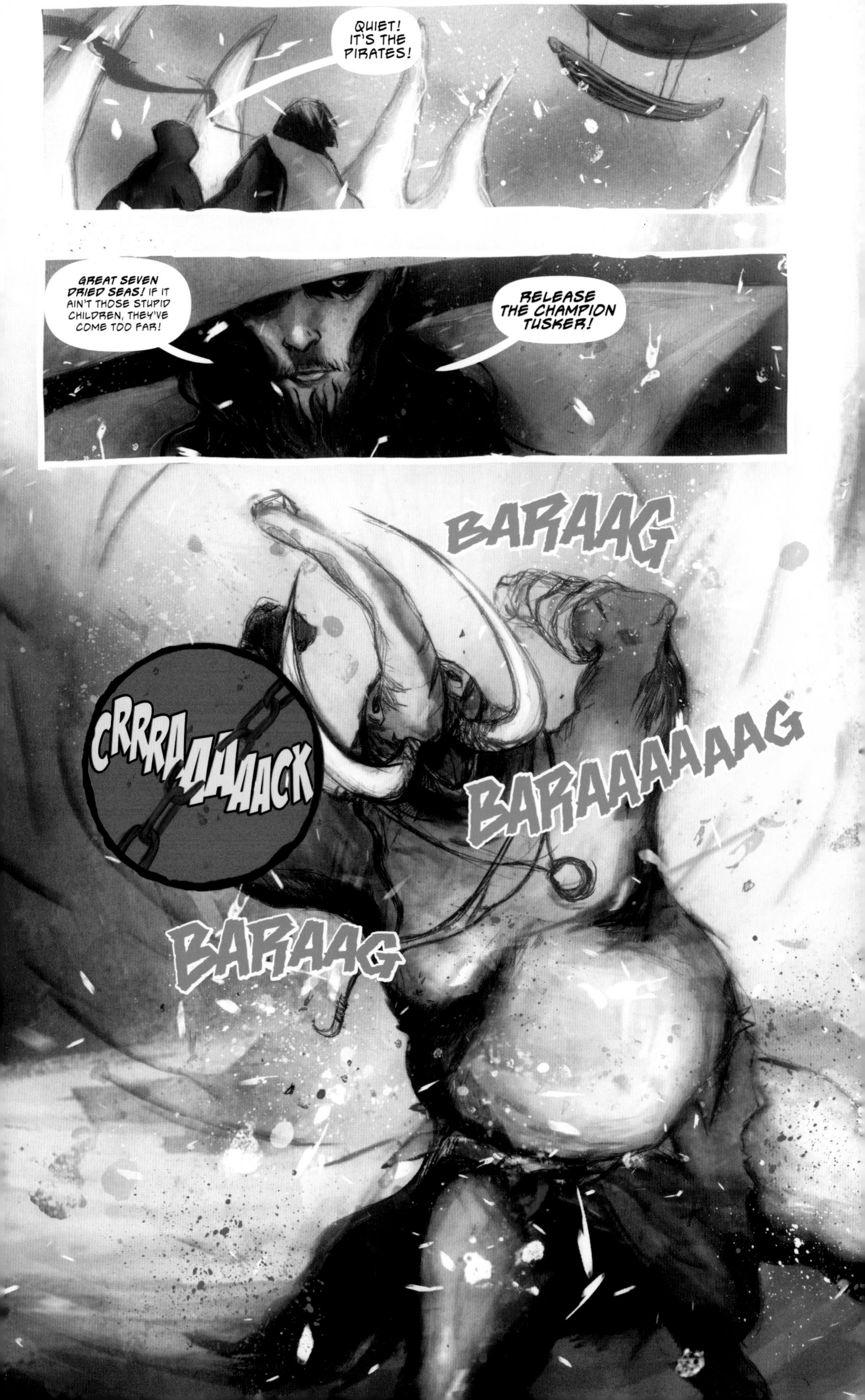
QUIET! IT'S THE PIRATES!
GREAT SEVEN DRIED SEAS! IF IT AIN'T THOSE STUPID CHILDREN, THEY'VE COME TOO FAR!
RELEASE THE CHAMPION TUSKER!
BARAAG
CRRRAAAAACK
BARAAAAAAG
BARAAG

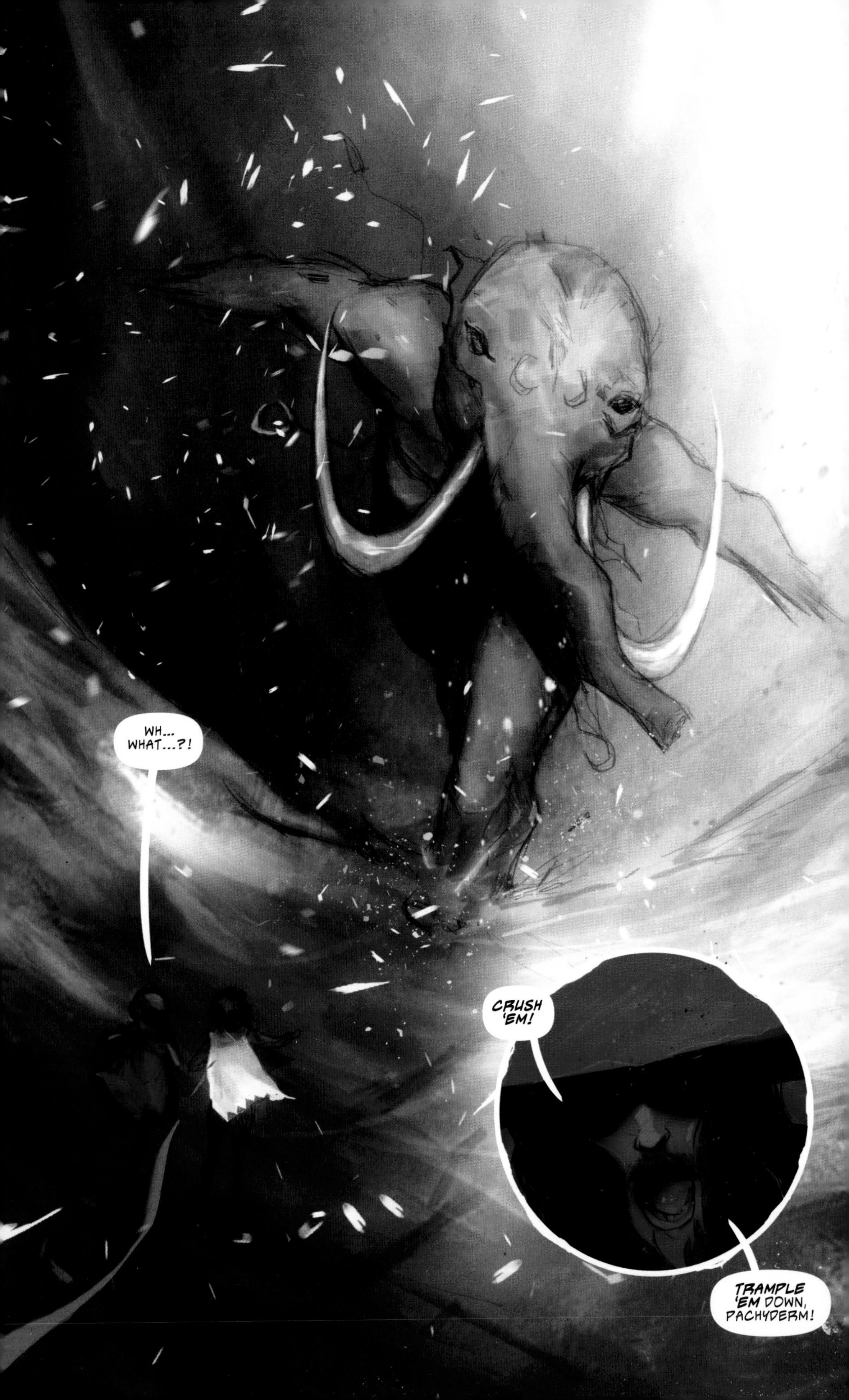
WH... WHAT...?!
CRUSH 'EM!
TRAMPLE 'EM DOWN, PACHYDERM!

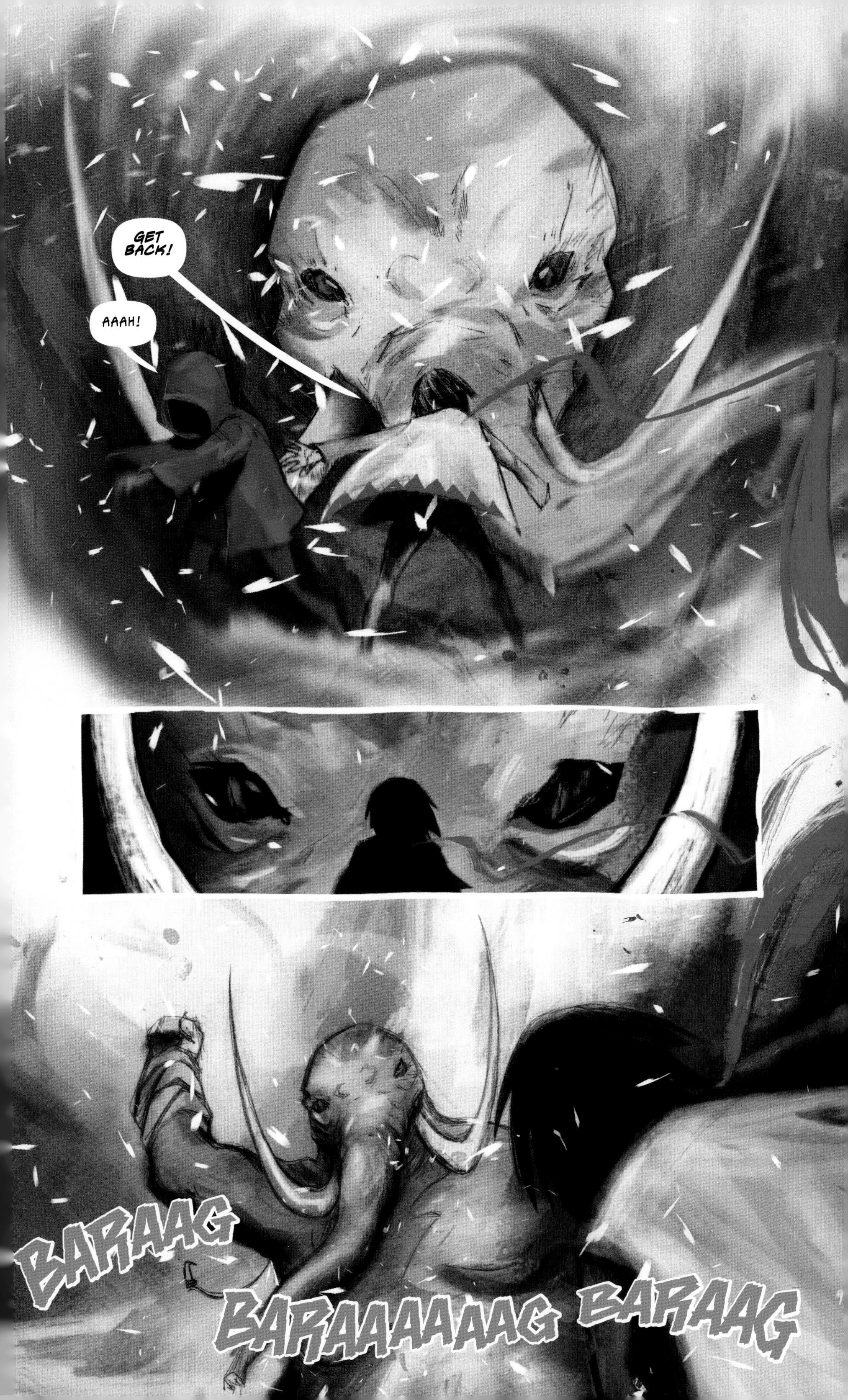
GET BACK!
AAAH!
BARAAG
BARAAAAAAG BARAAG

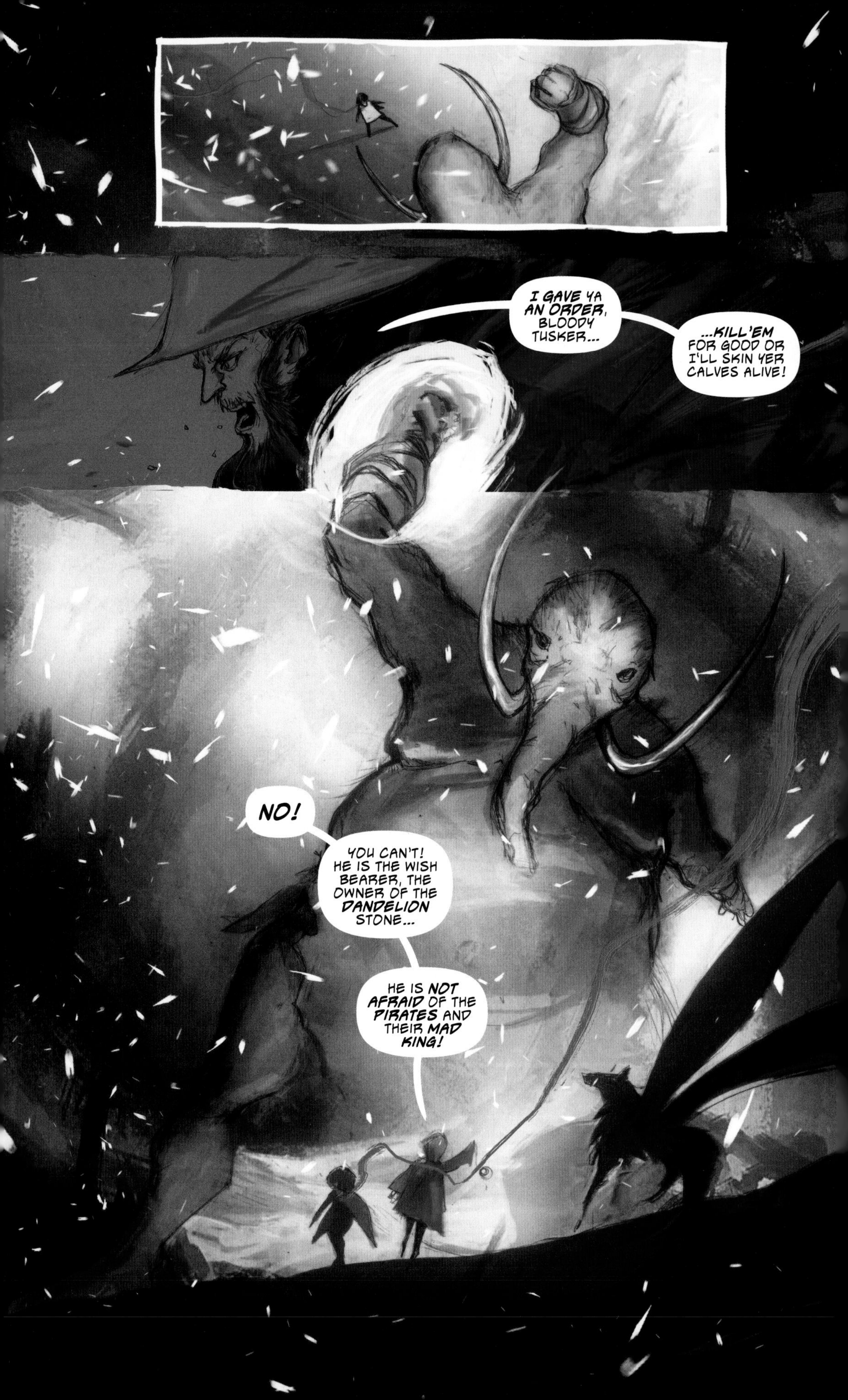
I GAVE YA AN ORDER, BLOODY TUSKER...
...KILL'EM FOR GOOD OR I'LL SKIN YER CALVES ALIVE!
NO!
YOU CAN'T! HE IS THE WISH BEARER, THE OWNER OF THE DANDELION STONE...
HE IS NOT AFRAID OF THE PIRATES AND THEIR MAD KING!

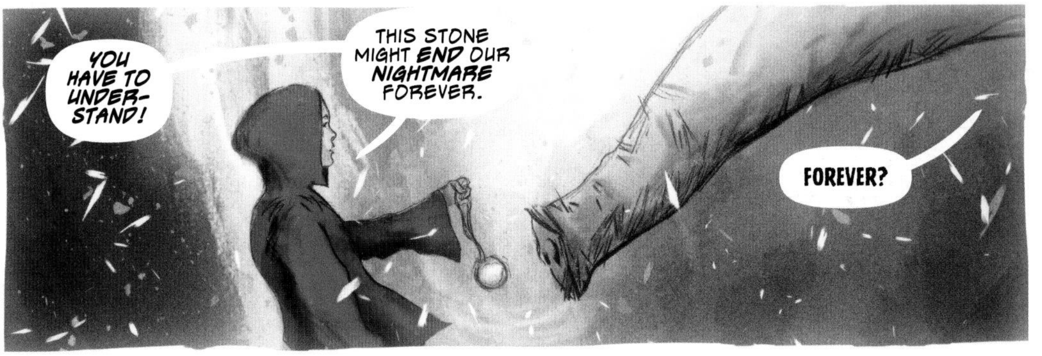
YOU HAVE TO UNDER-STAND!
THIS STONE MIGHT END OUR NIGHTMARE FOREVER.
FOREVER?

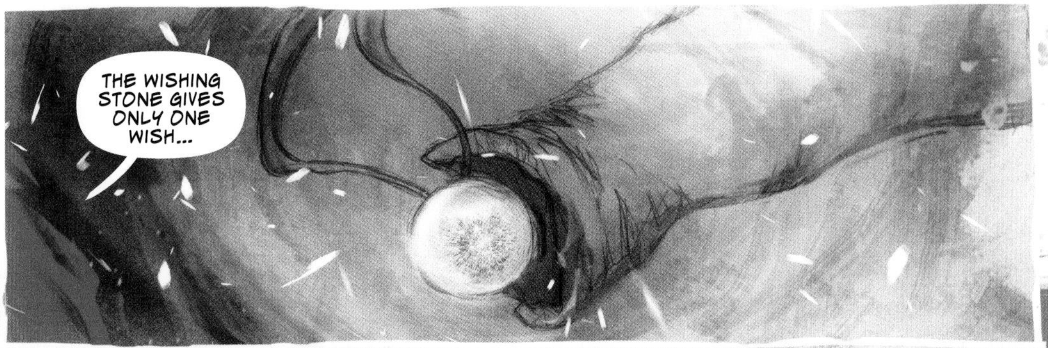
THE WISHING STONE GIVES ONLY ONE WISH...

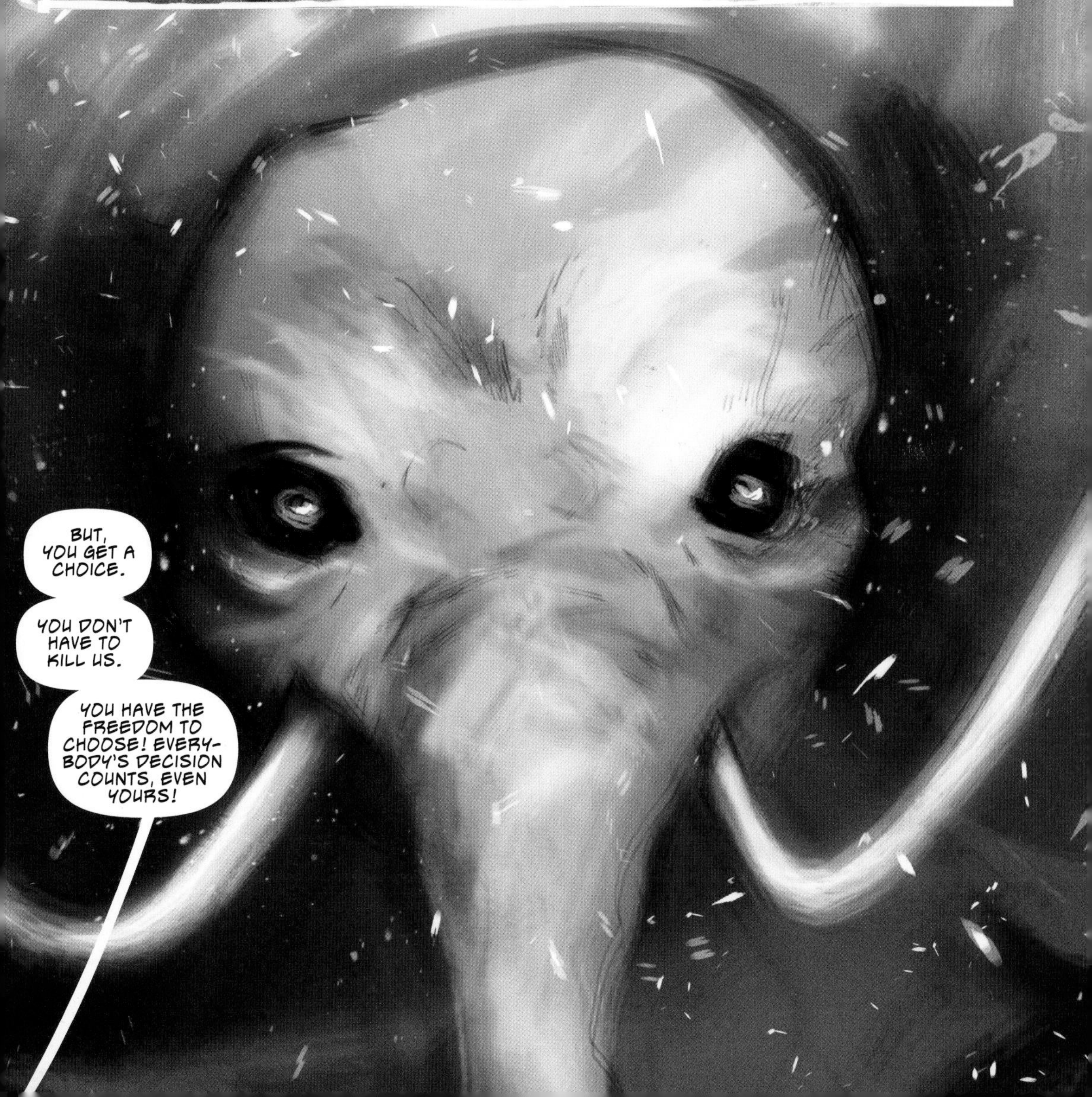
BUT, YOU GET A CHOICE.
YOU DON'T HAVE TO KILL US.
YOU HAVE THE FREEDOM TO CHOOSE! EVERY-BODY'S DECISION COUNTS, EVEN YOURS!

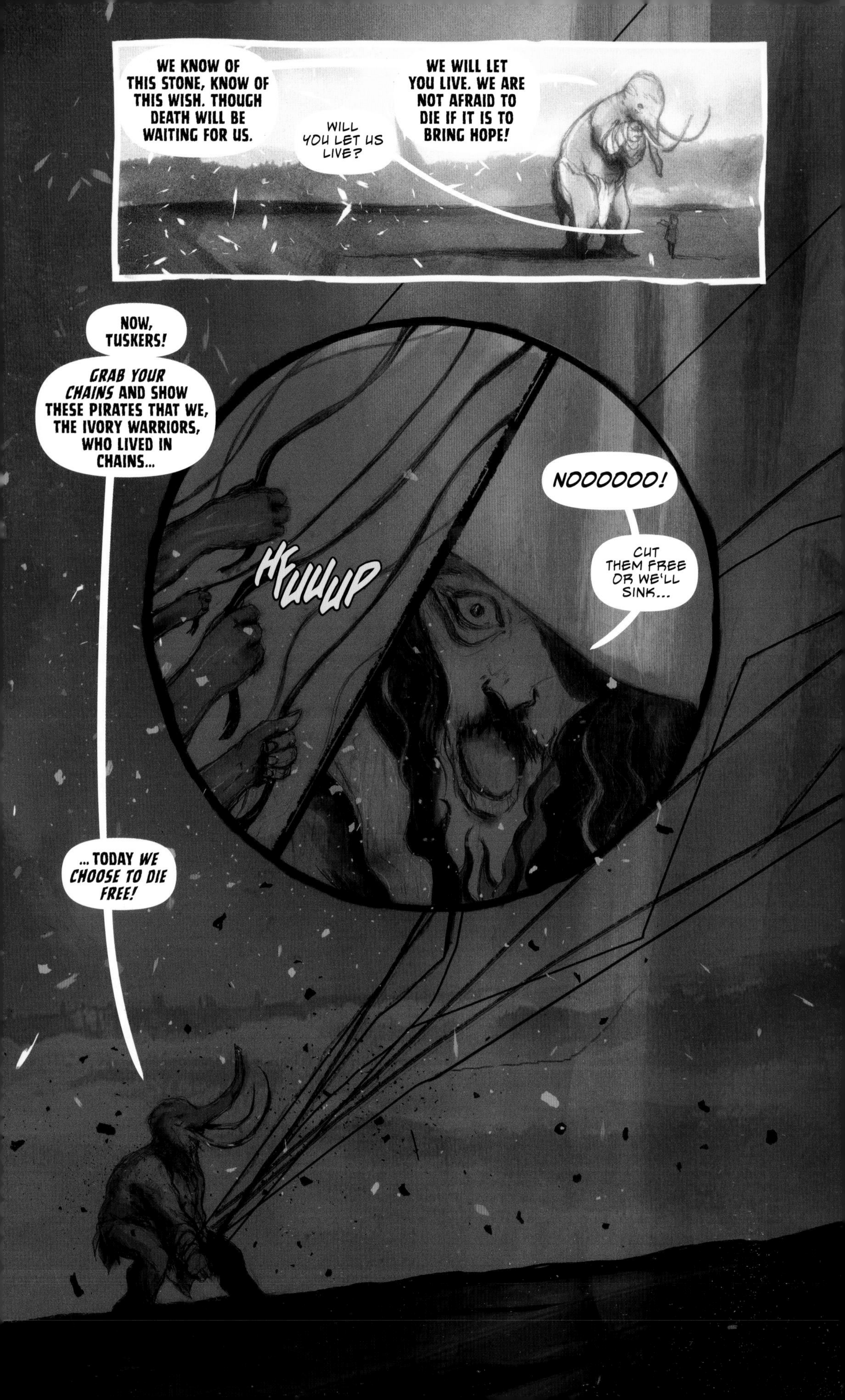
WE KNOW OF THIS STONE, KNOW OF THIS WISH. THOUGH DEATH WILL BE WAITING FOR US.
WILL YOU LET US LIVE?
WE WILL LET YOU LIVE. WE ARE NOT AFRAID TO DIE IF IT IS TO BRING HOPE!
NOW, TUSKERS!
GRAB YOUR CHAINS AND SHOW THESE PIRATES THAT WE, THE IVORY WARRIORS, WHO LIVED IN CHAINS...
HYUUUP
NOOOOOO!
CUT THEM FREE OR WE'LL SINK...
...TODAY WE CHOOSE TO DIE FREE!

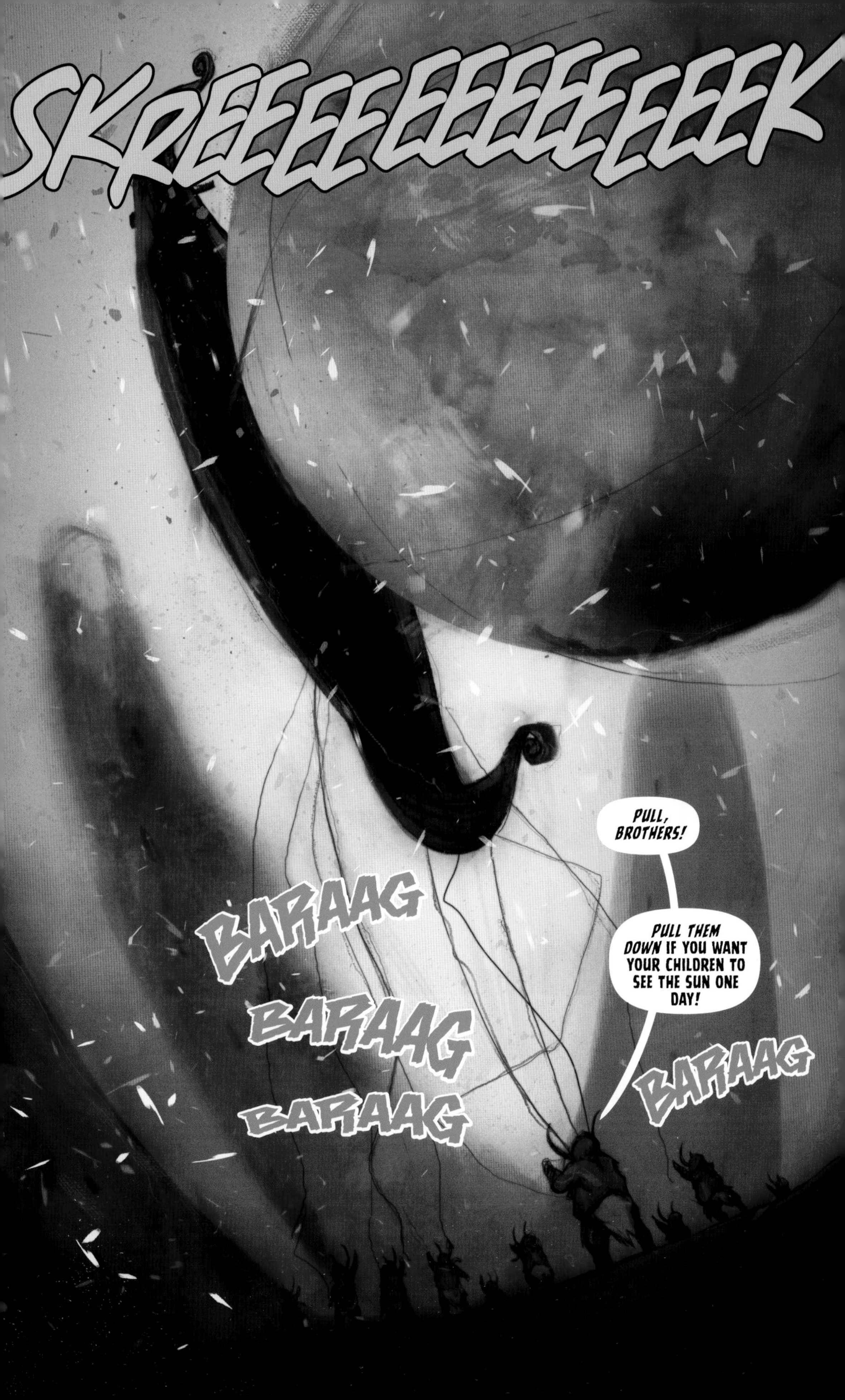
SKREEEEEEEEEEEEK
PULL, BROTHERS!
PULL THEM DOWN IF YOU WANT YOUR CHILDREN TO SEE THE SUN ONE DAY!
BARAAG
BARAAG
BARAAG
BARAAG

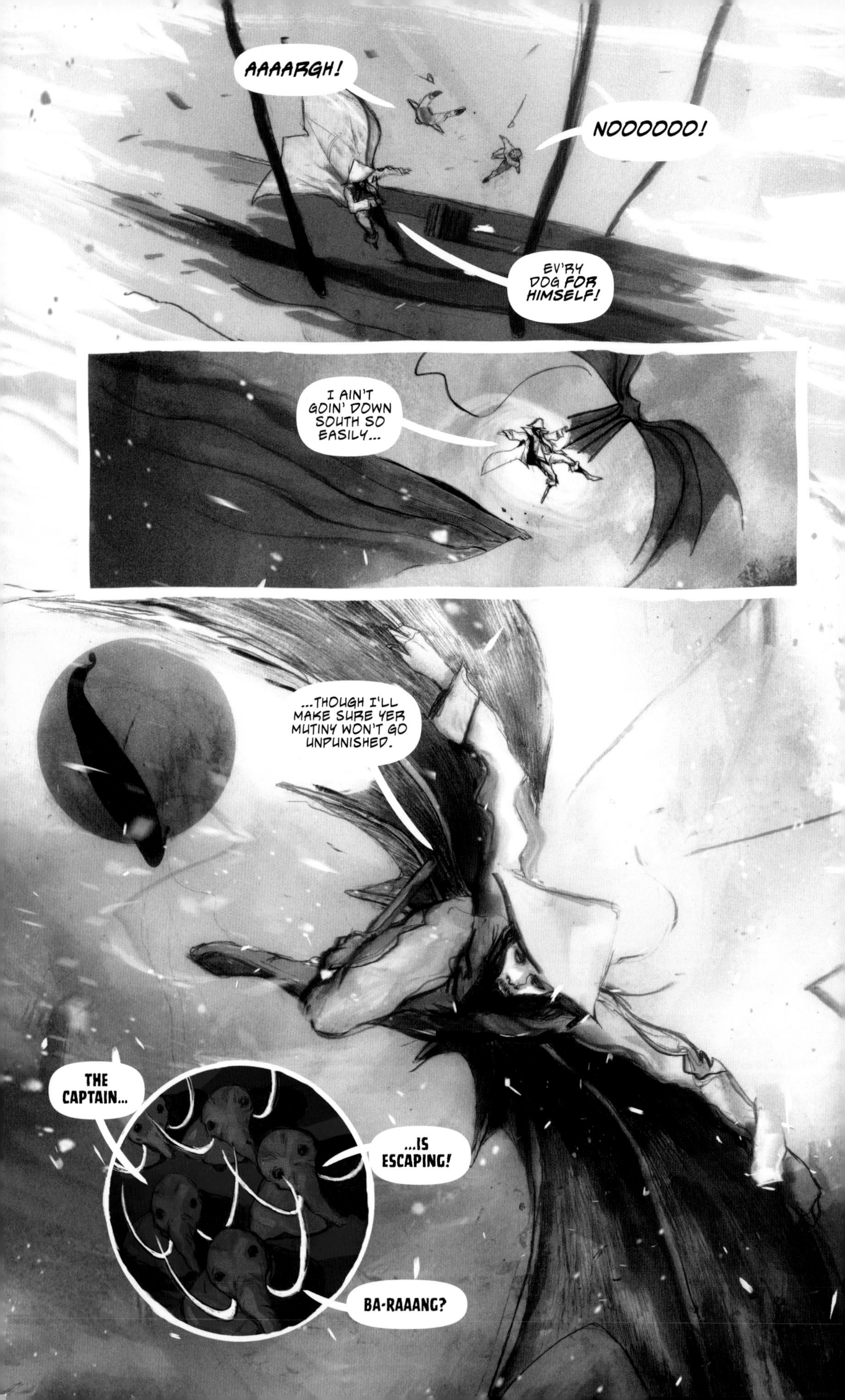

AAAARGH!
NOOOOOO!
EV'RY DOG FOR HIMSELF!
I AIN'T GOIN' DOWN SOUTH SO EASILY...
...THOUGH I'LL MAKE SURE YER MUTINY WON'T GO UNPUNISHED.
THE CAPTAIN...
...IS ESCAPING!
BA-RAAANG?

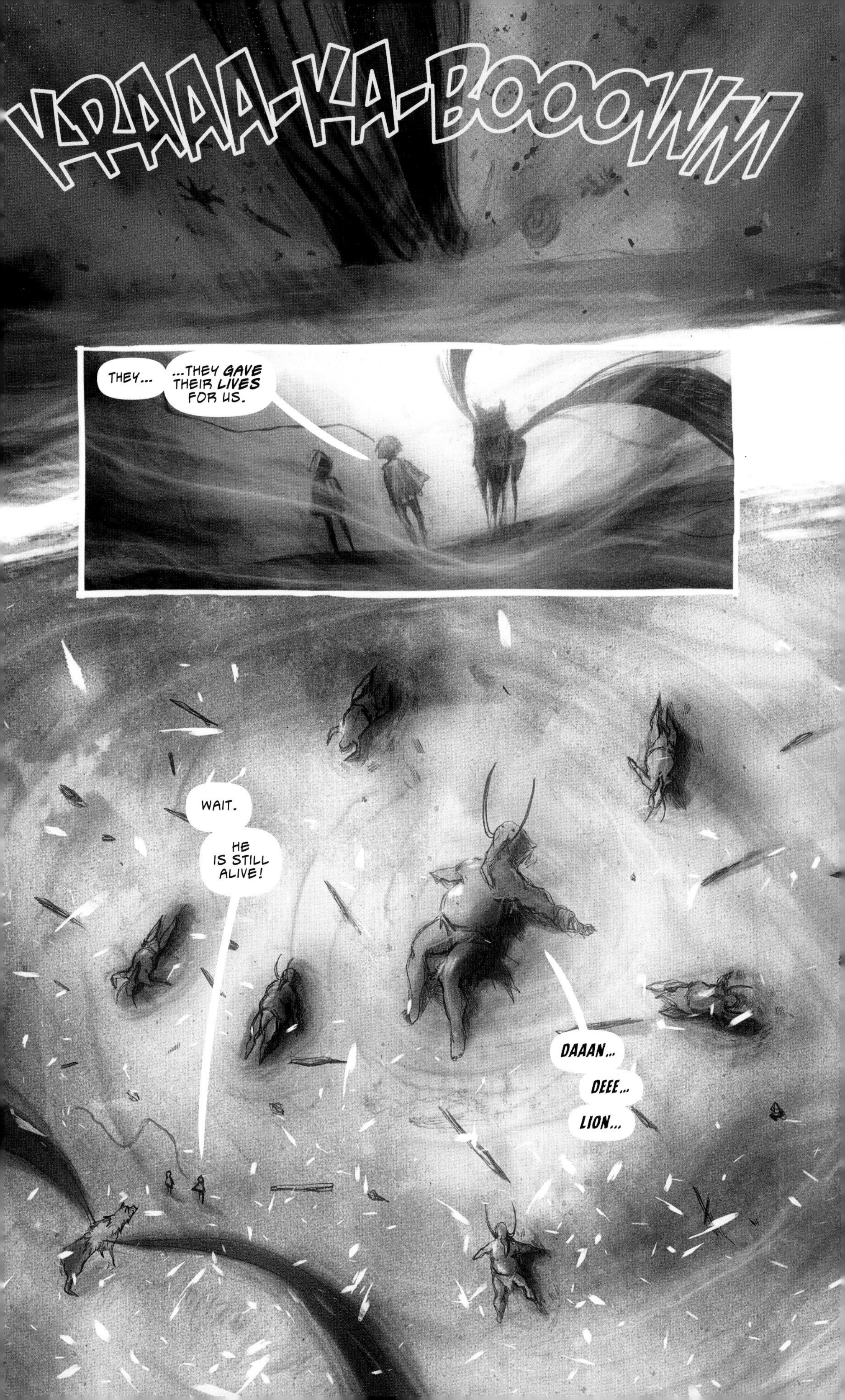
KRAAA-KA-BOOOWM
THEY...
...THEY GAVE THEIR LIVES FOR US.
WAIT.
HE IS STILL ALIVE!
DAAAN...
DEEE...
LION...

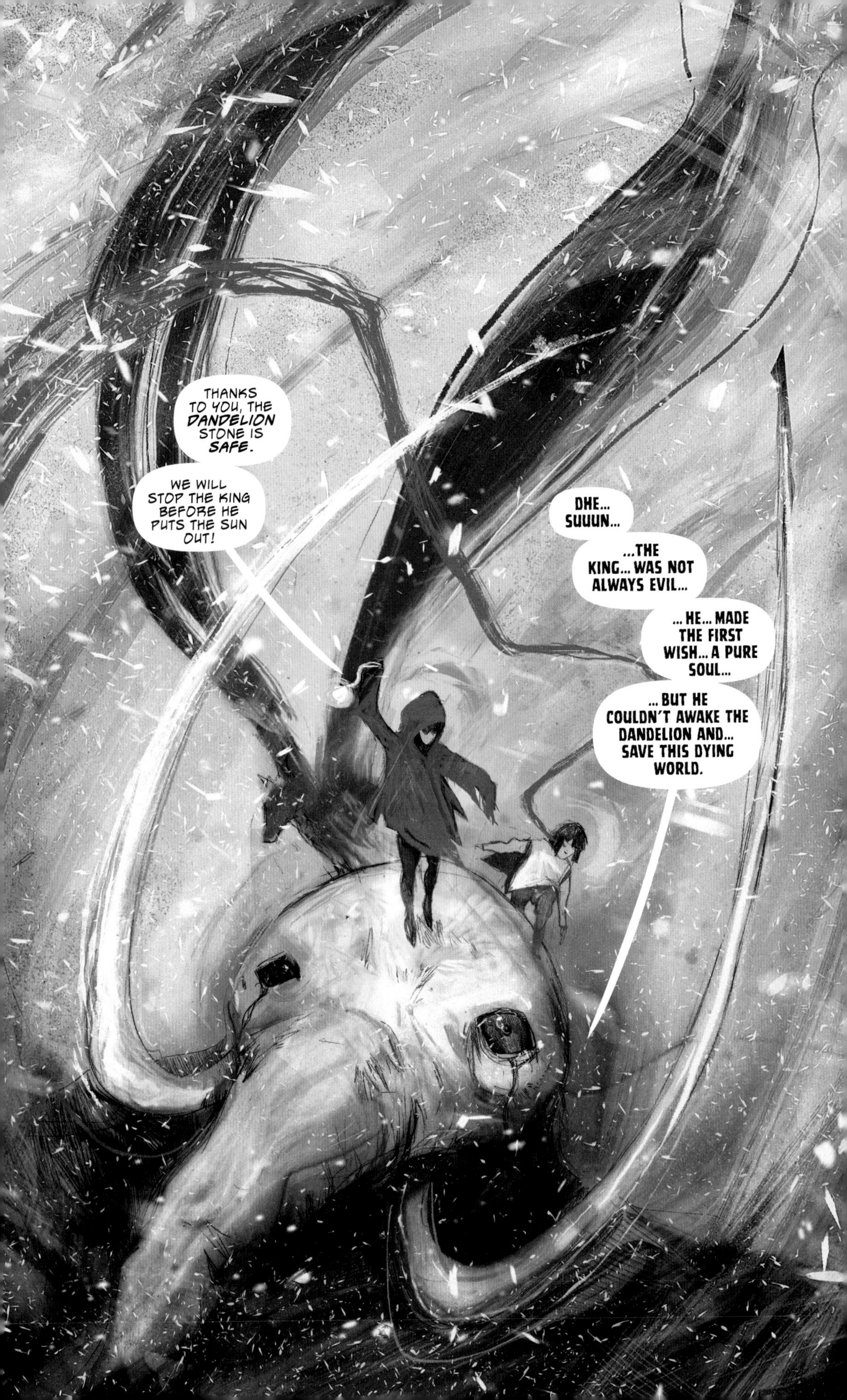
THANKS TO YOU, THE DANDELION STONE IS SAFE.
WE WILL STOP THE KING BEFORE HE PUTS THE SUN OUT!
DHE... SUUUN...
...THE KING... WAS NOT ALWAYS EVIL...
... HE... MADE THE FIRST WISH... A PURE SOUL...
... BUT HE COULDN'T AWAKE THE DANDELION AND... SAVE THIS DYING WORLD.

BETRAYED BY THE SKYBORNS...*FALLEN*...HE *PROMISED* TO TAKE HIS *REVENGE* BY PUTTING THEIR GREAT SHINY GODDESS OUT...

...HE...*MADE US BUILD A TOWER* SO HIGH THAT COULD PIERCE THE CLOUDS...

...AND PENETRATE HER BURNING HEART...

THEN HE BROUGHT *CAPTIVES* FROM THE *SKYWORLD*... AND MADE THEM WORK LIKE SLAVES.

THEY TOLD US THAT THE *GODDESS ABOVE THE CLOUDS* WAS... *WARM* AND *SOFT* LIKE A *MOTHER'S* ARM.

YOU KIDS ARE THIS WORLD'S *LAST HOPE*.

...GO AND *DON'T FORGET* THAT EARTHBORN OR SKYBORN...

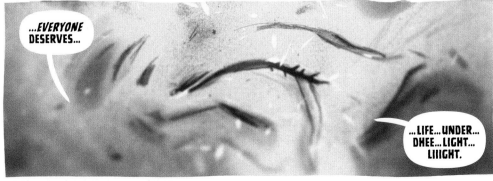

...*EVERYONE* DESERVES...

...LIFE...UNDER... DHEE...LIGHT... LIIIGHT.

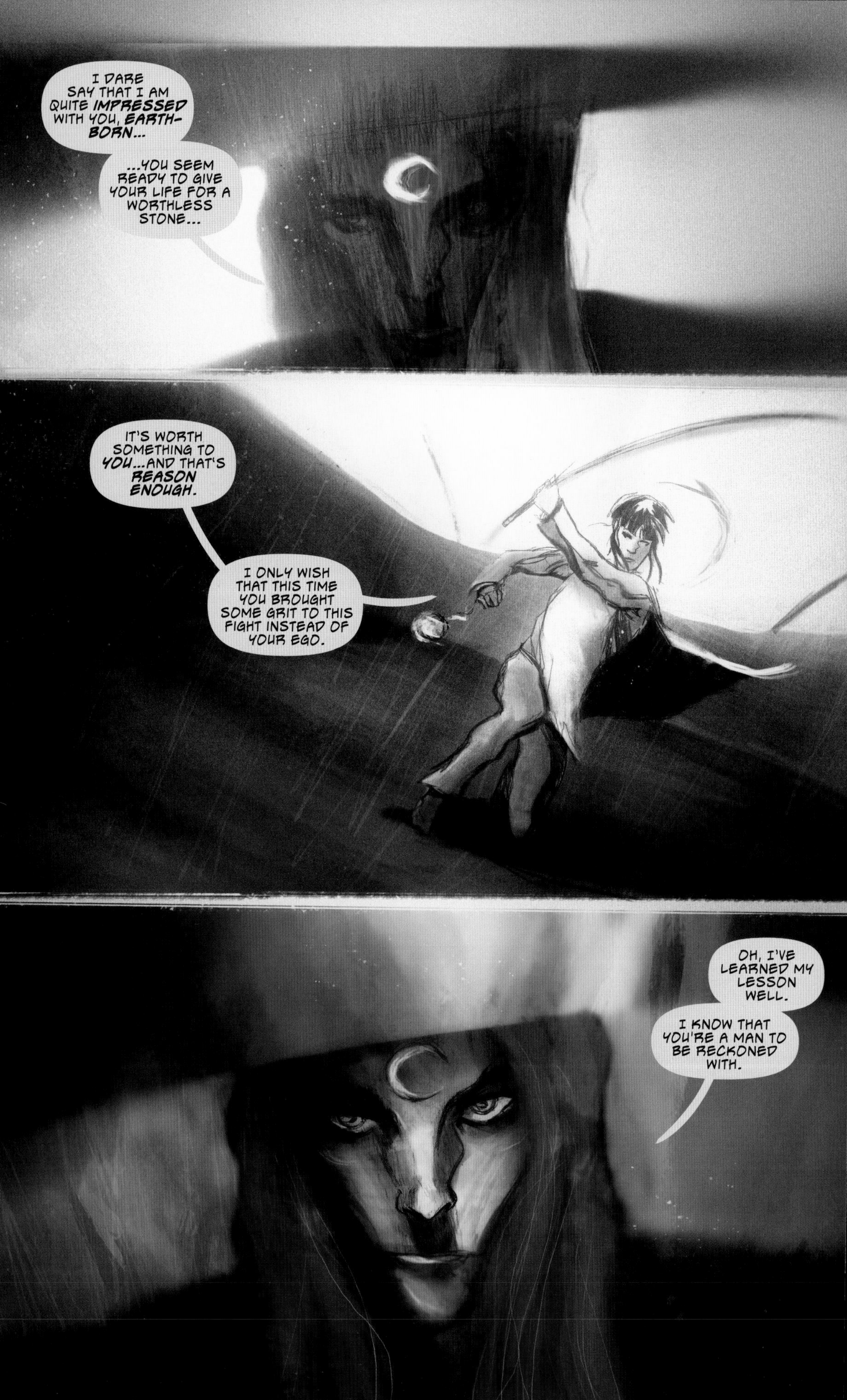
I DARE SAY THAT I AM QUITE IMPRESSED WITH YOU, EARTH-BORN...
...YOU SEEM READY TO GIVE YOUR LIFE FOR A WORTHLESS STONE...
IT'S WORTH SOMETHING TO YOU...AND THAT'S REASON ENOUGH.
I ONLY WISH THAT THIS TIME YOU BROUGHT SOME GRIT TO THIS FIGHT INSTEAD OF YOUR EGO.
OH, I'VE LEARNED MY LESSON WELL.
I KNOW THAT YOU'RE A MAN TO BE RECKONED WITH.

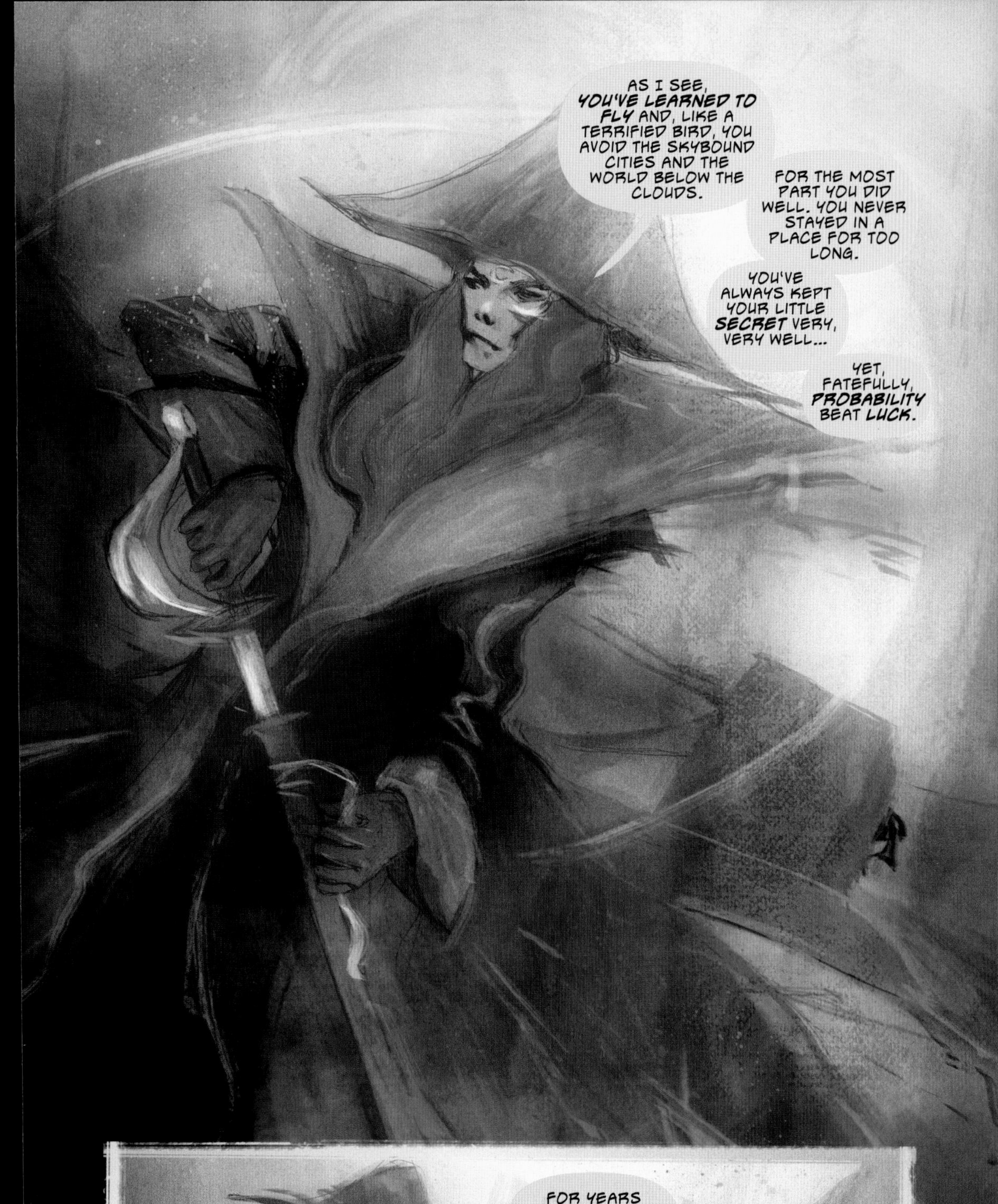
AS I SEE, YOU'VE LEARNED TO FLY AND, LIKE A TERRIFIED BIRD, YOU AVOID THE SKYBOUND CITIES AND THE WORLD BELOW THE CLOUDS.
FOR THE MOST PART YOU DID WELL. YOU NEVER STAYED IN A PLACE FOR TOO LONG.
YOU'VE ALWAYS KEPT YOUR LITTLE SECRET VERY, VERY WELL...
YET, FATEFULLY, PROBABILITY BEAT LUCK.

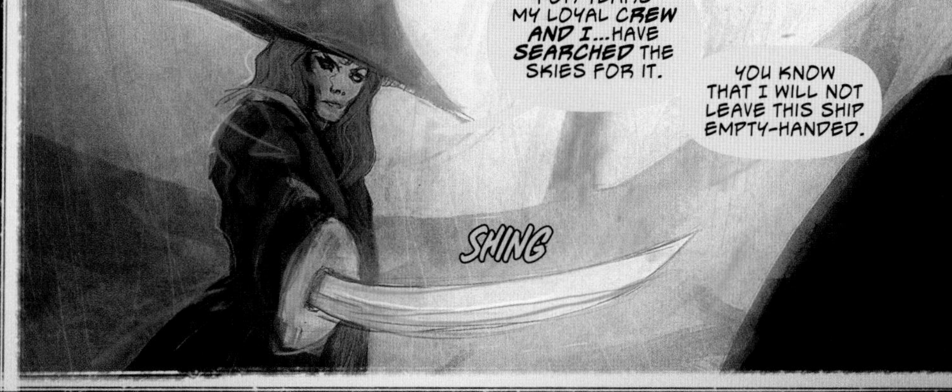
FOR YEARS MY LOYAL CREW AND I...HAVE SEARCHED THE SKIES FOR IT.
YOU KNOW THAT I WILL NOT LEAVE THIS SHIP EMPTY-HANDED.
SHING

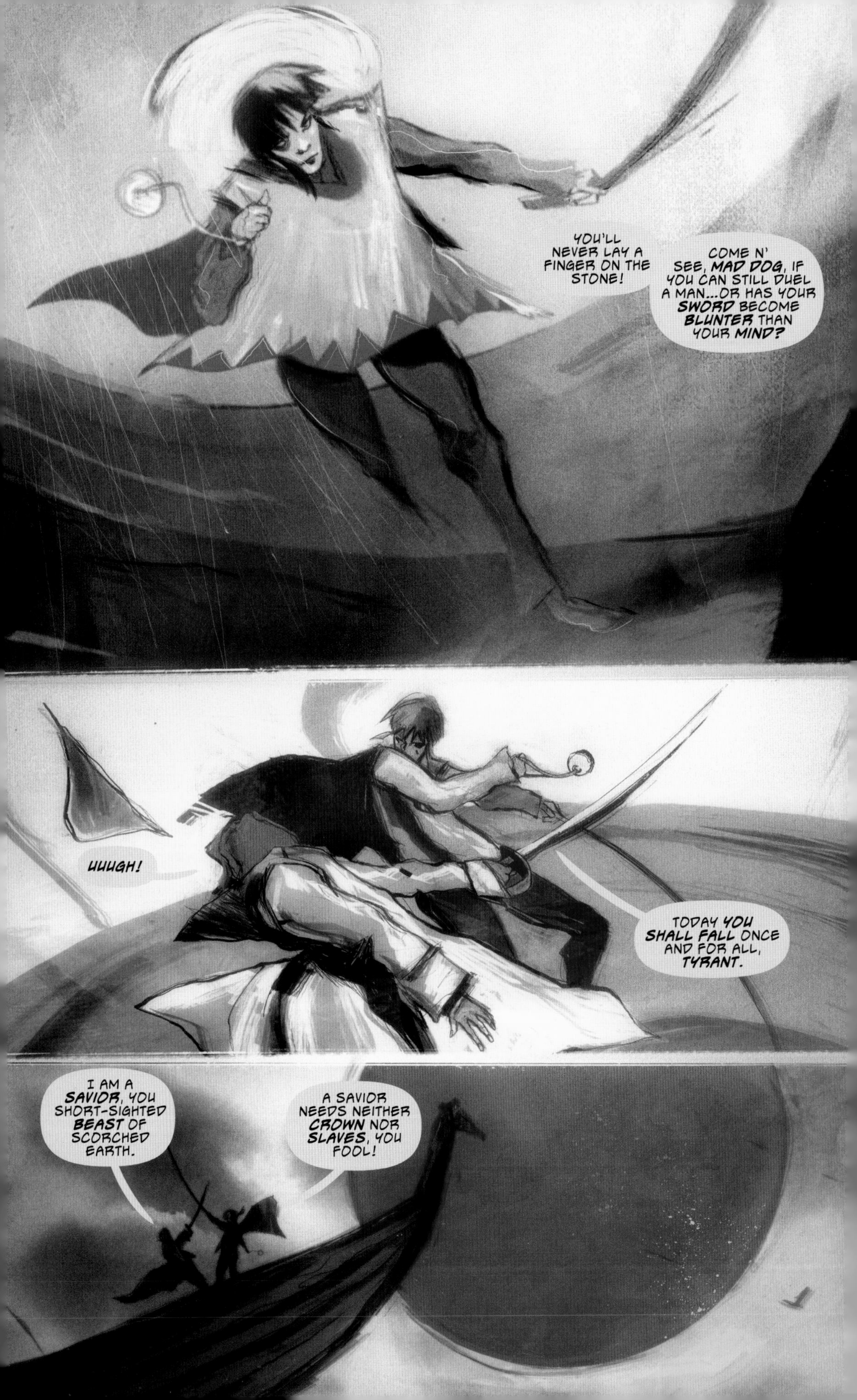
YOU'LL NEVER LAY A FINGER ON THE STONE!
COME N' SEE, MAD DOG, IF YOU CAN STILL DUEL A MAN...OR HAS YOUR SWORD BECOME BLUNTER THAN YOUR MIND?
UUUGH!
TODAY YOU SHALL FALL ONCE AND FOR ALL, TYRANT.
I AM A SAVIOR, YOU SHORT-SIGHTED BEAST OF SCORCHED EARTH.
A SAVIOR NEEDS NEITHER CROWN NOR SLAVES, YOU FOOL!

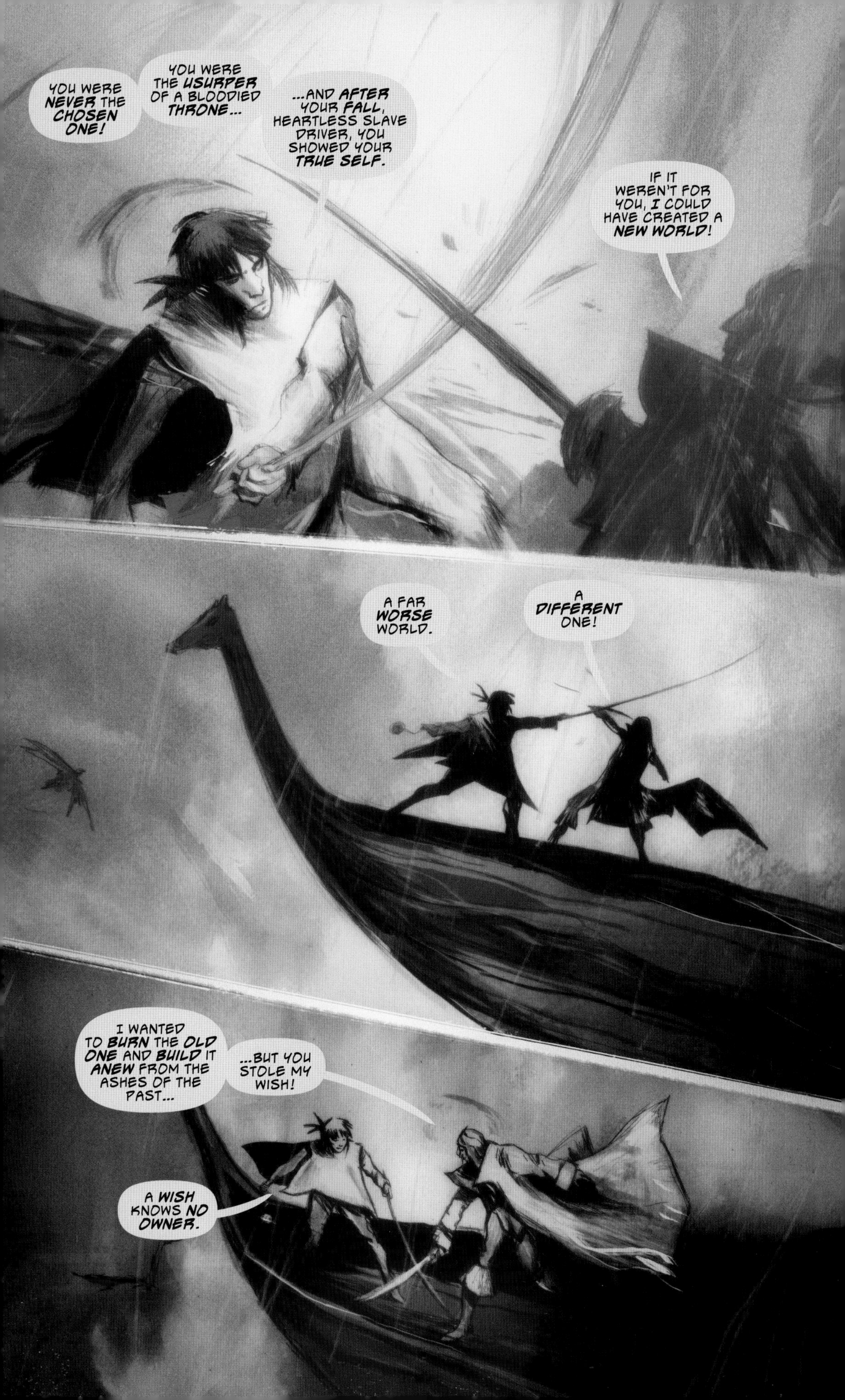
YOU WERE NEVER THE CHOSEN ONE!
YOU WERE THE USURPER OF A BLOODIED THRONE...
...AND AFTER YOUR FALL, HEARTLESS SLAVE DRIVER, YOU SHOWED YOUR TRUE SELF.
IF IT WEREN'T FOR YOU, I COULD HAVE CREATED A NEW WORLD!
A FAR WORSE WORLD.
A DIFFERENT ONE!
I WANTED TO BURN THE OLD ONE AND BUILD IT ANEW FROM THE ASHES OF THE PAST...
...BUT YOU STOLE MY WISH!
A WISH KNOWS NO OWNER.

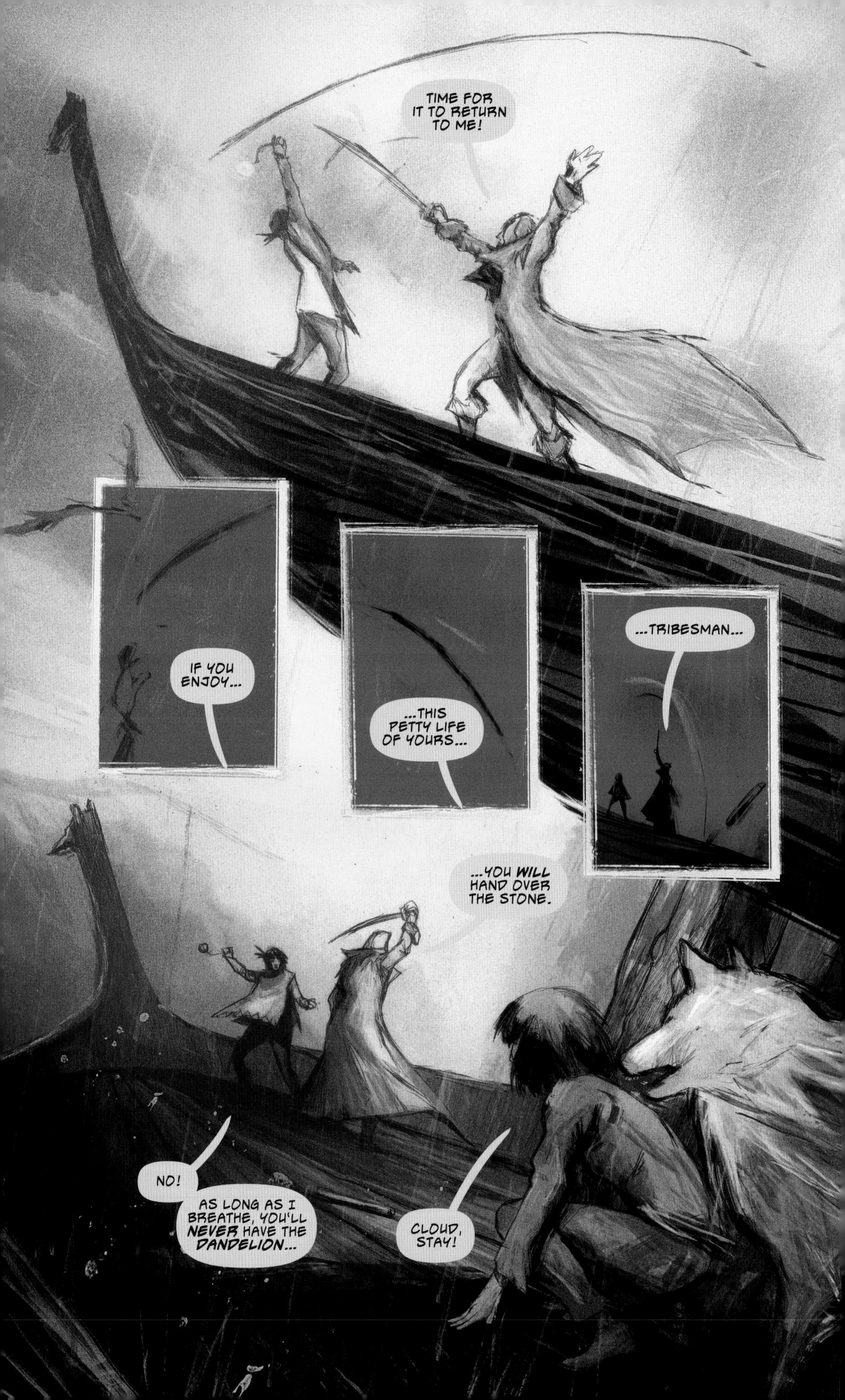

TIME FOR IT TO RETURN TO ME!
IF YOU ENJOY...
...THIS PETTY LIFE OF YOURS...
...TRIBESMAN...
...YOU **WILL** HAND OVER THE STONE.
NO!
AS LONG AS I BREATHE, YOU'LL ***NEVER*** HAVE THE ***DANDELION***...
CLOUD, STAY!

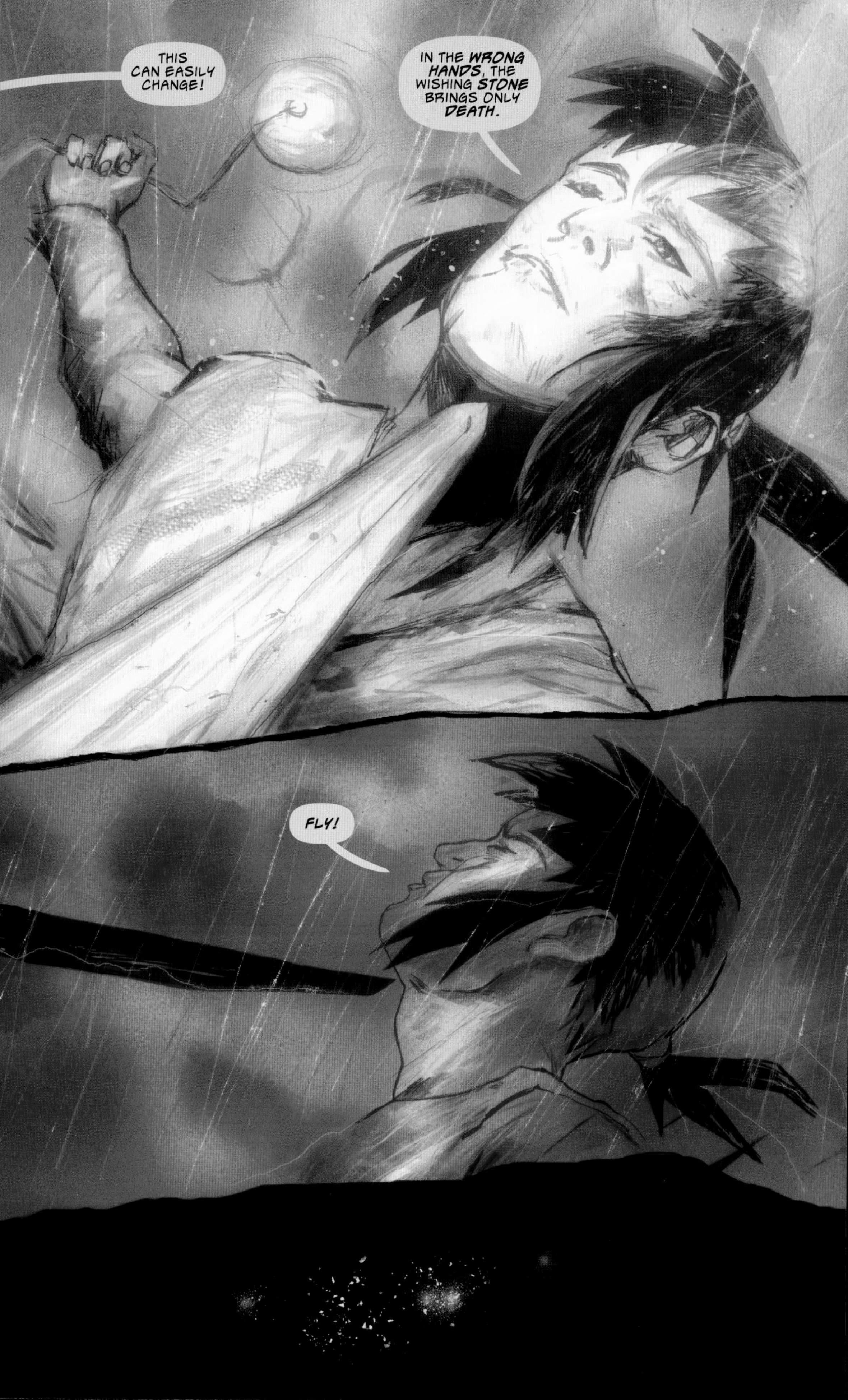
THIS CAN EASILY CHANGE!
IN THE WRONG HANDS, THE WISHING STONE BRINGS ONLY DEATH.
FLY!

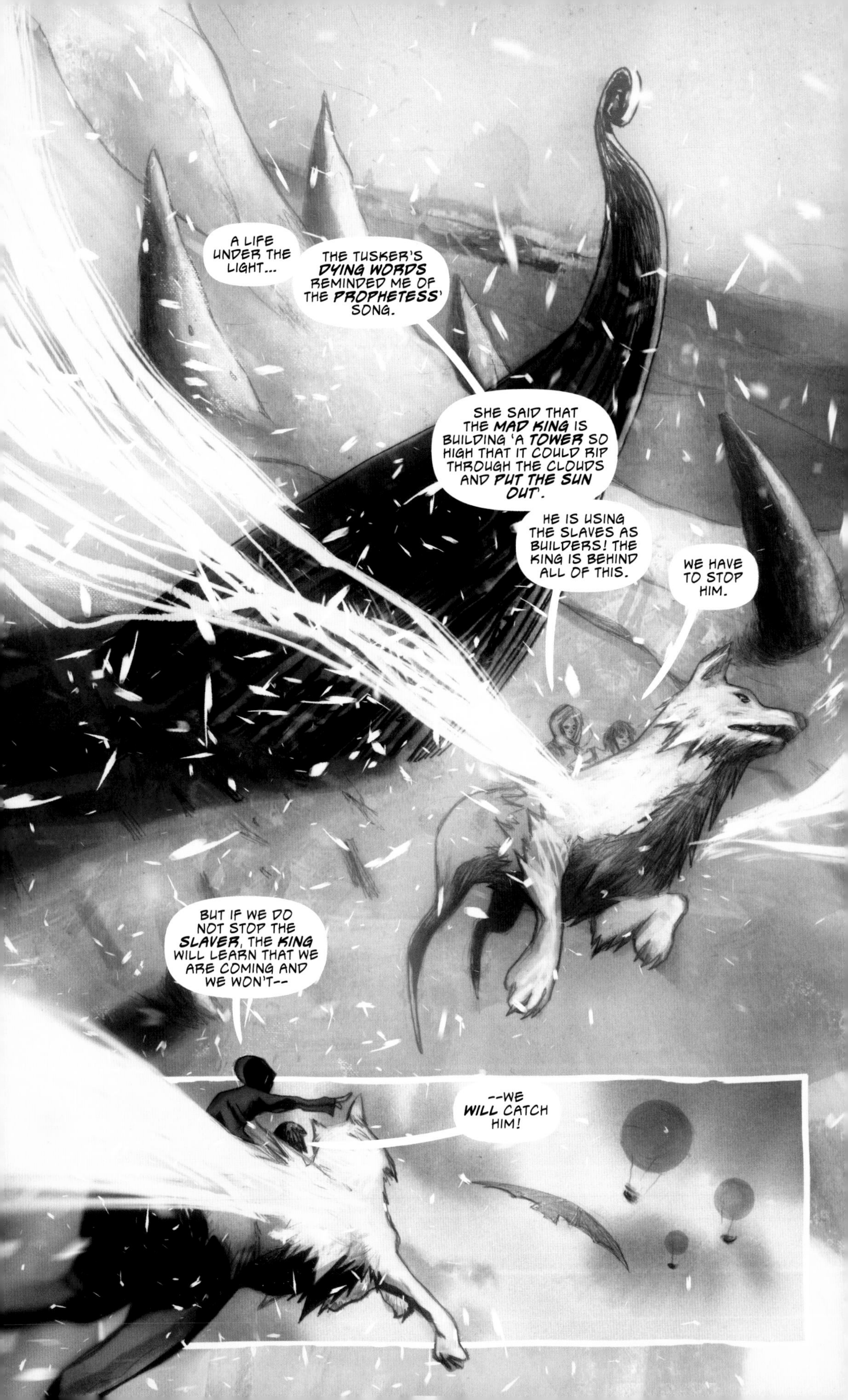
A LIFE UNDER THE LIGHT...
THE TUSKER'S DYING WORDS REMINDED ME OF THE PROPHETESS' SONG.
SHE SAID THAT THE MAD KING IS BUILDING 'A TOWER SO HIGH THAT IT COULD RIP THROUGH THE CLOUDS AND PUT THE SUN OUT'.
HE IS USING THE SLAVES AS BUILDERS! THE KING IS BEHIND ALL OF THIS.
WE HAVE TO STOP HIM.
BUT IF WE DO NOT STOP THE SLAVER, THE KING WILL LEARN THAT WE ARE COMING AND WE WON'T--
--WE WILL CATCH HIM!

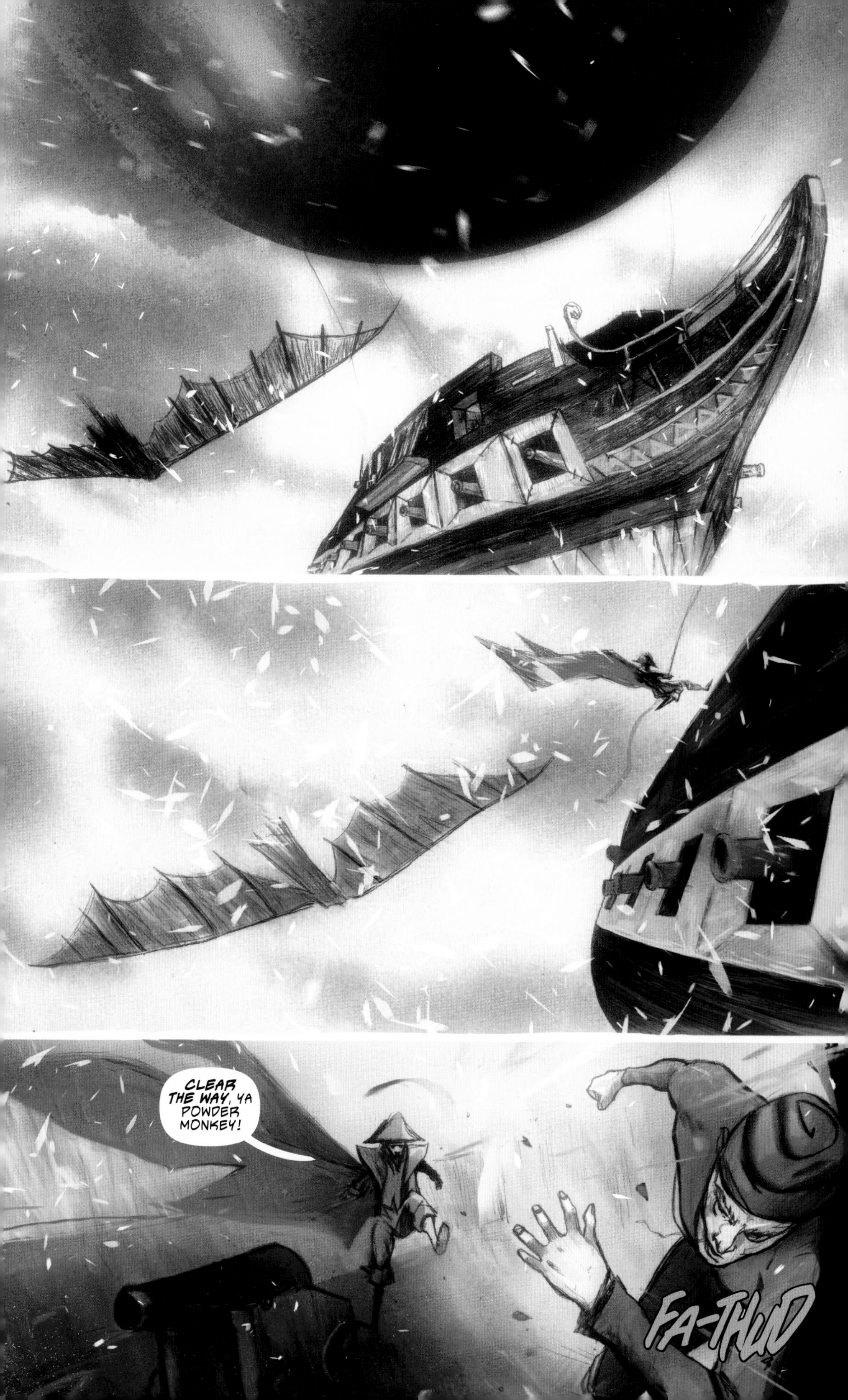
CLEAR THE WAY, YA POWDER MONKEY!
FA-THUD

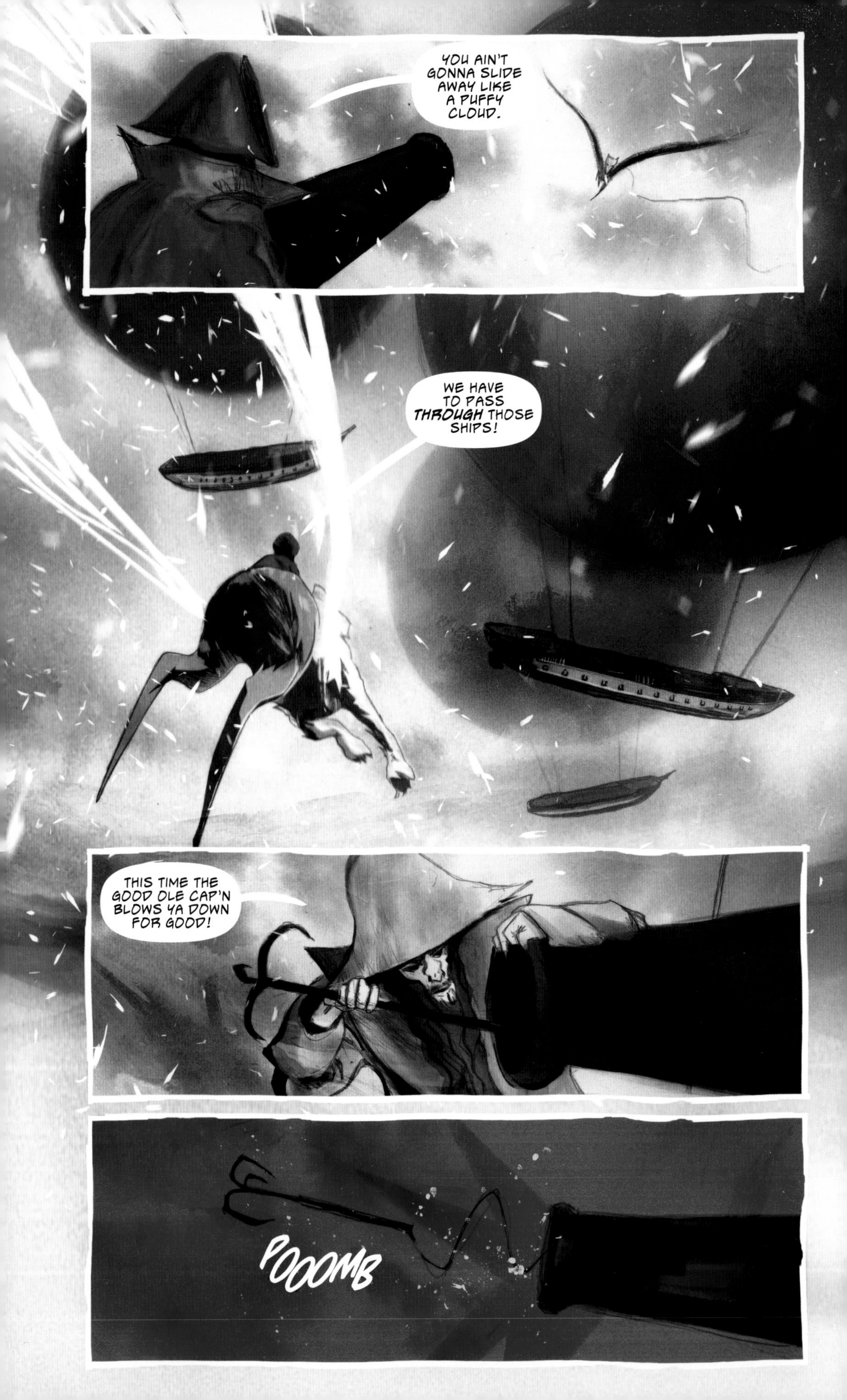
YOU AIN'T GONNA SLIDE AWAY LIKE A PUFFY CLOUD.
WE HAVE TO PASS *THROUGH* THOSE SHIPS!
THIS TIME THE GOOD OLE CAP'N BLOWS YA DOWN FOR GOOD!
POOOMB

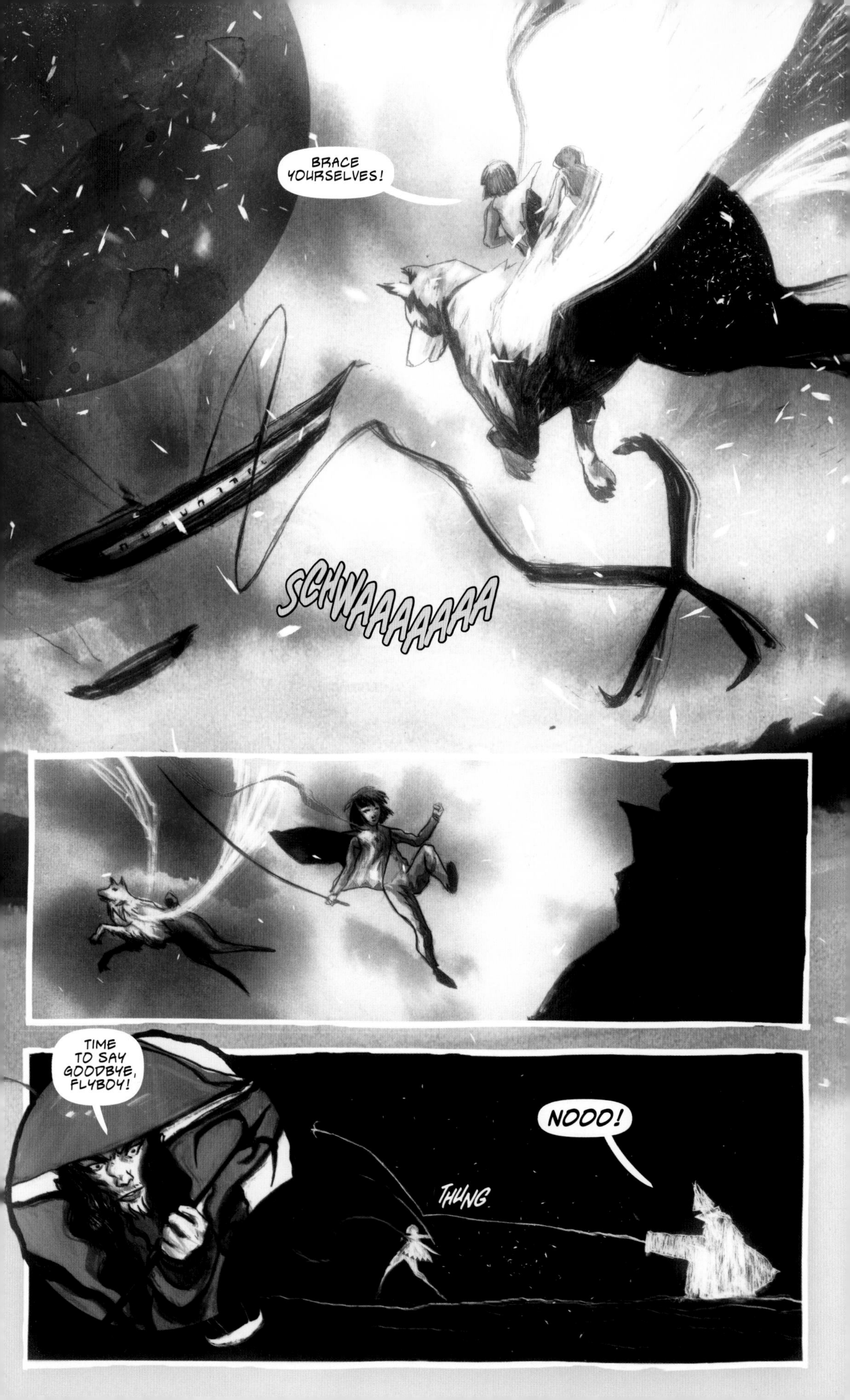
BRACE YOURSELVES!
SCHWAAAAAAAA
TIME TO SAY GOODBYE, FLYBOY!
NOOO!
THUNG

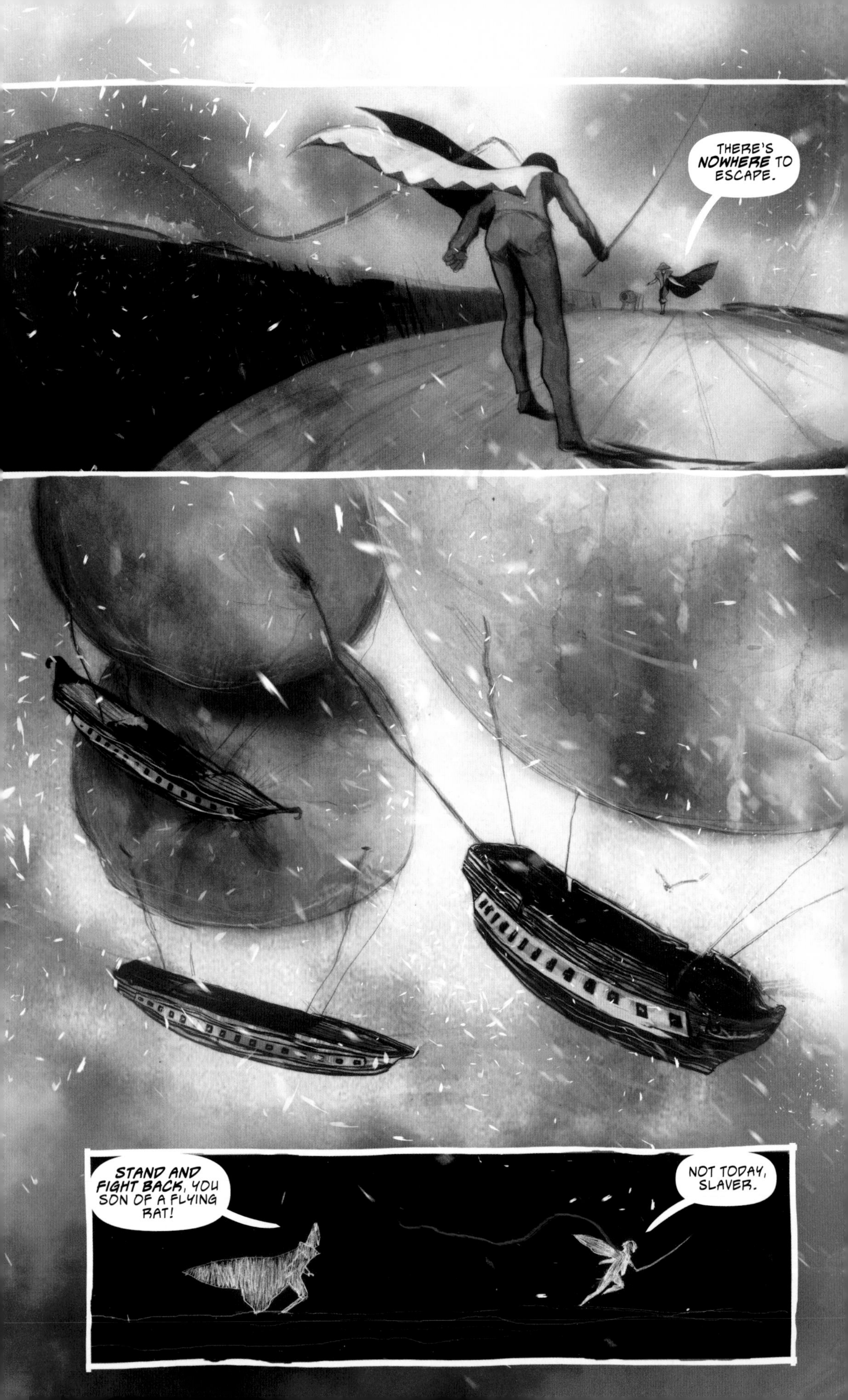
THERE'S NOWHERE TO ESCAPE.
STAND AND FIGHT BACK, YOU SON OF A FLYING RAT!
NOT TODAY, SLAVER.

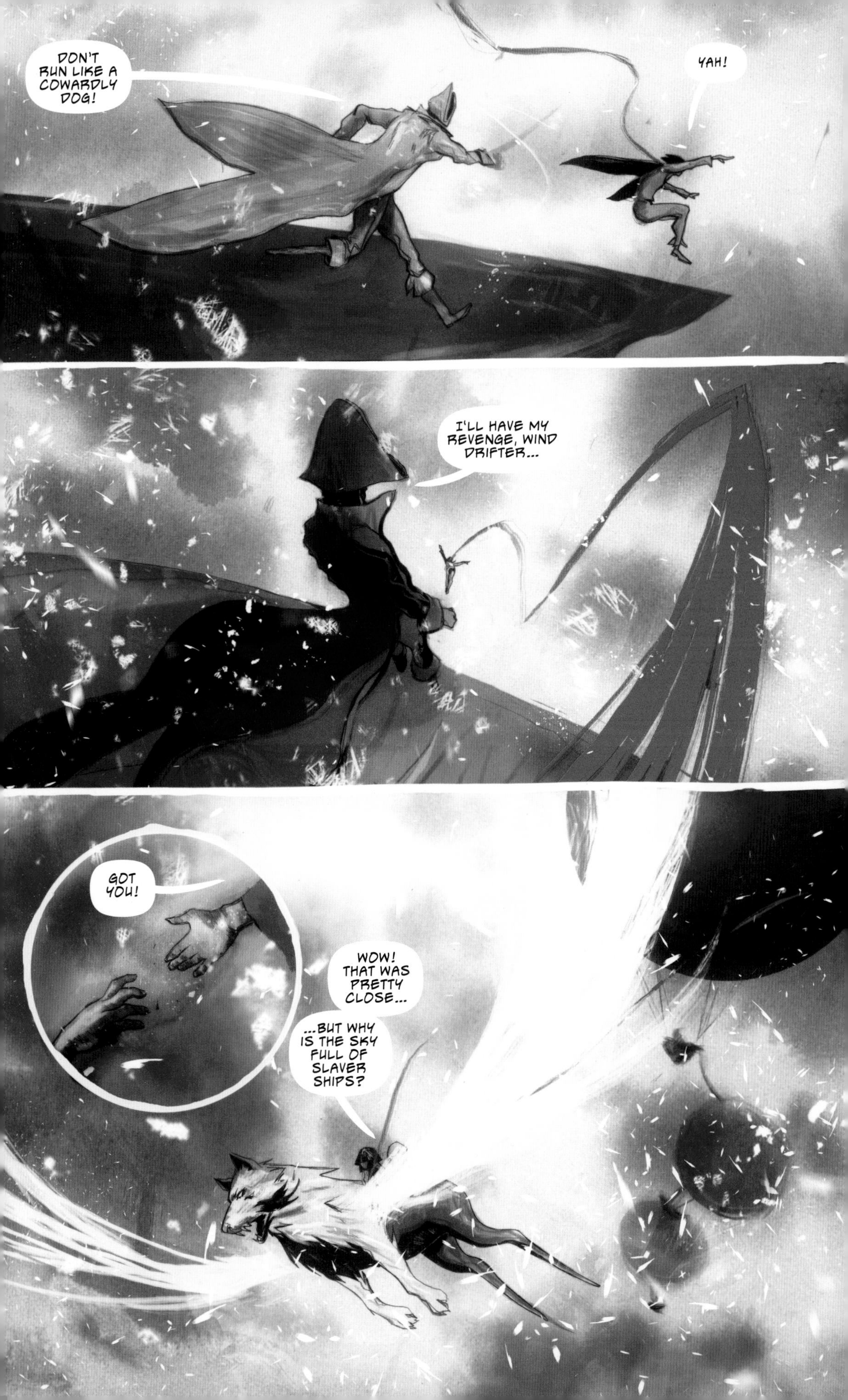
DON'T RUN LIKE A COWARDLY DOG!
YAH!
I'LL HAVE MY REVENGE, WIND DRIFTER...
GOT YOU!
WOW! THAT WAS PRETTY CLOSE...
...BUT WHY IS THE SKY FULL OF SLAVER SHIPS?

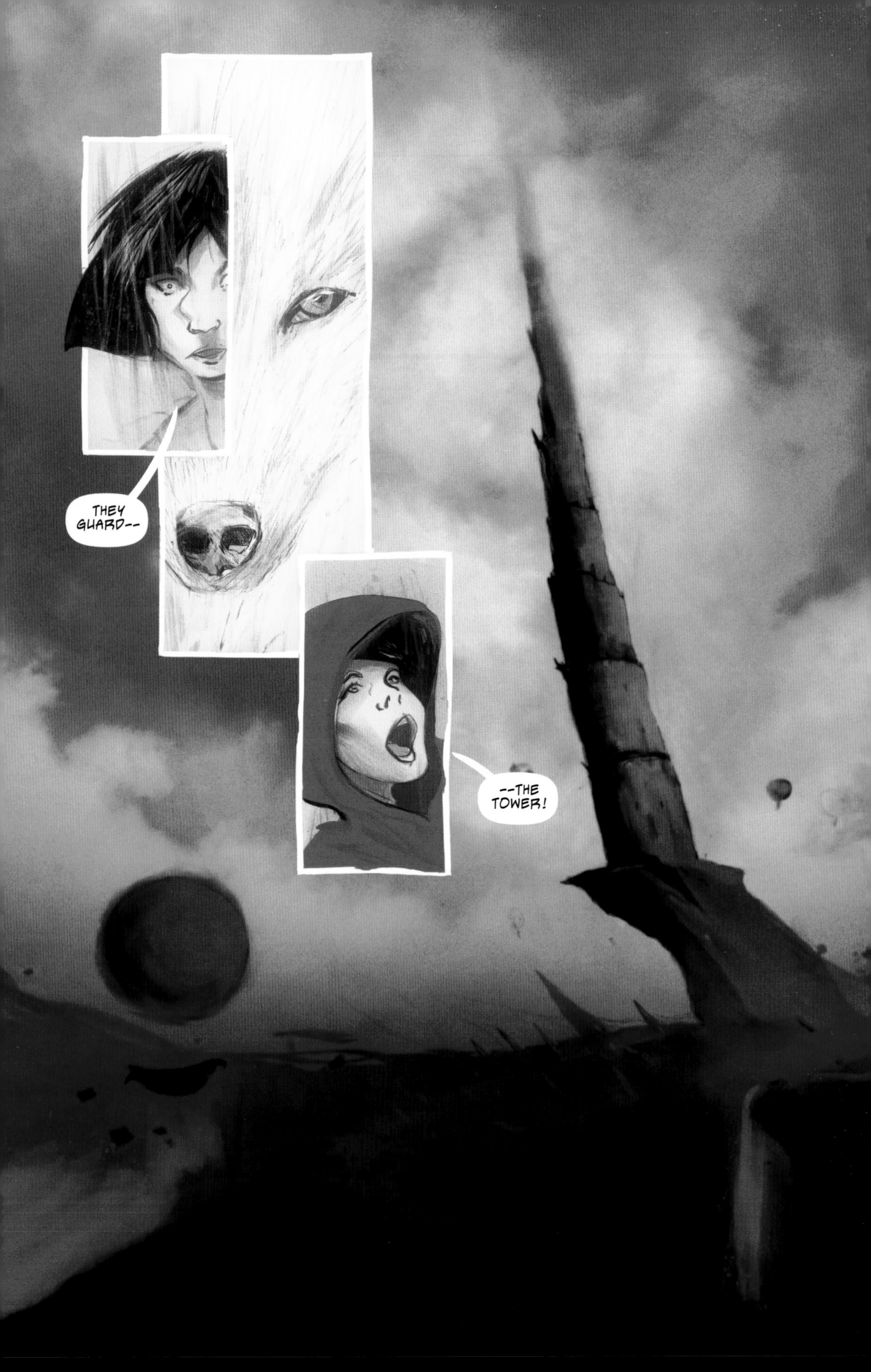
THEY GUARD--
--THE TOWER!

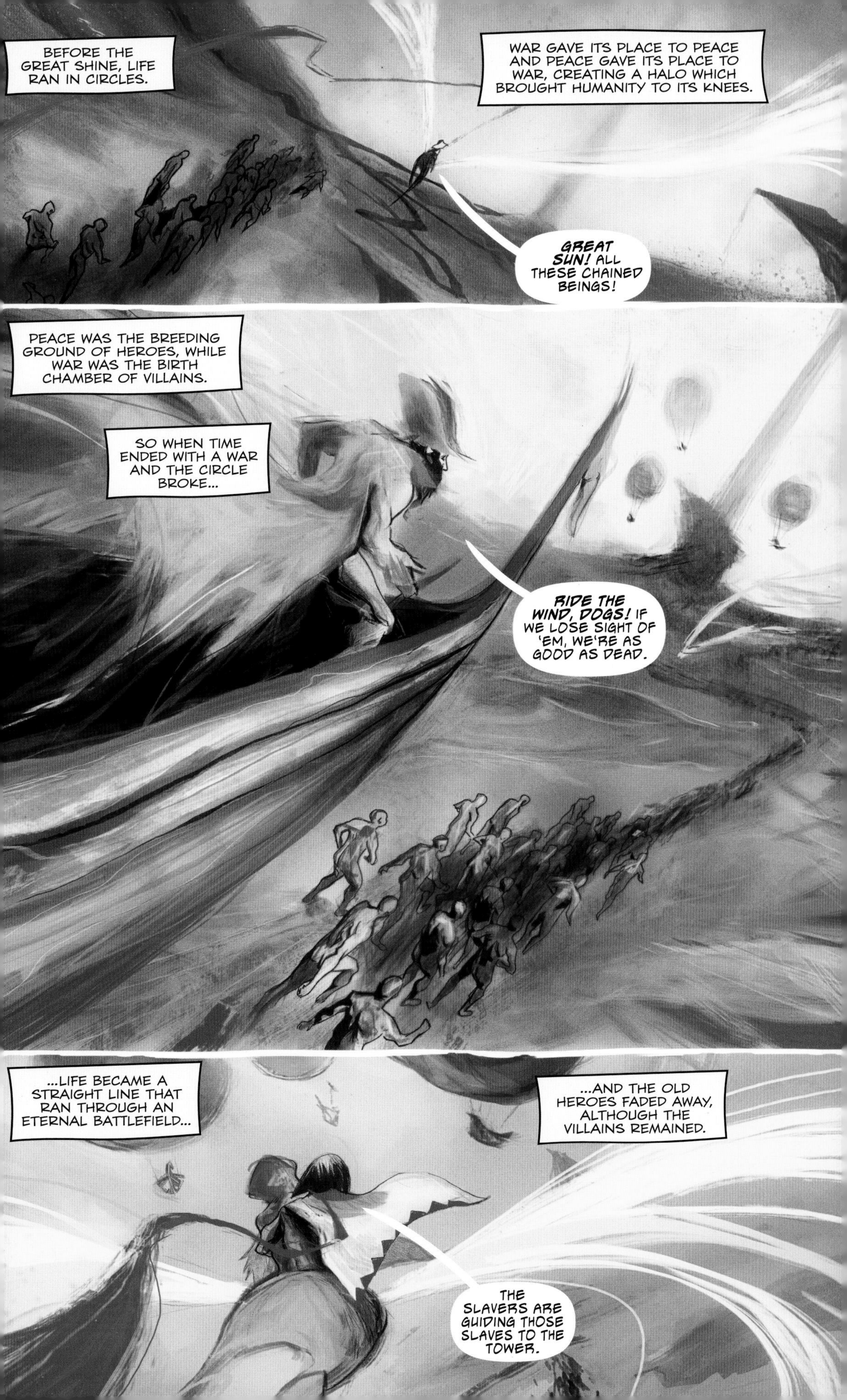
BEFORE THE GREAT SHINE, LIFE RAN IN CIRCLES.
WAR GAVE ITS PLACE TO PEACE AND PEACE GAVE ITS PLACE TO WAR, CREATING A HALO WHICH BROUGHT HUMANITY TO ITS KNEES.
GREAT SUN! ALL THESE CHAINED BEINGS!
PEACE WAS THE BREEDING GROUND OF HEROES, WHILE WAR WAS THE BIRTH CHAMBER OF VILLAINS.
SO WHEN TIME ENDED WITH A WAR AND THE CIRCLE BROKE...
RIDE THE WIND, DOGS! IF WE LOSE SIGHT OF 'EM, WE'RE AS GOOD AS DEAD.
...LIFE BECAME A STRAIGHT LINE THAT RAN THROUGH AN ETERNAL BATTLEFIELD...
...AND THE OLD HEROES FADED AWAY, ALTHOUGH THE VILLAINS REMAINED.
THE SLAVERS ARE GUIDING THOSE SLAVES TO THE TOWER.

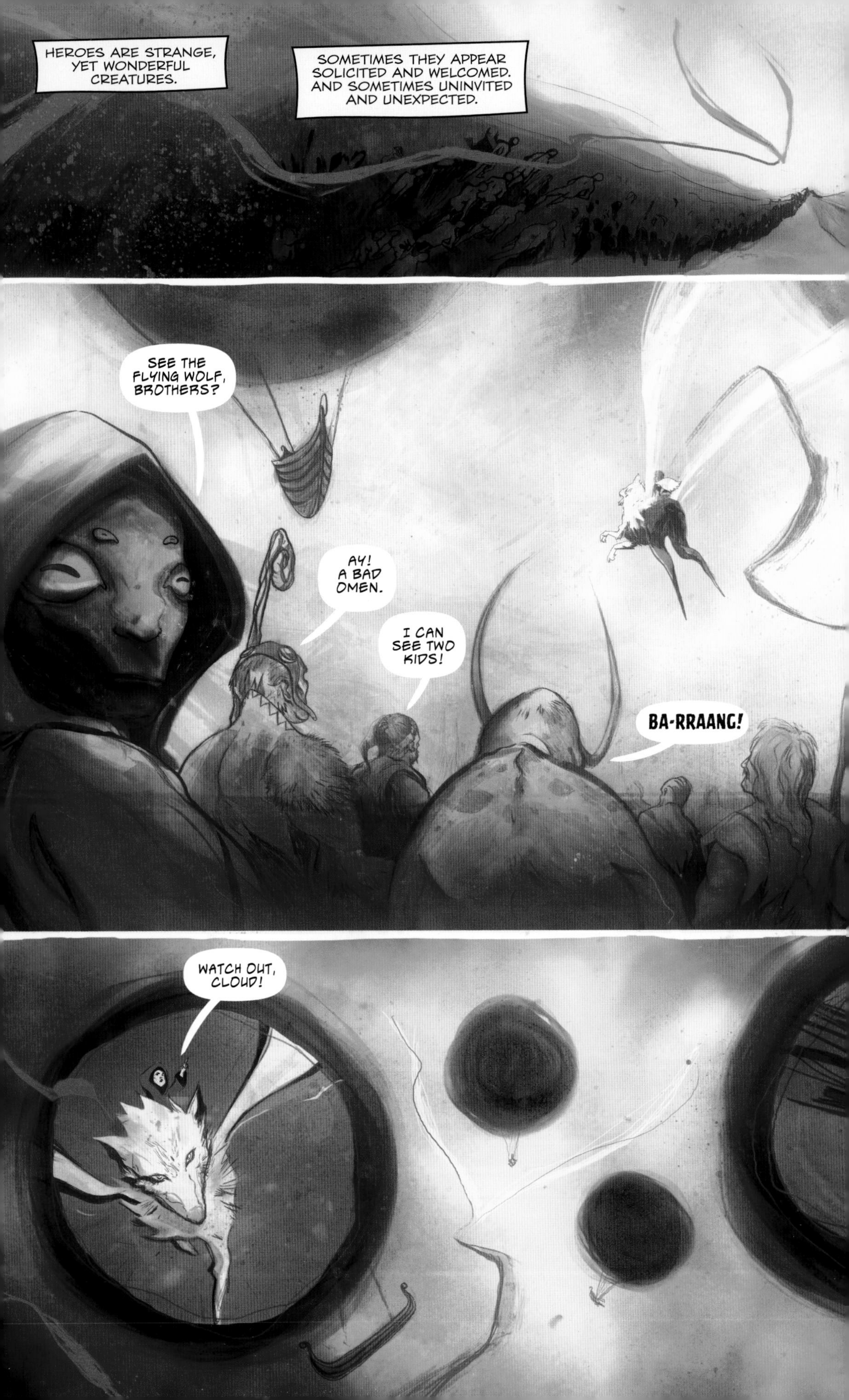
HEROES ARE STRANGE, YET WONDERFUL CREATURES.
SOMETIMES THEY APPEAR SOLICITED AND WELCOMED. AND SOMETIMES UNINVITED AND UNEXPECTED.
SEE THE FLYING WOLF, BROTHERS?
AY! A BAD OMEN.
I CAN SEE TWO KIDS!
BA-RRAANG!
WATCH OUT, CLOUD!

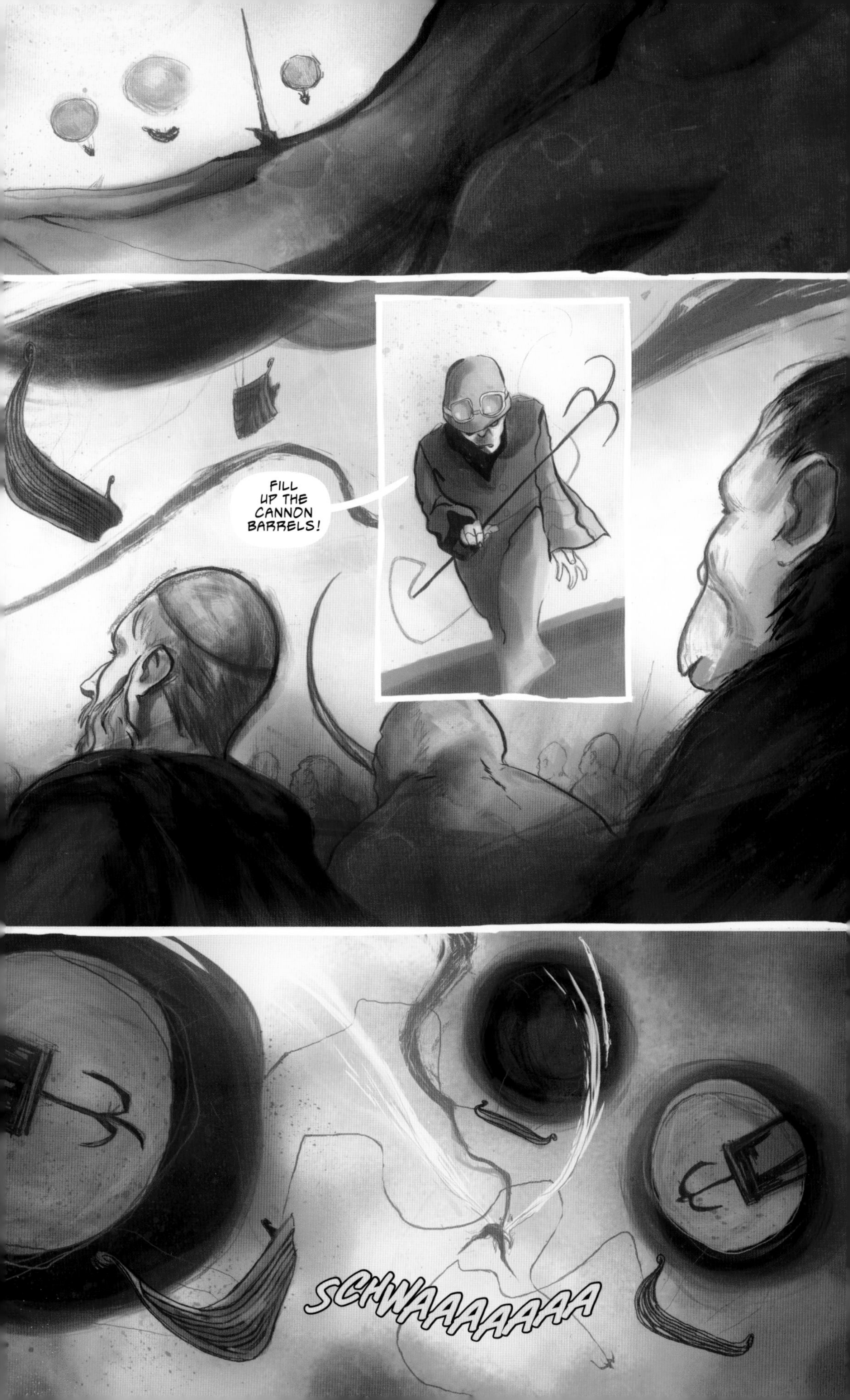
FILL UP THE CANNON BARRELS!
SCHWAAAAAAAA

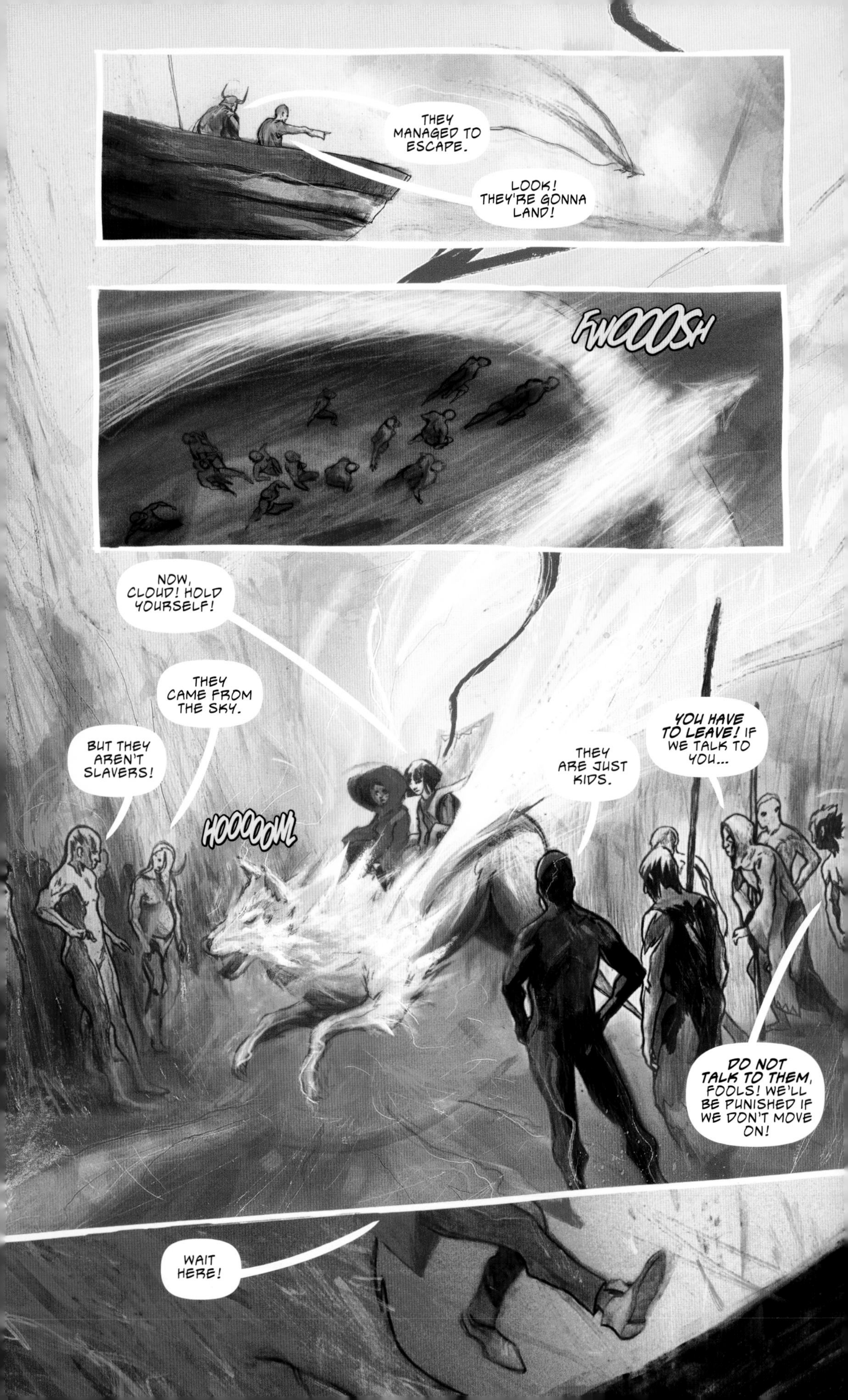
THEY MANAGED TO ESCAPE.
LOOK! THEY'RE GONNA LAND!
FWOOOSH
NOW, CLOUD! HOLD YOURSELF!
THEY CAME FROM THE SKY.
BUT THEY AREN'T SLAVERS!
HOOOOOWL
THEY ARE JUST KIDS.
YOU HAVE TO LEAVE! IF WE TALK TO YOU...
DO NOT TALK TO THEM, FOOLS! WE'LL BE PUNISHED IF WE DON'T MOVE ON!
WAIT HERE!

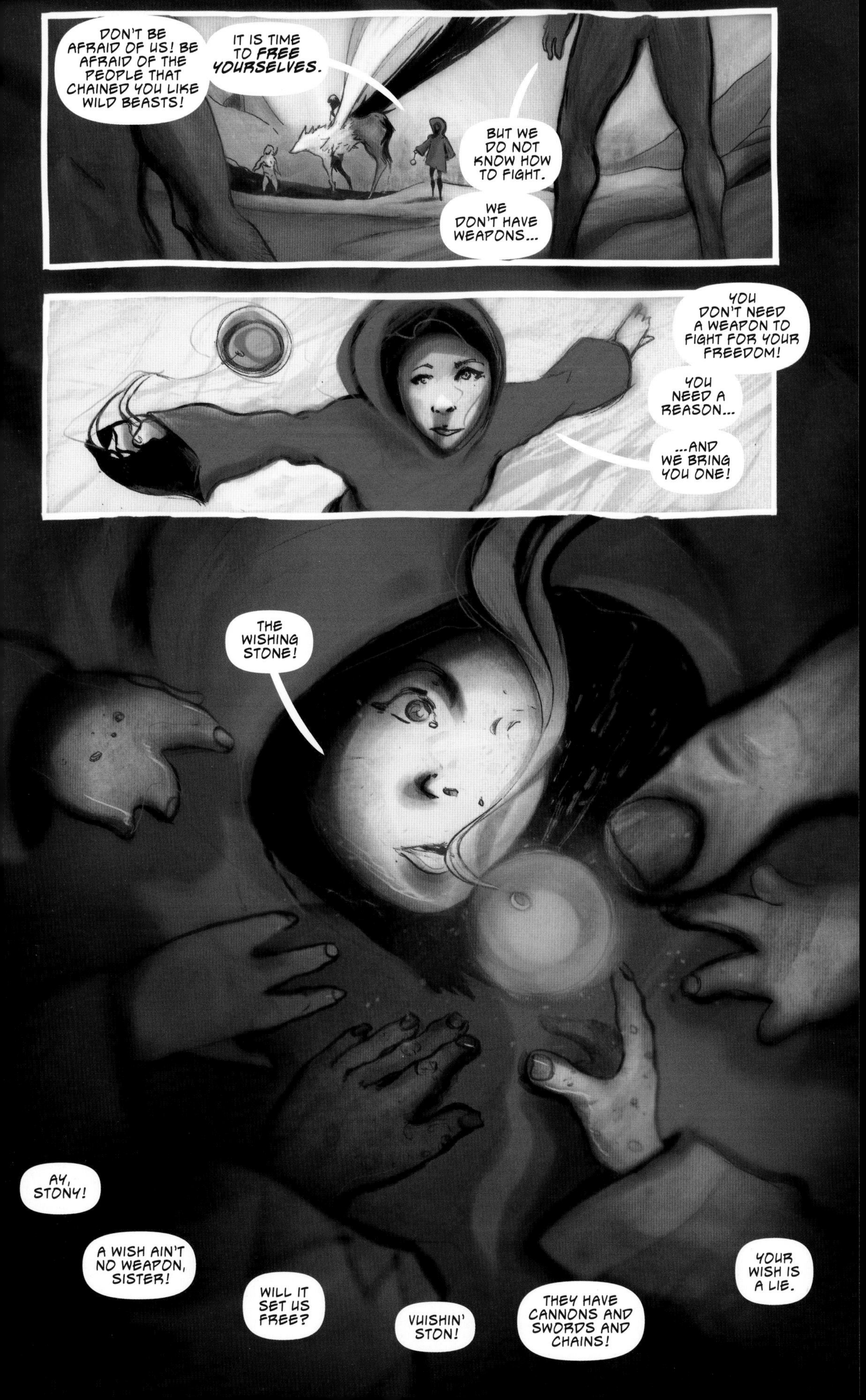
DON'T BE AFRAID OF US! BE AFRAID OF THE PEOPLE THAT CHAINED YOU LIKE WILD BEASTS!
IT IS TIME TO **FREE YOURSELVES.**
BUT WE DO NOT KNOW HOW TO FIGHT.
WE DON'T HAVE WEAPONS...
YOU DON'T NEED A WEAPON TO FIGHT FOR YOUR FREEDOM!
YOU NEED A REASON...
...AND WE BRING YOU ONE!
THE WISHING STONE!
AY, STONY!
A WISH AIN'T NO WEAPON, SISTER!
WILL IT SET US FREE?
VUISHIN' STON!
THEY HAVE CANNONS AND SWORDS AND CHAINS!
YOUR WISH IS A LIE.

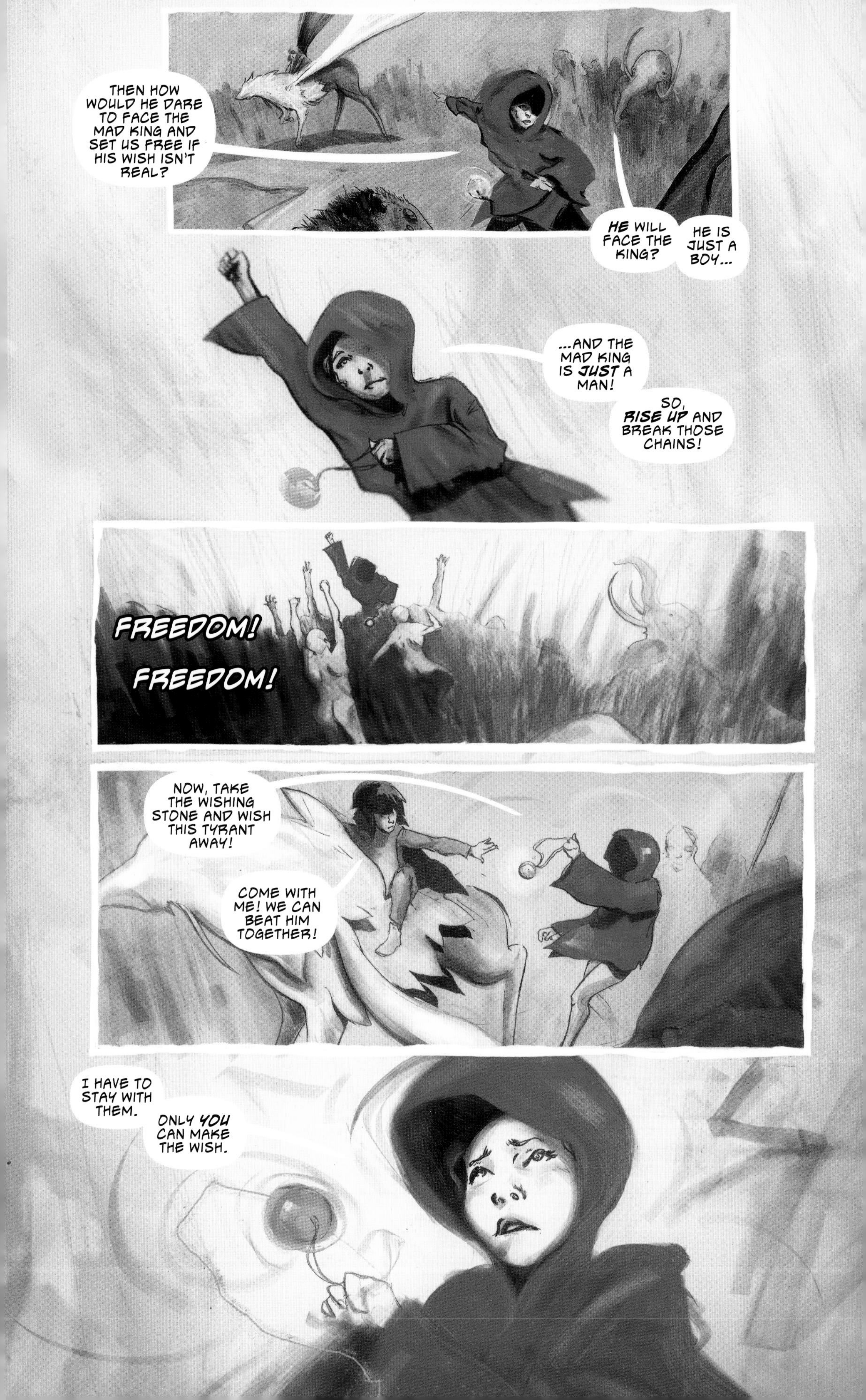
THEN HOW WOULD HE DARE TO FACE THE MAD KING AND SET US FREE IF HIS WISH ISN'T REAL?
HE WILL FACE THE KING?
HE IS JUST A BOY...
...AND THE MAD KING IS JUST A MAN!
SO, RISE UP AND BREAK THOSE CHAINS!
FREEDOM!
FREEDOM!
NOW, TAKE THE WISHING STONE AND WISH THIS TYRANT AWAY!
COME WITH ME! WE CAN BEAT HIM TOGETHER!
I HAVE TO STAY WITH THEM.
ONLY YOU CAN MAKE THE WISH.

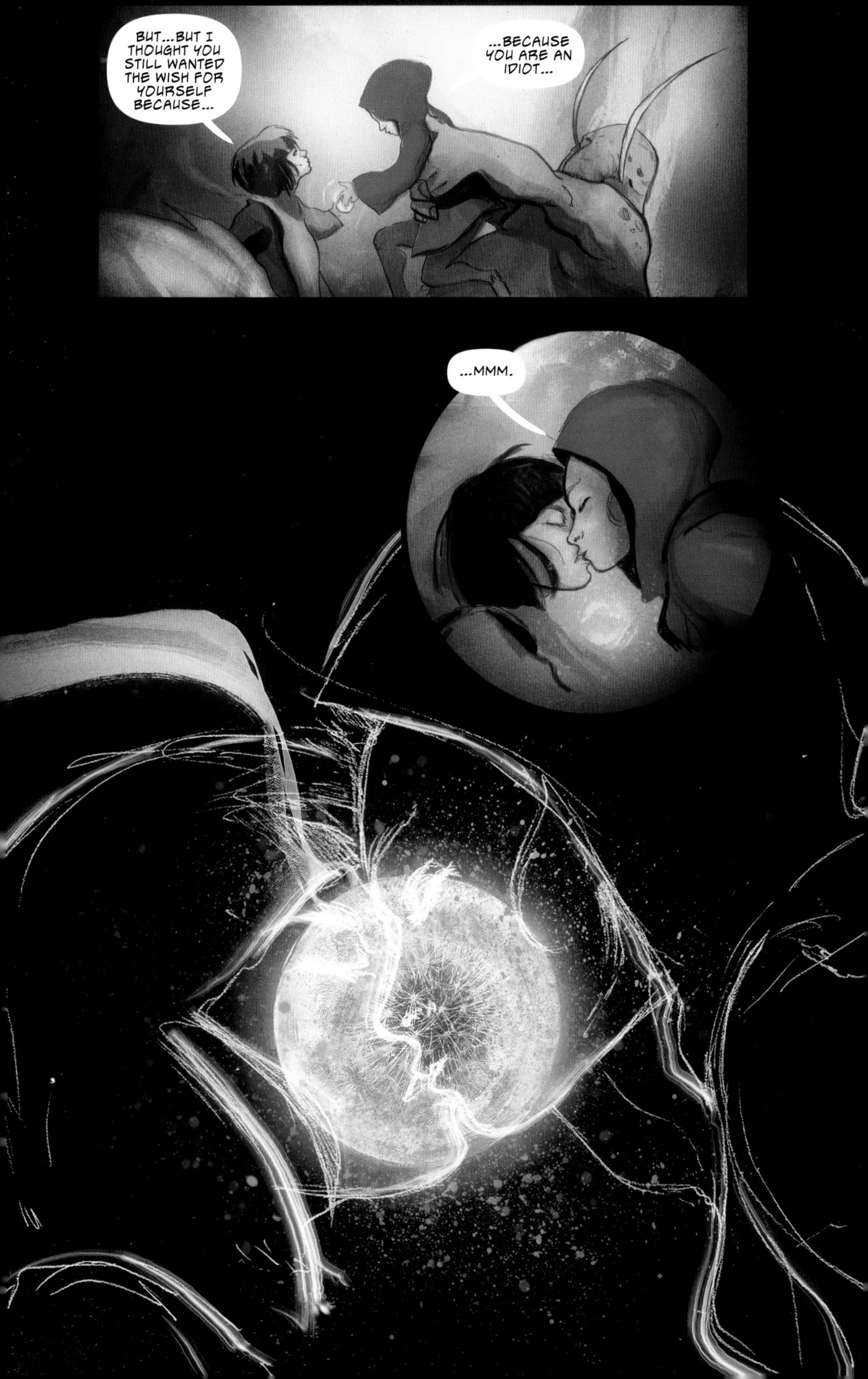
BUT...BUT I THOUGHT YOU STILL WANTED THE WISH FOR YOURSELF BECAUSE...
...BECAUSE YOU ARE AN IDIOT...
...MMM.

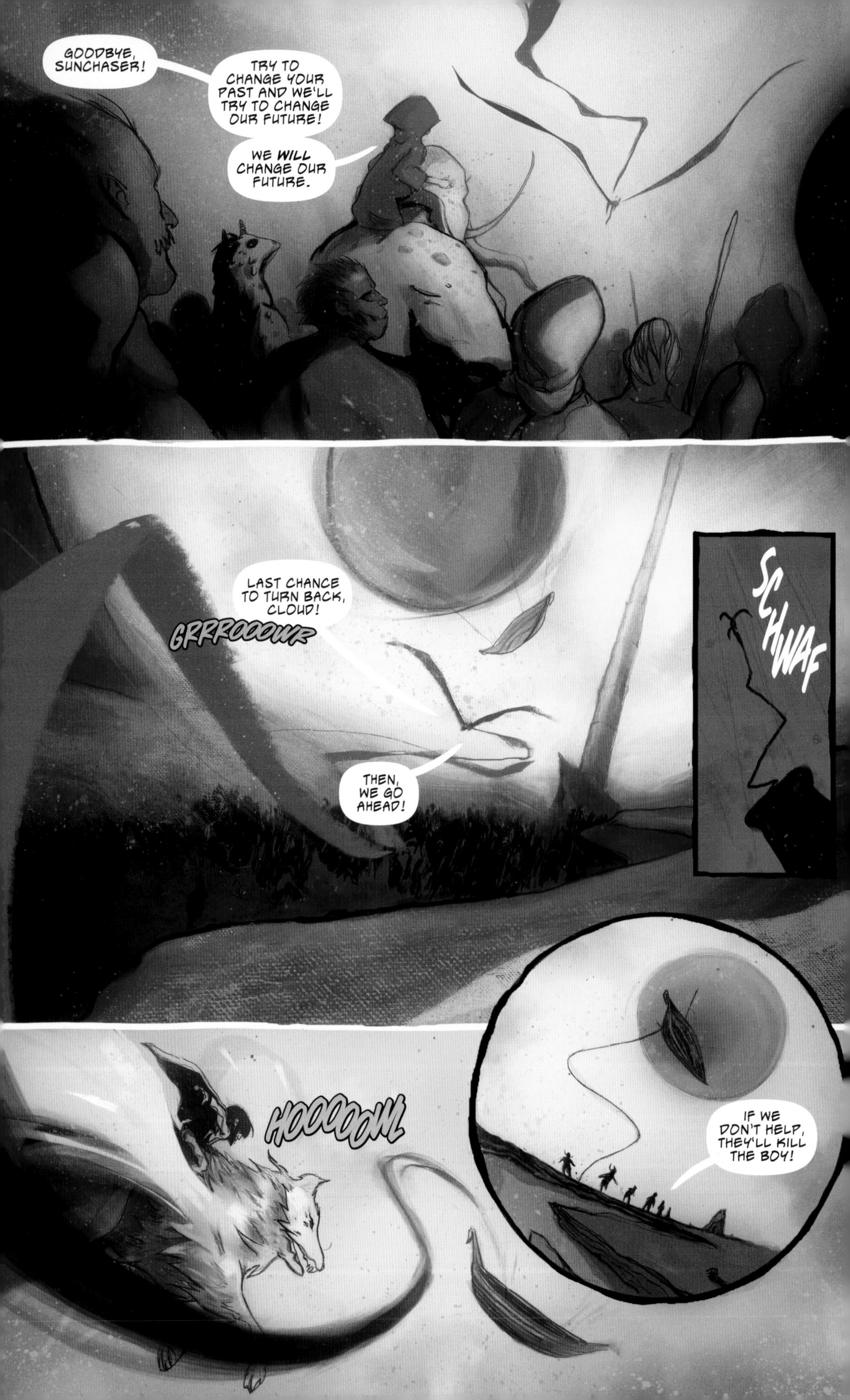
GOODBYE, SUNCHASER!
TRY TO CHANGE YOUR PAST AND WE'LL TRY TO CHANGE OUR FUTURE!
WE WILL CHANGE OUR FUTURE.
GRRROOOOWR
LAST CHANCE TO TURN BACK, CLOUD!
THEN, WE GO AHEAD!
SCHWAF
HOOOOOWL
IF WE DON'T HELP, THEY'LL KILL THE BOY!

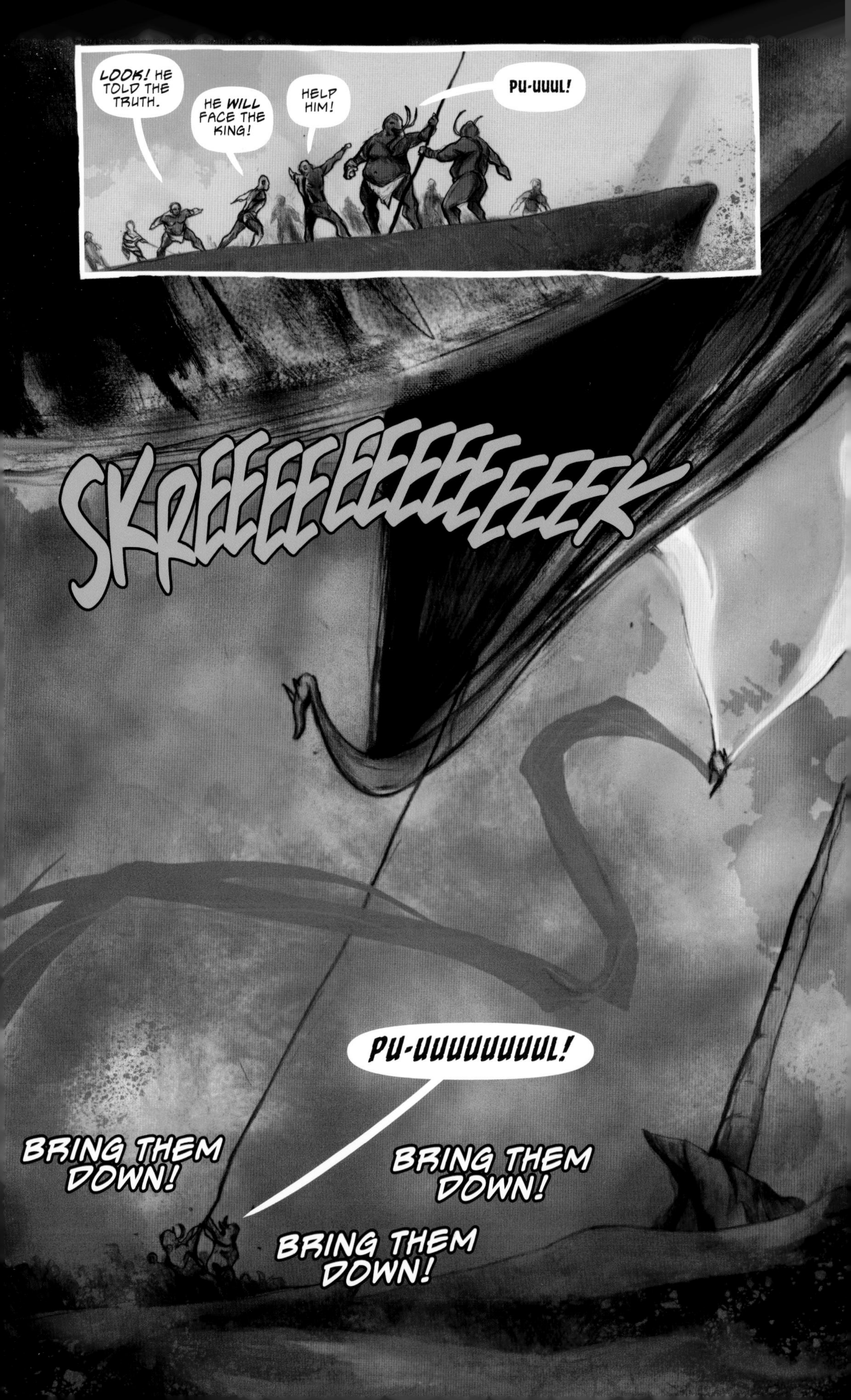

LOOK! HE TOLD THE TRUTH.
HE WILL FACE THE KING!
HELP HIM!
PU-UUUL!
SKREEEEEEEEEEEEEK
PU-UUUUUUUUL!
BRING THEM DOWN!
BRING THEM DOWN!
BRING THEM DOWN!

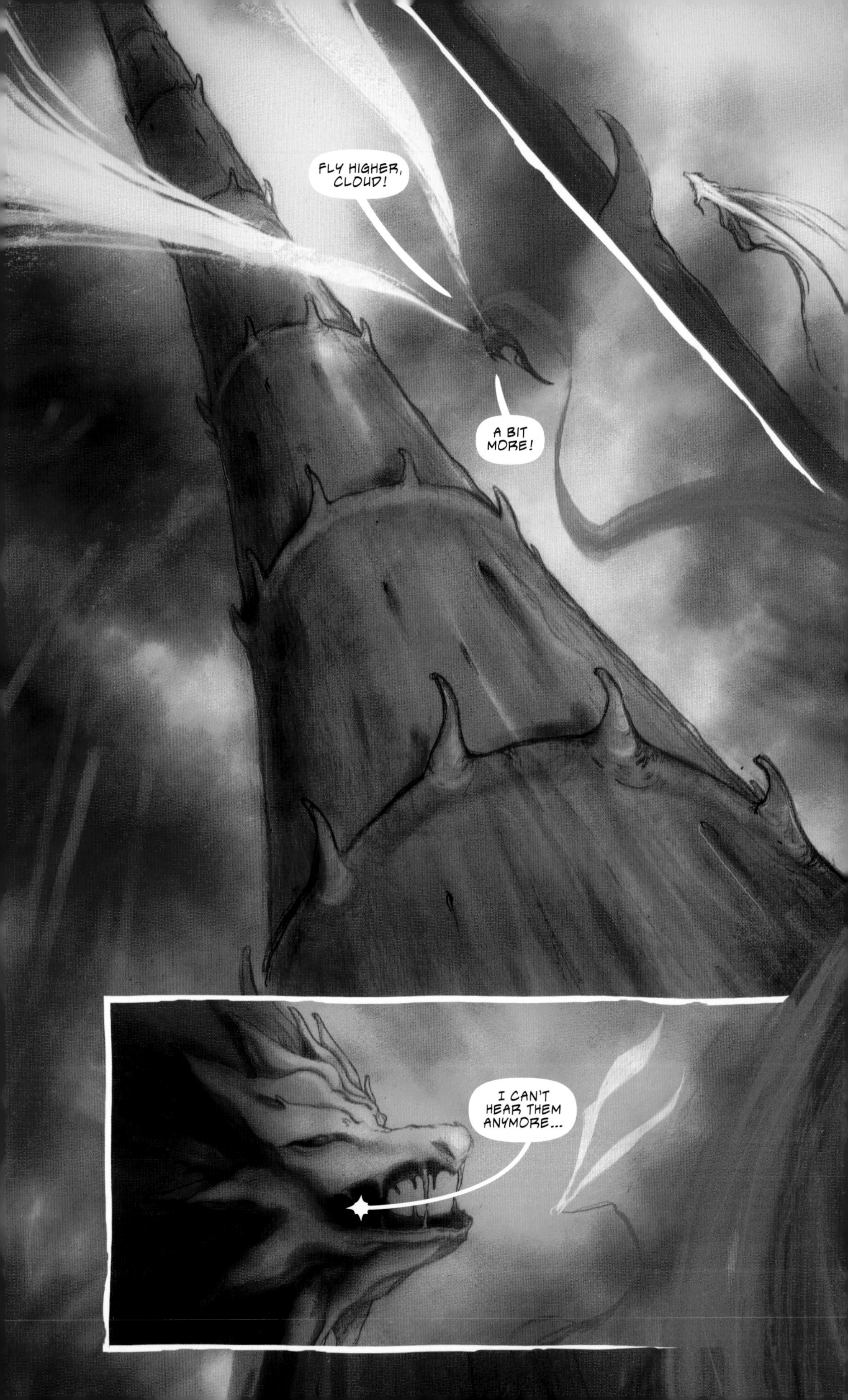
FLY HIGHER, CLOUD!
A BIT MORE!
I CAN'T HEAR THEM ANYMORE...

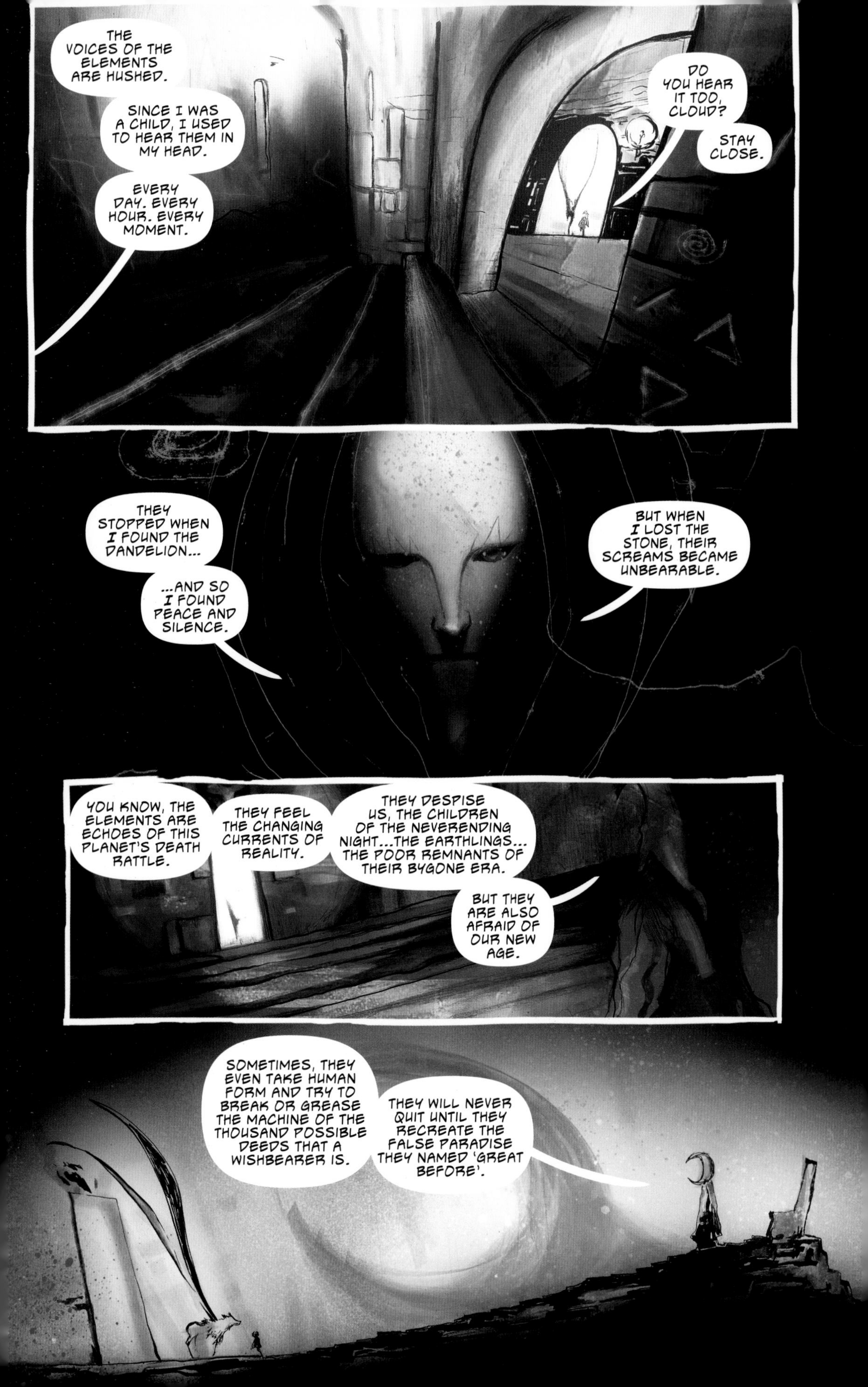
THE VOICES OF THE ELEMENTS ARE HUSHED.
SINCE I WAS A CHILD, I USED TO HEAR THEM IN MY HEAD.
EVERY DAY. EVERY HOUR. EVERY MOMENT.
DO YOU HEAR IT TOO, CLOUD?
STAY CLOSE.
THEY STOPPED WHEN I FOUND THE DANDELION...
...AND SO I FOUND PEACE AND SILENCE.
BUT WHEN I LOST THE STONE, THEIR SCREAMS BECAME UNBEARABLE.
YOU KNOW, THE ELEMENTS ARE ECHOES OF THIS PLANET'S DEATH BATTLE.
THEY FEEL THE CHANGING CURRENTS OF REALITY.
THEY DESPISE US, THE CHILDREN OF THE NEVERENDING NIGHT...THE EARTHLINGS... THE POOR REMNANTS OF THEIR BYGONE ERA.
BUT THEY ARE ALSO AFRAID OF OUR NEW AGE.
SOMETIMES, THEY EVEN TAKE HUMAN FORM AND TRY TO BREAK OR GREASE THE MACHINE OF THE THOUSAND POSSIBLE DEEDS THAT A WISHBEARER IS.
THEY WILL NEVER QUIT UNTIL THEY RECREATE THE FALSE PARADISE THEY NAMED 'GREAT BEFORE'.

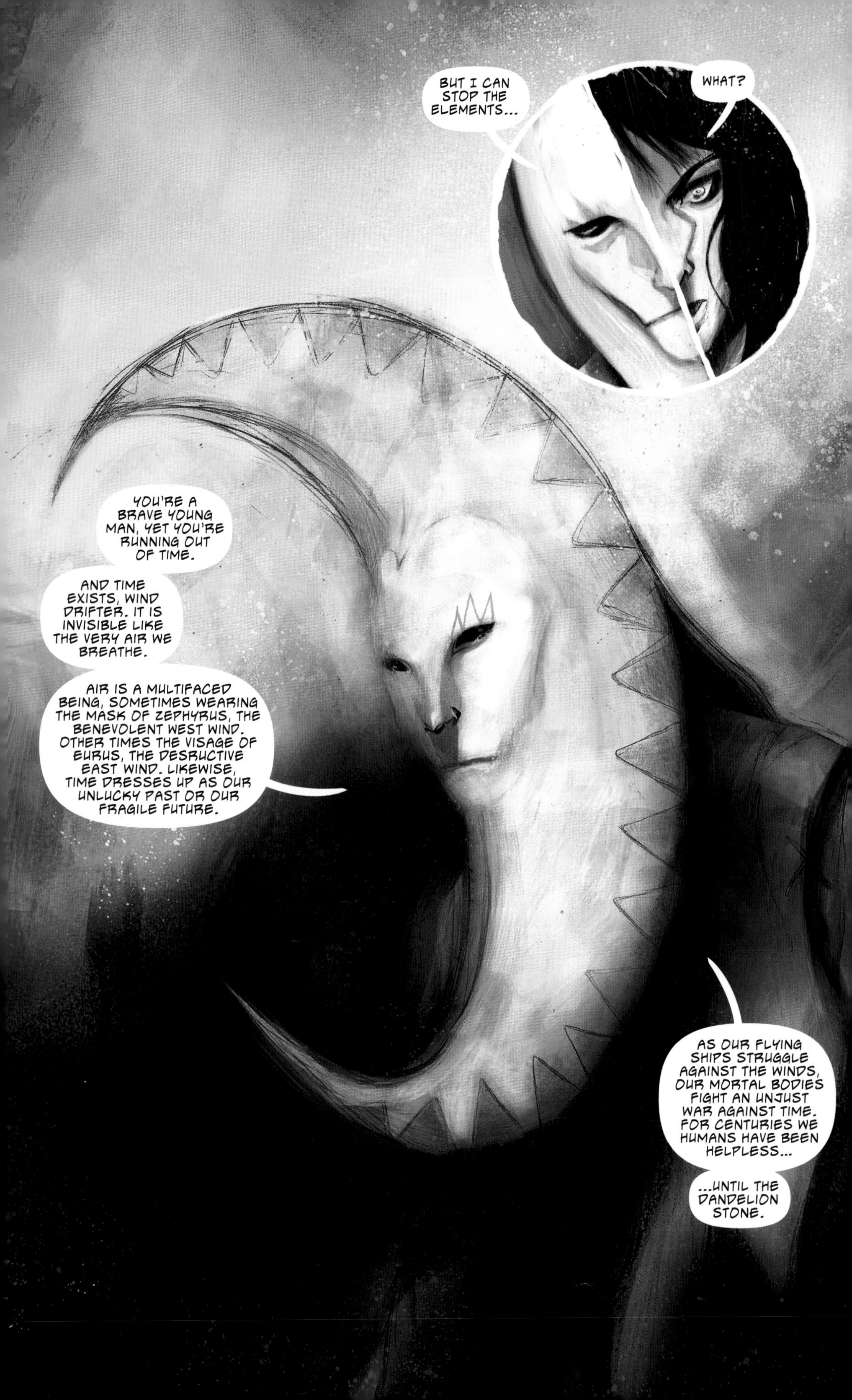
BUT I CAN STOP THE ELEMENTS...
WHAT?
YOU'RE A BRAVE YOUNG MAN, YET YOU'RE RUNNING OUT OF TIME.
AND TIME EXISTS, WIND DRIFTER. IT IS INVISIBLE LIKE THE VERY AIR WE BREATHE.
AIR IS A MULTIFACED BEING, SOMETIMES WEARING THE MASK OF ZEPHYRUS, THE BENEVOLENT WEST WIND. OTHER TIMES THE VISAGE OF EURUS, THE DESRUCTIVE EAST WIND. LIKEWISE, TIME DRESSES UP AS OUR UNLUCKY PAST OR OUR FRAGILE FUTURE.
AS OUR FLYING SHIPS STRUGGLE AGAINST THE WINDS, OUR MORTAL BODIES FIGHT AN UNJUST WAR AGAINST TIME. FOR CENTURIES WE HUMANS HAVE BEEN HELPLESS...
...UNTIL THE DANDELION STONE.

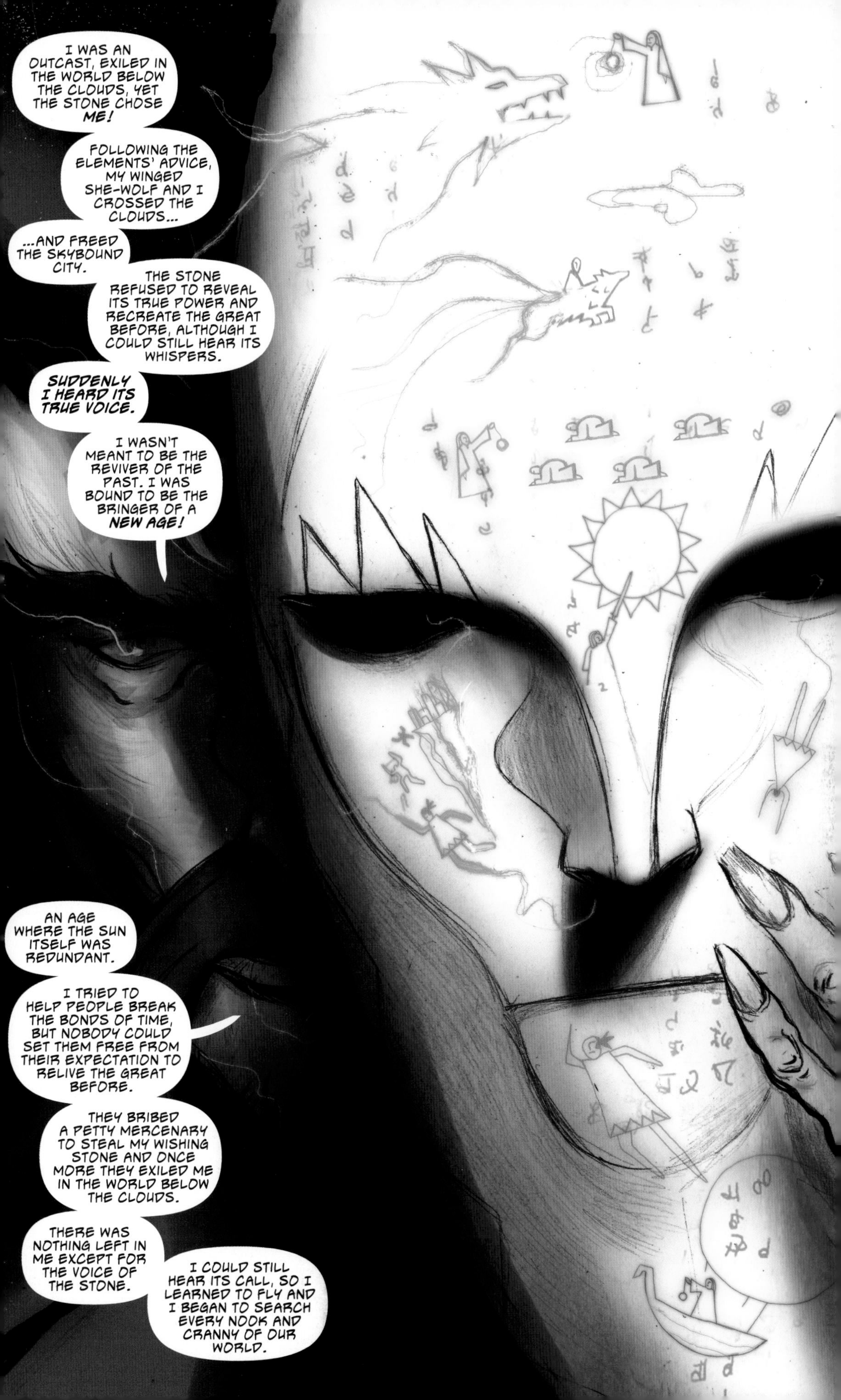
I WAS AN OUTCAST, EXILED IN THE WORLD BELOW THE CLOUDS, YET THE STONE CHOSE ***ME!***
FOLLOWING THE ELEMENTS' ADVICE, MY WINGED SHE-WOLF AND I CROSSED THE CLOUDS...
...AND FREED THE SKYBOUND CITY.
THE STONE REFUSED TO REVEAL ITS TRUE POWER AND RECREATE THE GREAT BEFORE, ALTHOUGH I COULD STILL HEAR ITS WHISPERS.
SUDDENLY I HEARD ITS TRUE VOICE.
I WASN'T MEANT TO BE THE REVIVER OF THE PAST. I WAS BOUND TO BE THE BRINGER OF A ***NEW AGE!***
AN AGE WHERE THE SUN ITSELF WAS REDUNDANT.
I TRIED TO HELP PEOPLE BREAK THE BONDS OF TIME, BUT NOBODY COULD SET THEM FREE FROM THEIR EXPECTATION TO RELIVE THE GREAT BEFORE.
THEY BRIBED A PETTY MERCENARY TO STEAL MY WISHING STONE AND ONCE MORE THEY EXILED ME IN THE WORLD BELOW THE CLOUDS.
THERE WAS NOTHING LEFT IN ME EXCEPT FOR THE VOICE OF THE STONE.
I COULD STILL HEAR ITS CALL, SO I LEARNED TO FLY AND I BEGAN TO SEARCH EVERY NOOK AND CRANNY OF OUR WORLD.

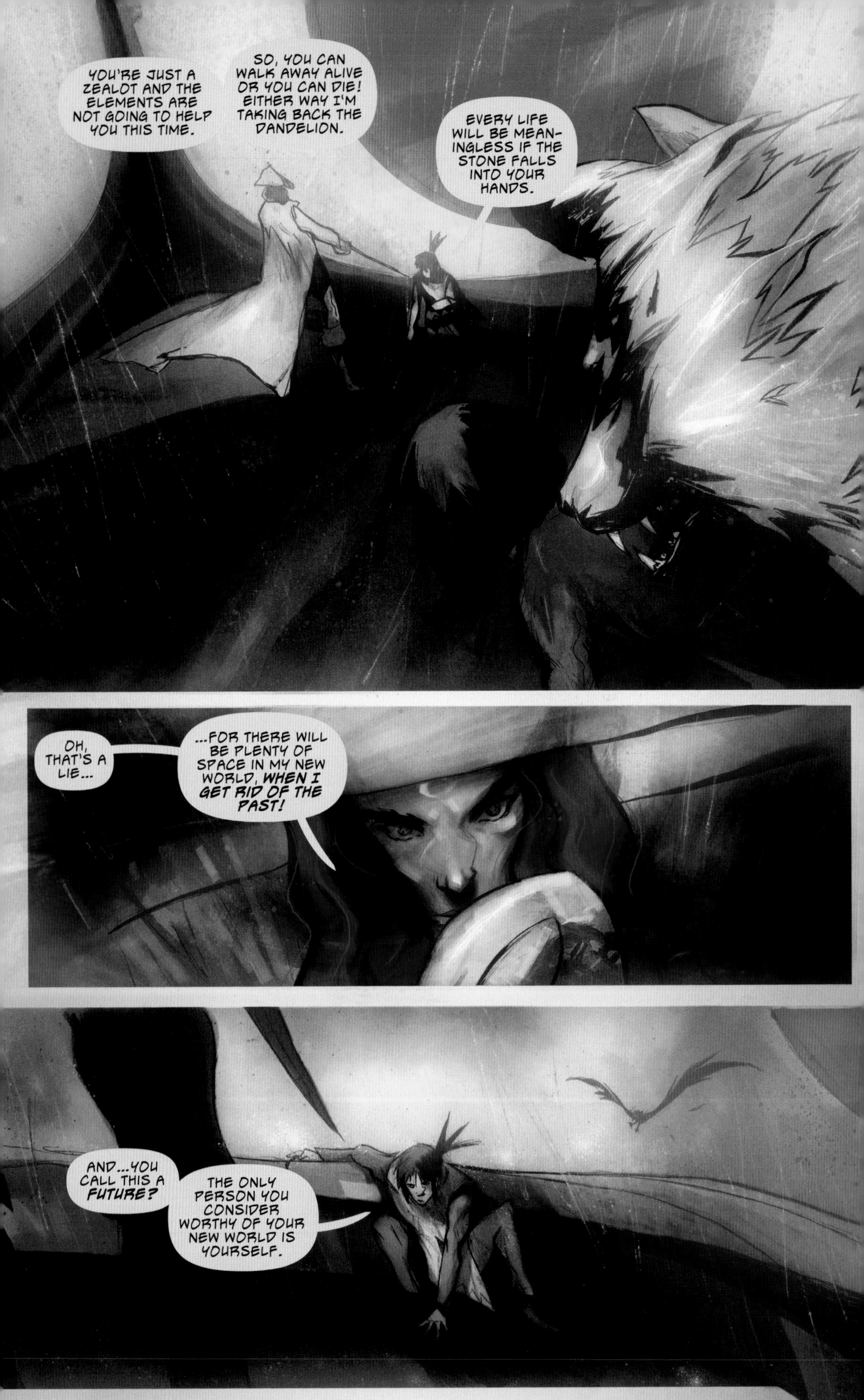
YOU'RE JUST A ZEALOT AND THE ELEMENTS ARE NOT GOING TO HELP YOU THIS TIME.
SO, YOU CAN WALK AWAY ALIVE OR YOU CAN DIE! EITHER WAY I'M TAKING BACK THE DANDELION.
EVERY LIFE WILL BE MEAN-INGLESS IF THE STONE FALLS INTO YOUR HANDS.
OH, THAT'S A LIE...
...FOR THERE WILL BE PLENTY OF SPACE IN MY NEW WORLD, ***WHEN I GET RID OF THE PAST!***
AND...YOU CALL THIS A ***FUTURE?***
THE ONLY PERSON YOU CONSIDER WORTHY OF YOUR NEW WORLD IS YOURSELF.

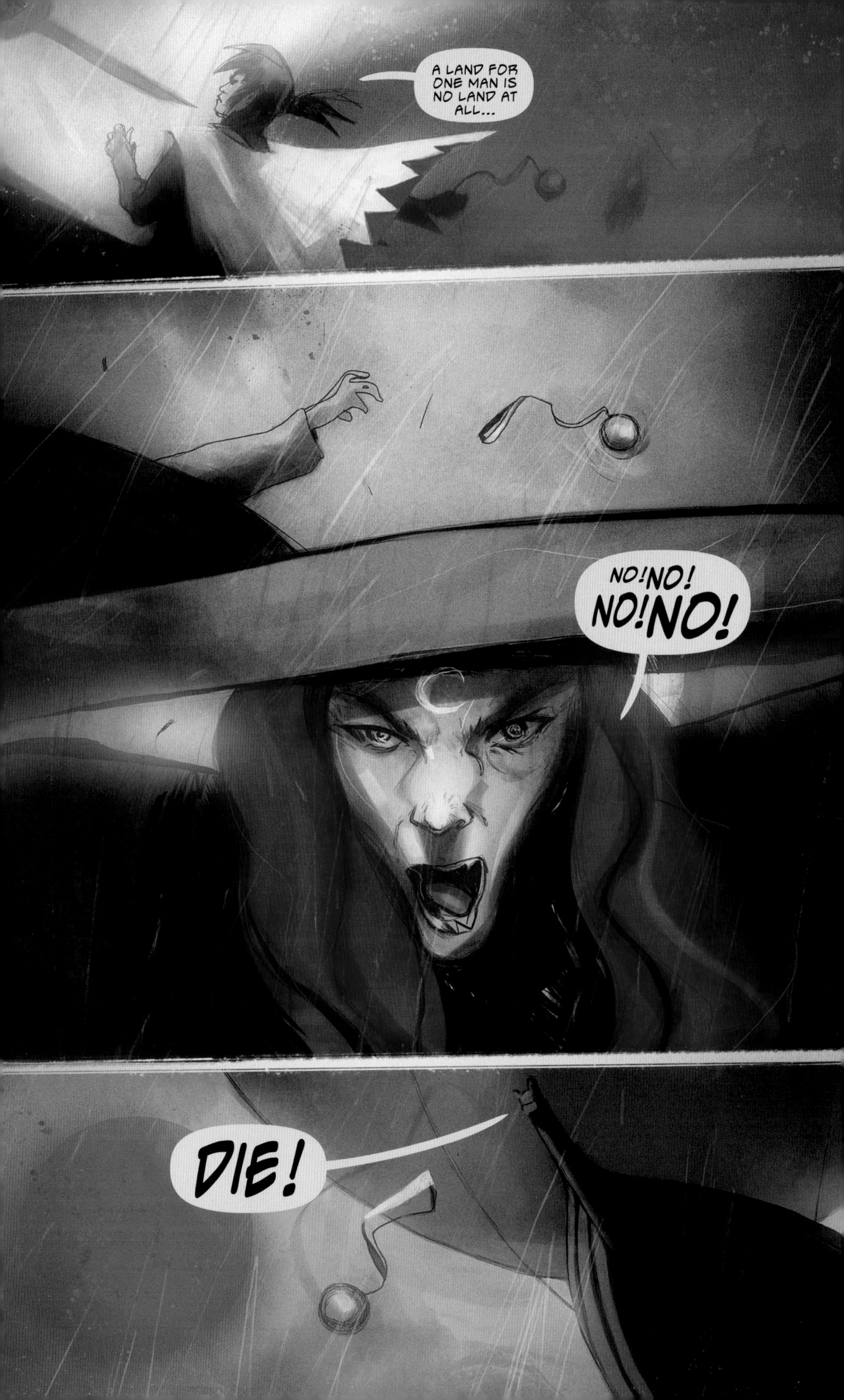
A LAND FOR ONE MAN IS NO LAND AT ALL...
NO! NO! NO! NO!
DIE!

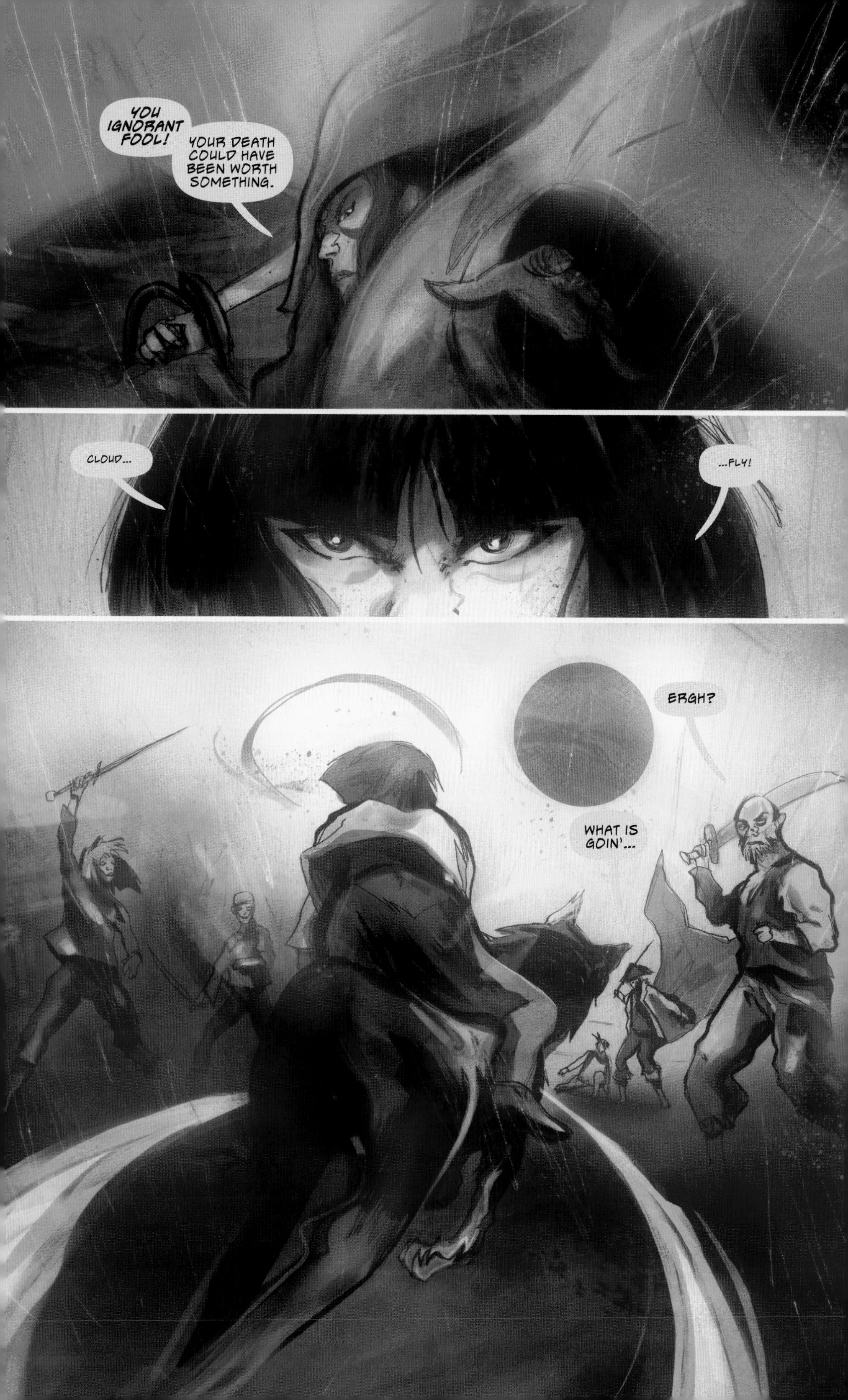
YOU IGNORANT FOOL!
YOUR DEATH COULD HAVE BEEN WORTH SOMETHING.
CLOUD...
...FLY!
ERGH?
WHAT IS GOIN'...

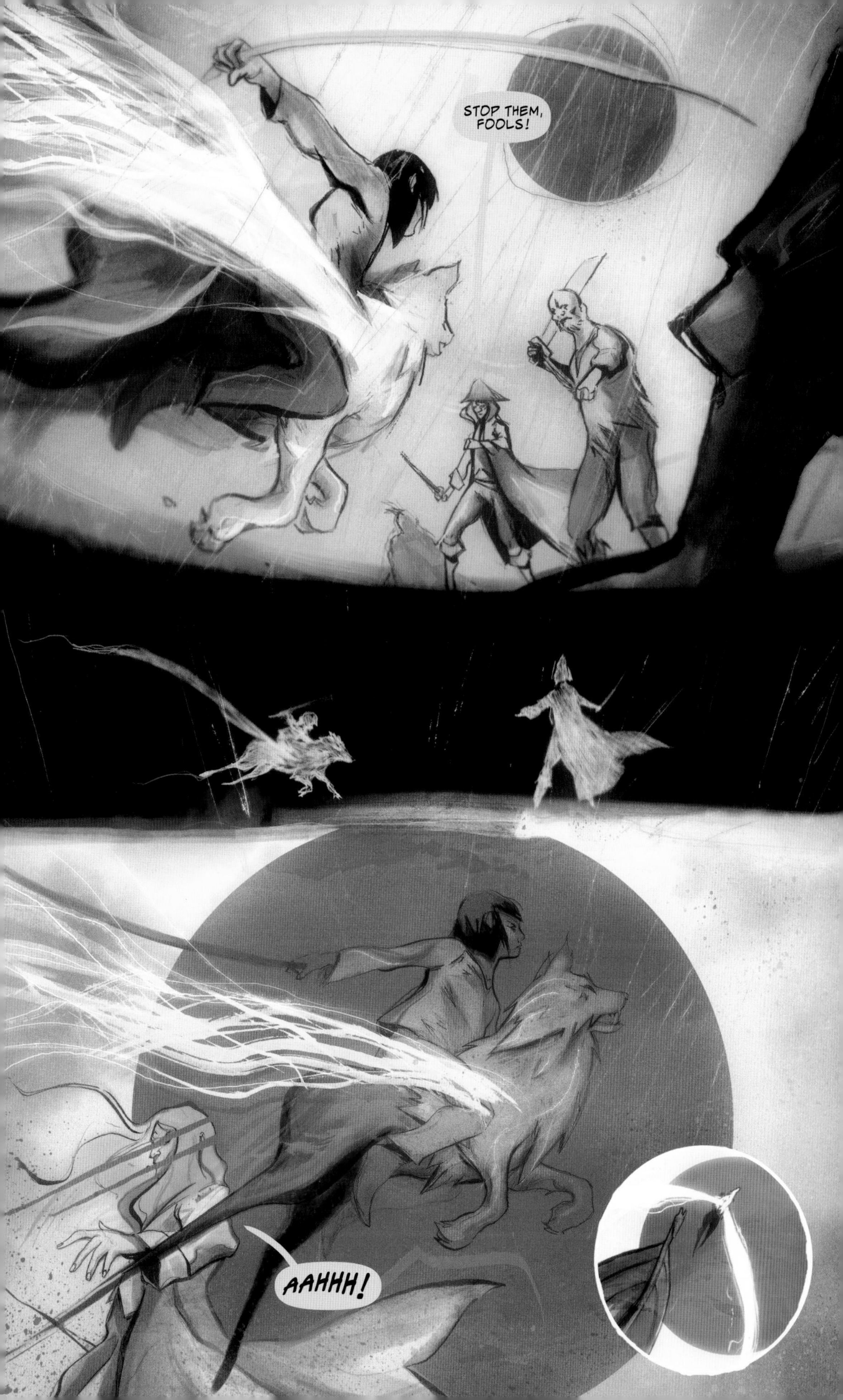
STOP THEM, FOOLS!
AAHHH!

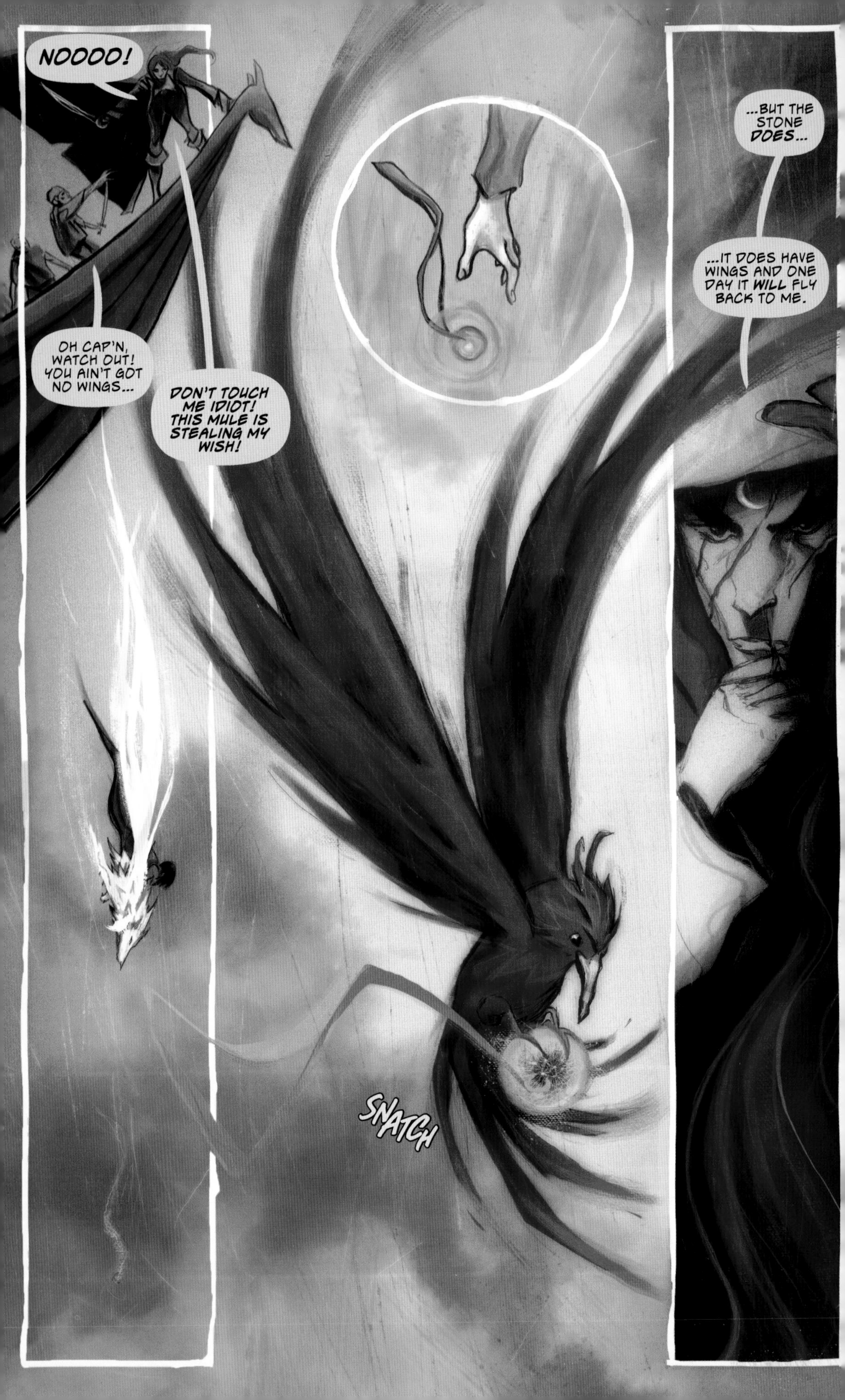
NOOOO!
OH CAP'N, WATCH OUT! YOU AIN'T GOT NO WINGS...
DON'T TOUCH ME IDIOT! THIS MULE IS STEALING MY WISH!
SNATCH
...BUT THE STONE DOES...
...IT DOES HAVE WINGS AND ONE DAY IT WILL FLY BACK TO ME.

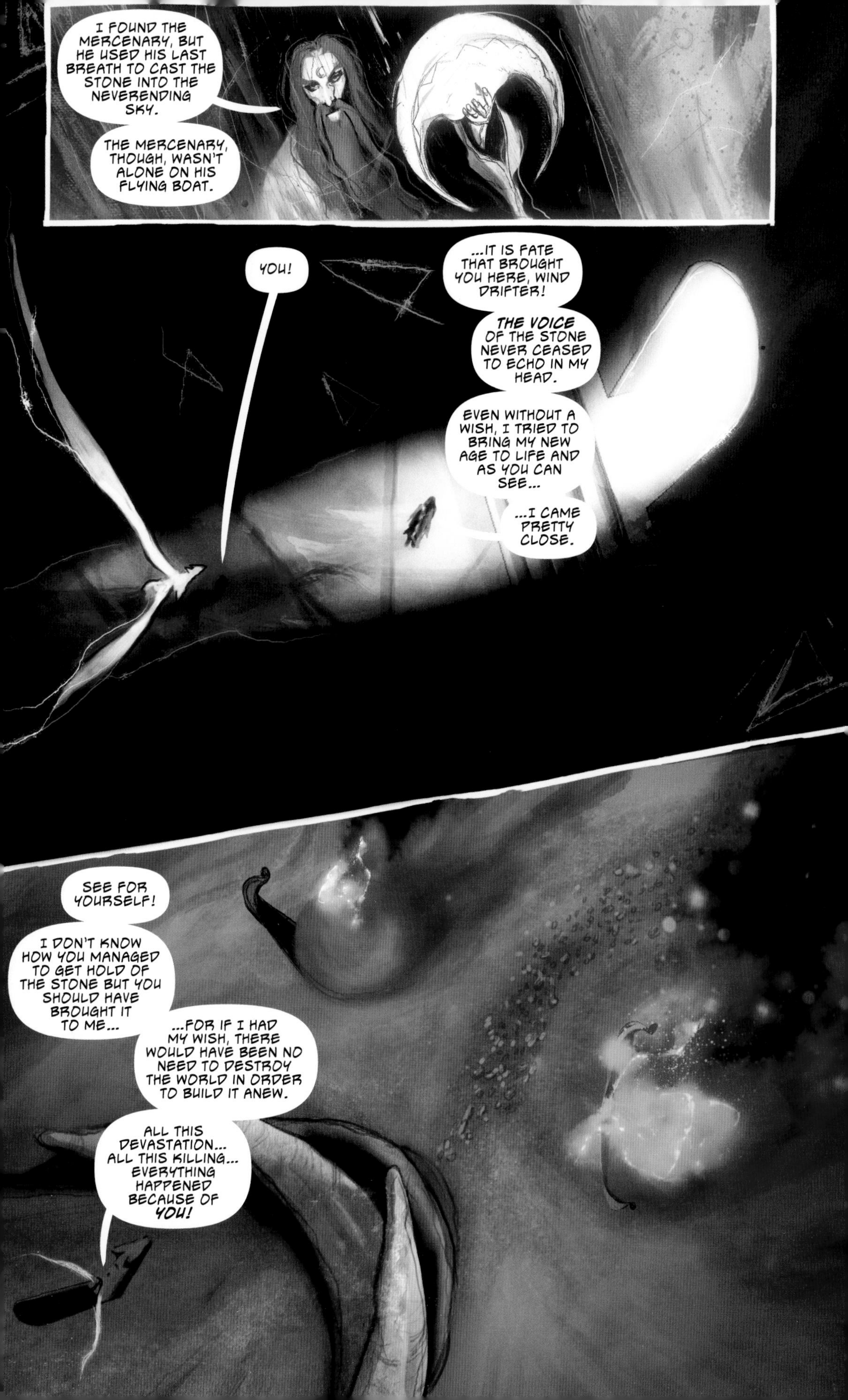
I FOUND THE MERCENARY, BUT HE USED HIS LAST BREATH TO CAST THE STONE INTO THE NEVERENDING SKY.
THE MERCENARY, THOUGH, WASN'T ALONE ON HIS FLYING BOAT.
YOU!
...IT IS FATE THAT BROUGHT YOU HERE, WIND DRIFTER!
THE VOICE OF THE STONE NEVER CEASED TO ECHO IN MY HEAD.
EVEN WITHOUT A WISH, I TRIED TO BRING MY NEW AGE TO LIFE AND AS YOU CAN SEE...
...I CAME PRETTY CLOSE.
SEE FOR YOURSELF!
I DON'T KNOW HOW YOU MANAGED TO GET HOLD OF THE STONE BUT YOU SHOULD HAVE BROUGHT IT TO ME...
...FOR IF I HAD MY WISH, THERE WOULD HAVE BEEN NO NEED TO DESTROY THE WORLD IN ORDER TO BUILD IT ANEW.
ALL THIS DEVASTATION... ALL THIS KILLING... EVERYTHING HAPPENED BECAUSE OF YOU!

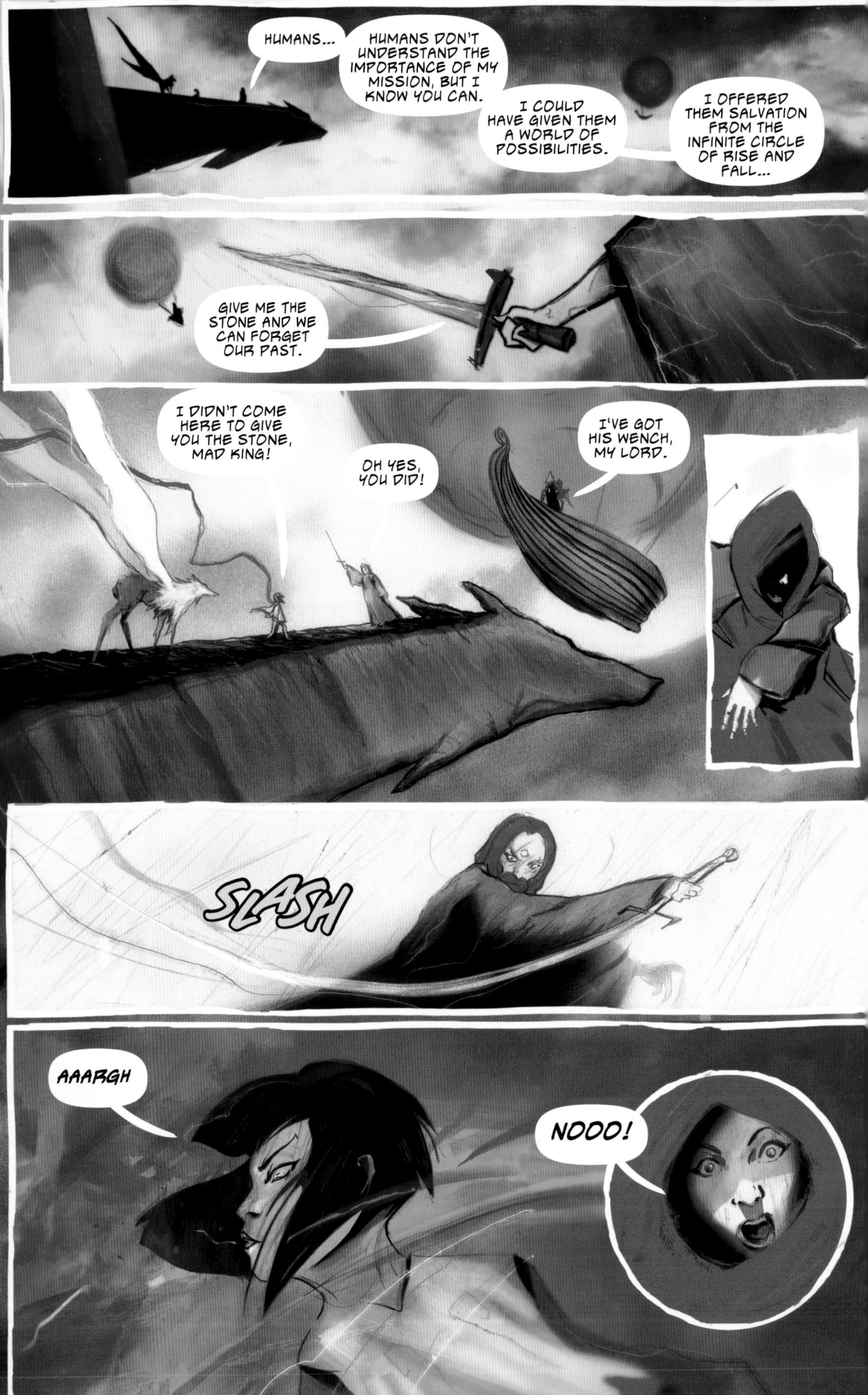
HUMANS...
HUMANS DON'T UNDERSTAND THE IMPORTANCE OF MY MISSION, BUT I KNOW YOU CAN.
I COULD HAVE GIVEN THEM A WORLD OF POSSIBILITIES.
I OFFERED THEM SALVATION FROM THE INFINITE CIRCLE OF RISE AND FALL...
GIVE ME THE STONE AND WE CAN FORGET OUR PAST.
I DIDN'T COME HERE TO GIVE YOU THE STONE, MAD KING!
OH YES, YOU DID!
I'VE GOT HIS WENCH, MY LORD.
SLASH
AAARGH
NOOO!

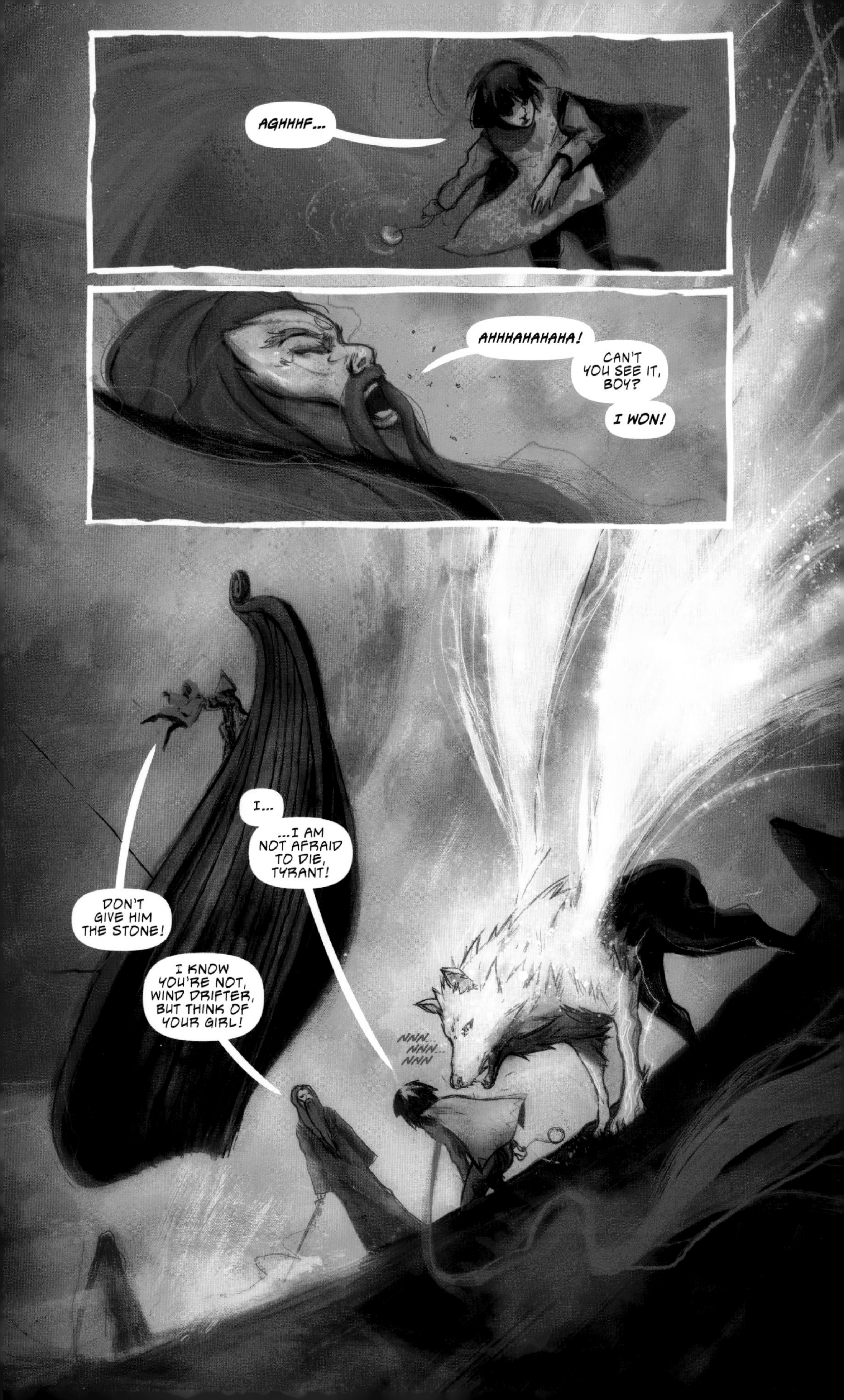
AGHHHF...
AHHHHAHAHAHA!
CAN'T YOU SEE IT, BOY?
I WON!
I...
...I AM NOT AFRAID TO DIE, TYRANT!
DON'T GIVE HIM THE STONE!
I KNOW YOU'RE NOT, WIND DRIFTER, BUT THINK OF YOUR GIRL!
NNN... NNN... NNN

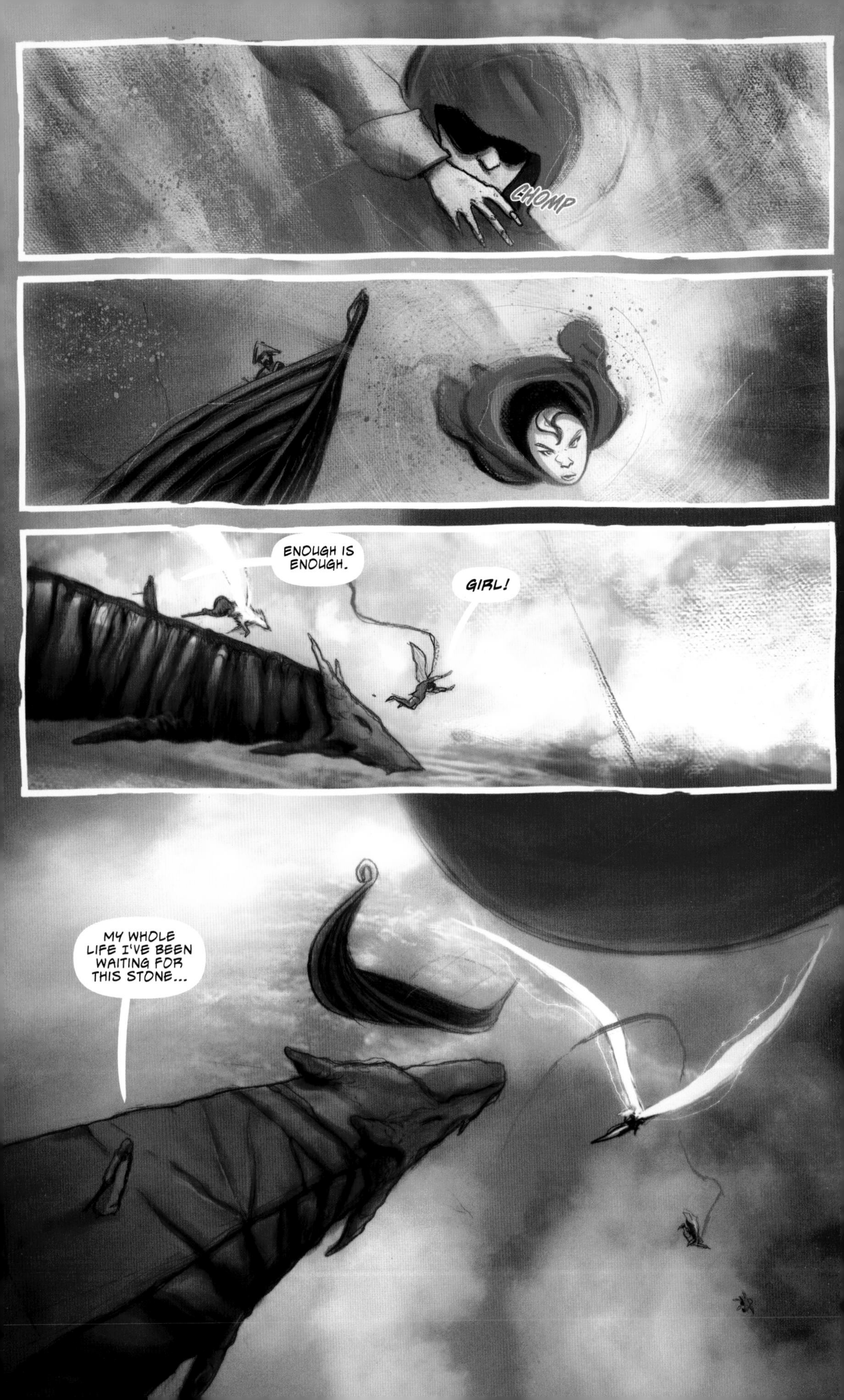
CHOMP
ENOUGH IS ENOUGH.
GIRL!
MY WHOLE LIFE I'VE BEEN WAITING FOR THIS STONE...

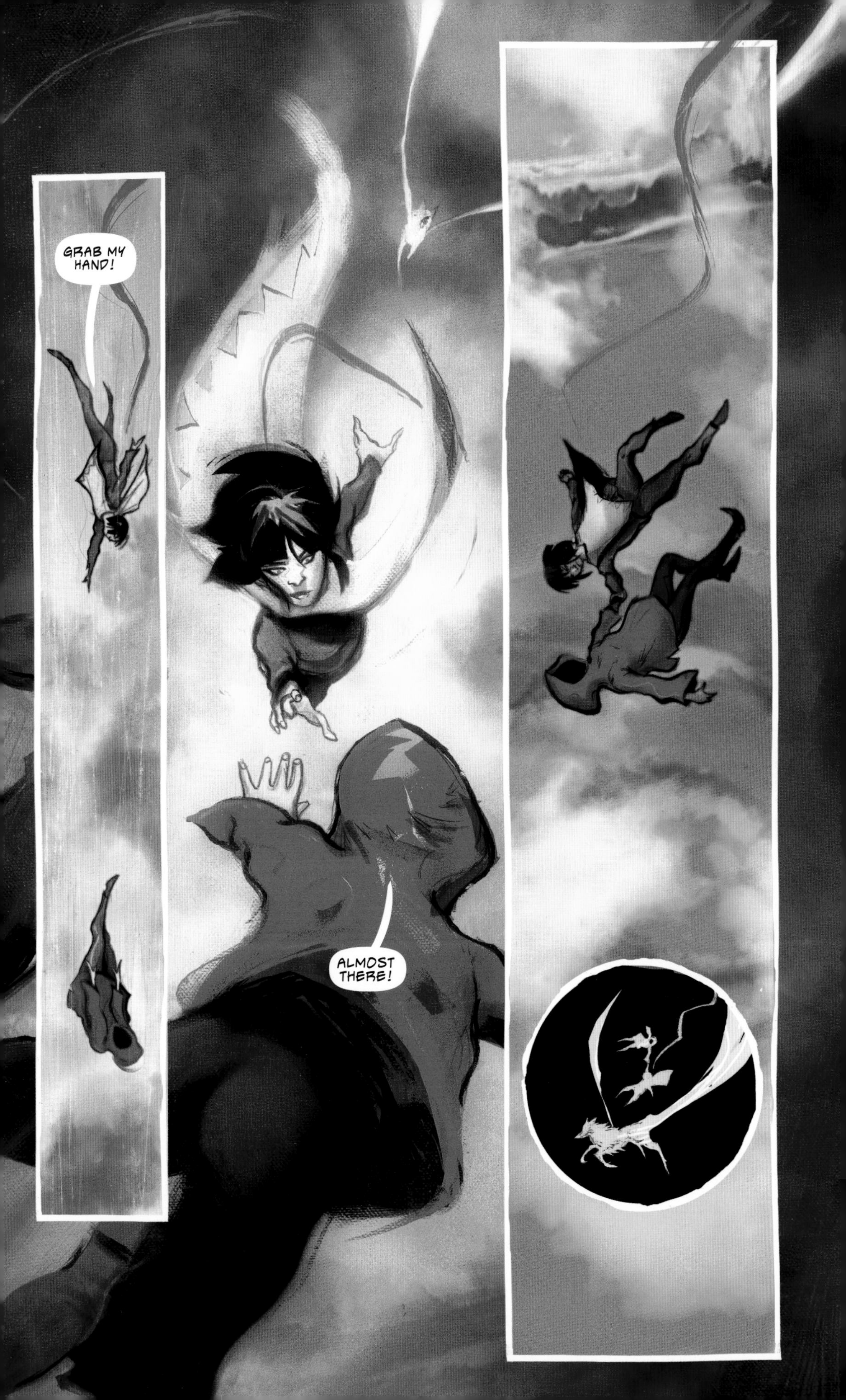
GRAB MY HAND!
ALMOST THERE!

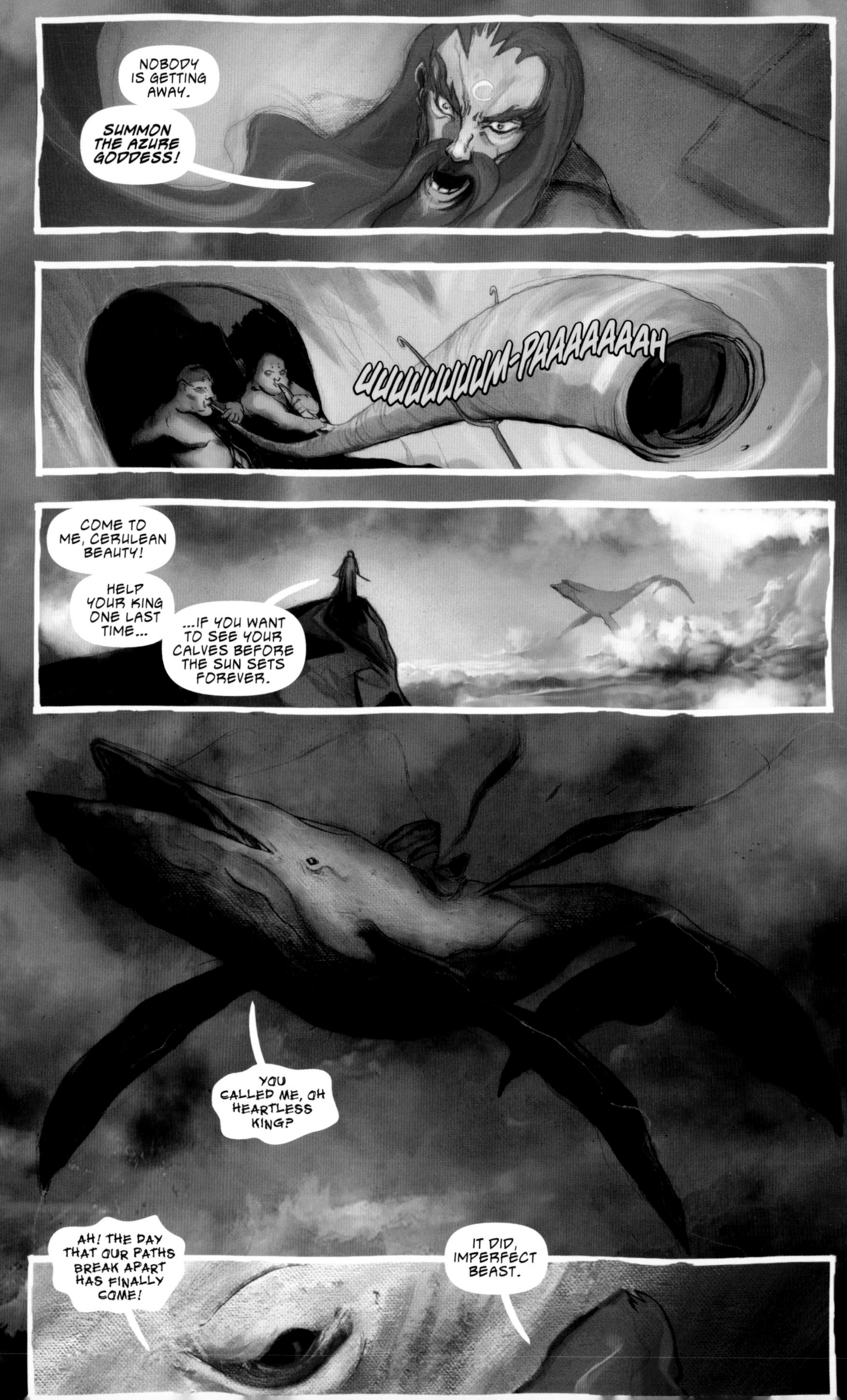
NOBODY IS GETTING AWAY.
SUMMON THE AZURE GODDESS!
UUUUUUUUUM-PAAAAAAAH
COME TO ME, CERULEAN BEAUTY!
HELP YOUR KING ONE LAST TIME...
...IF YOU WANT TO SEE YOUR CALVES BEFORE THE SUN SETS FOREVER.
YOU CALLED ME, OH HEARTLESS KING?
AH! THE DAY THAT OUR PATHS BREAK APART HAS FINALLY COME!
IT DID, IMPERFECT BEAST.

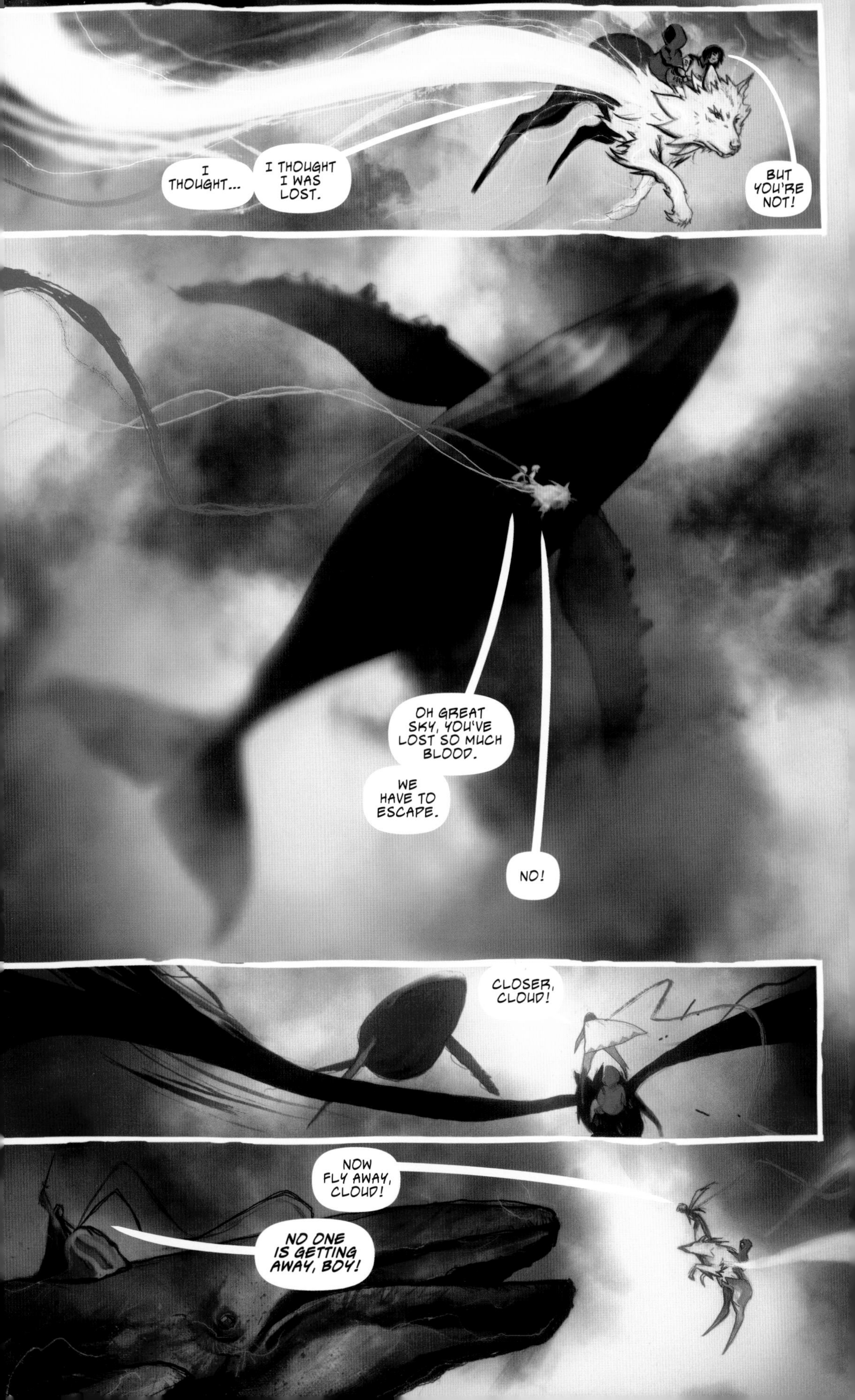

I THOUGHT...
I THOUGHT I WAS LOST.
BUT YOU'RE NOT!
OH GREAT SKY, YOU'VE LOST SO MUCH BLOOD.
WE HAVE TO ESCAPE.
NO!
CLOSER, CLOUD!
NOW FLY AWAY, CLOUD!
NO ONE IS GETTING AWAY, BOY!

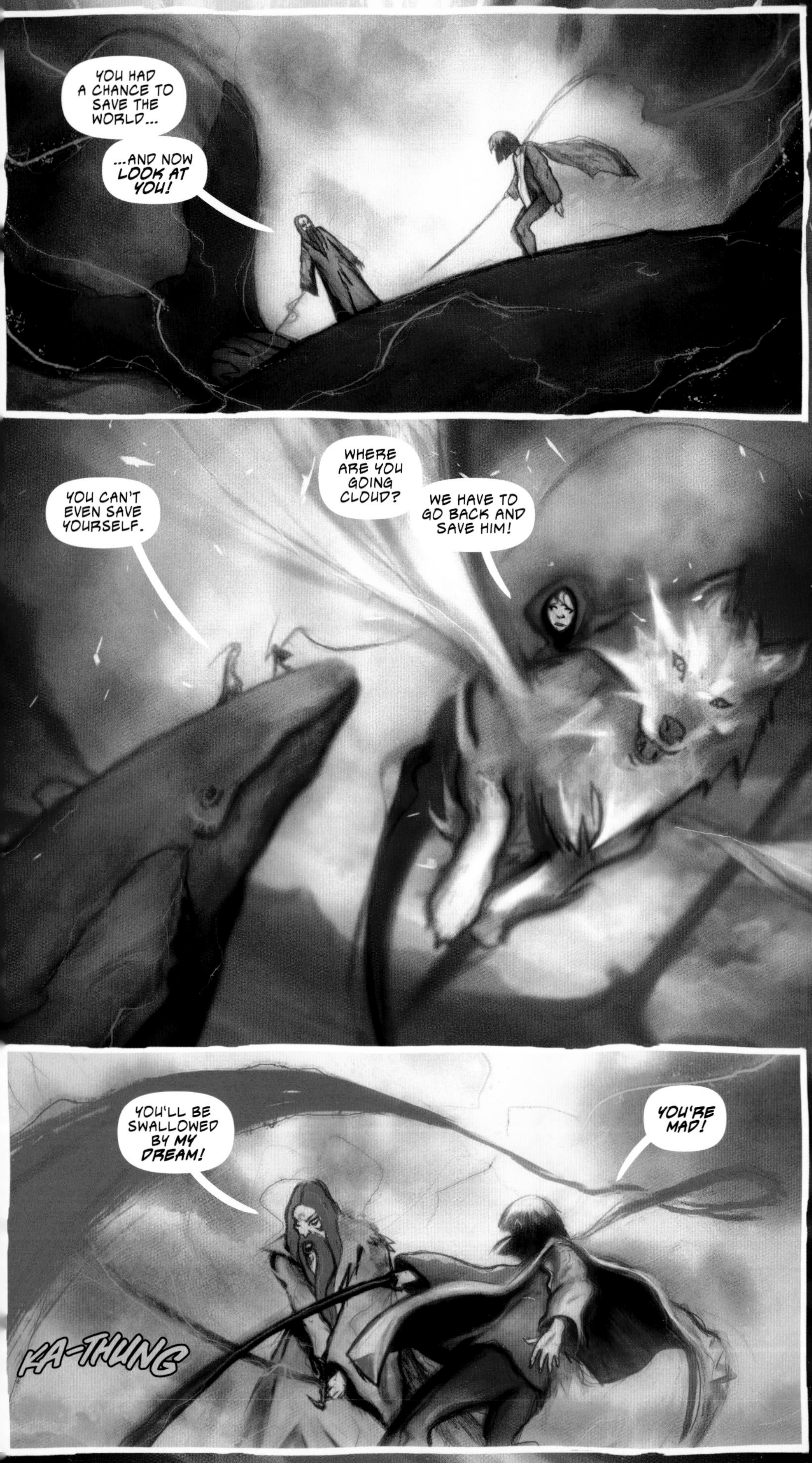
YOU HAD A CHANCE TO SAVE THE WORLD...
...AND NOW LOOK AT YOU!
YOU CAN'T EVEN SAVE YOURSELF.
WHERE ARE YOU GOING CLOUD?
WE HAVE TO GO BACK AND SAVE HIM!
YOU'LL BE SWALLOWED BY MY DREAM!
YOU'RE MAD!
KA-THUNG

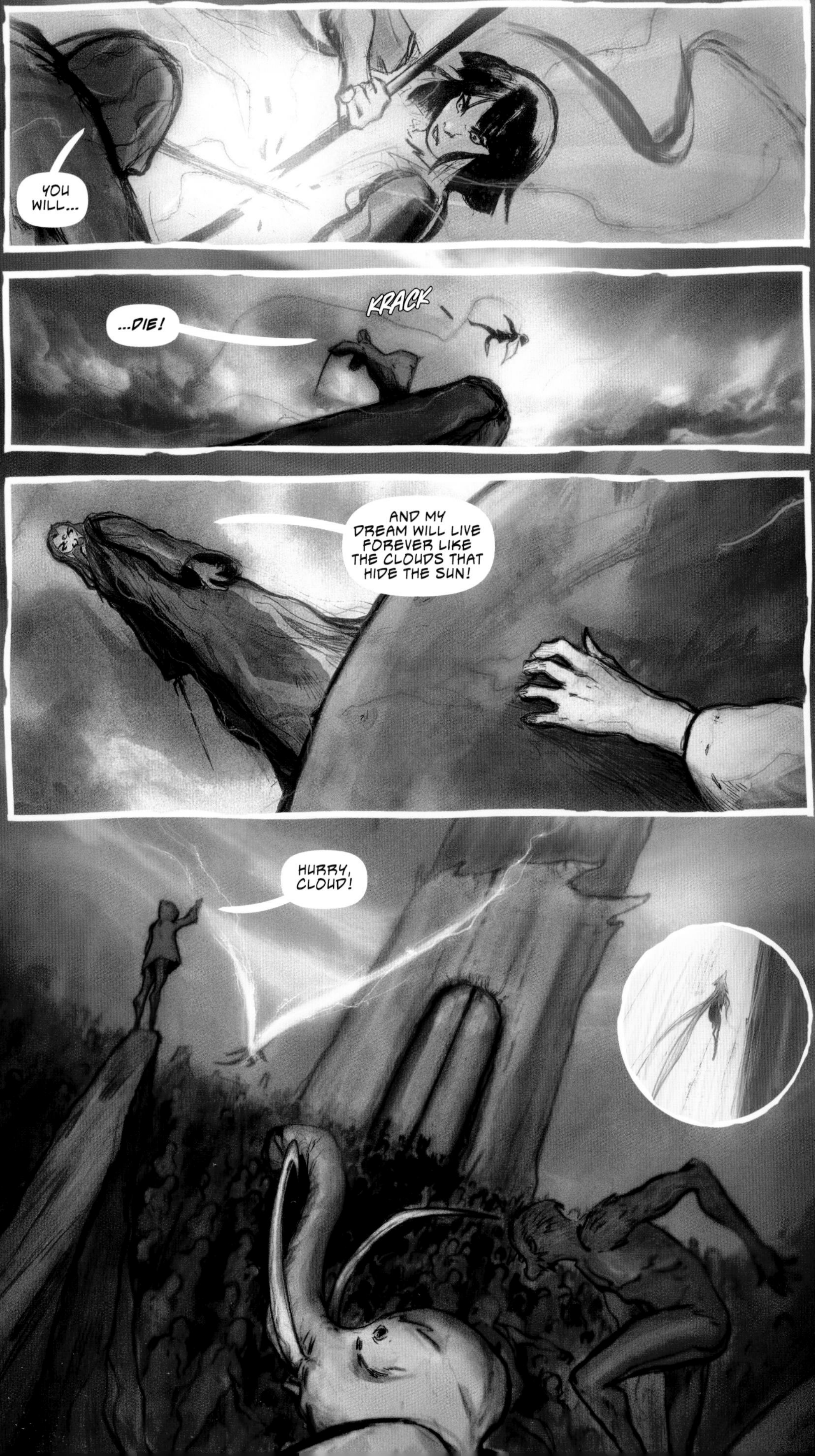
YOU WILL...
KRACK
...DIE!
AND MY DREAM WILL LIVE FOREVER LIKE THE CLOUDS THAT HIDE THE SUN!
HURRY, CLOUD!

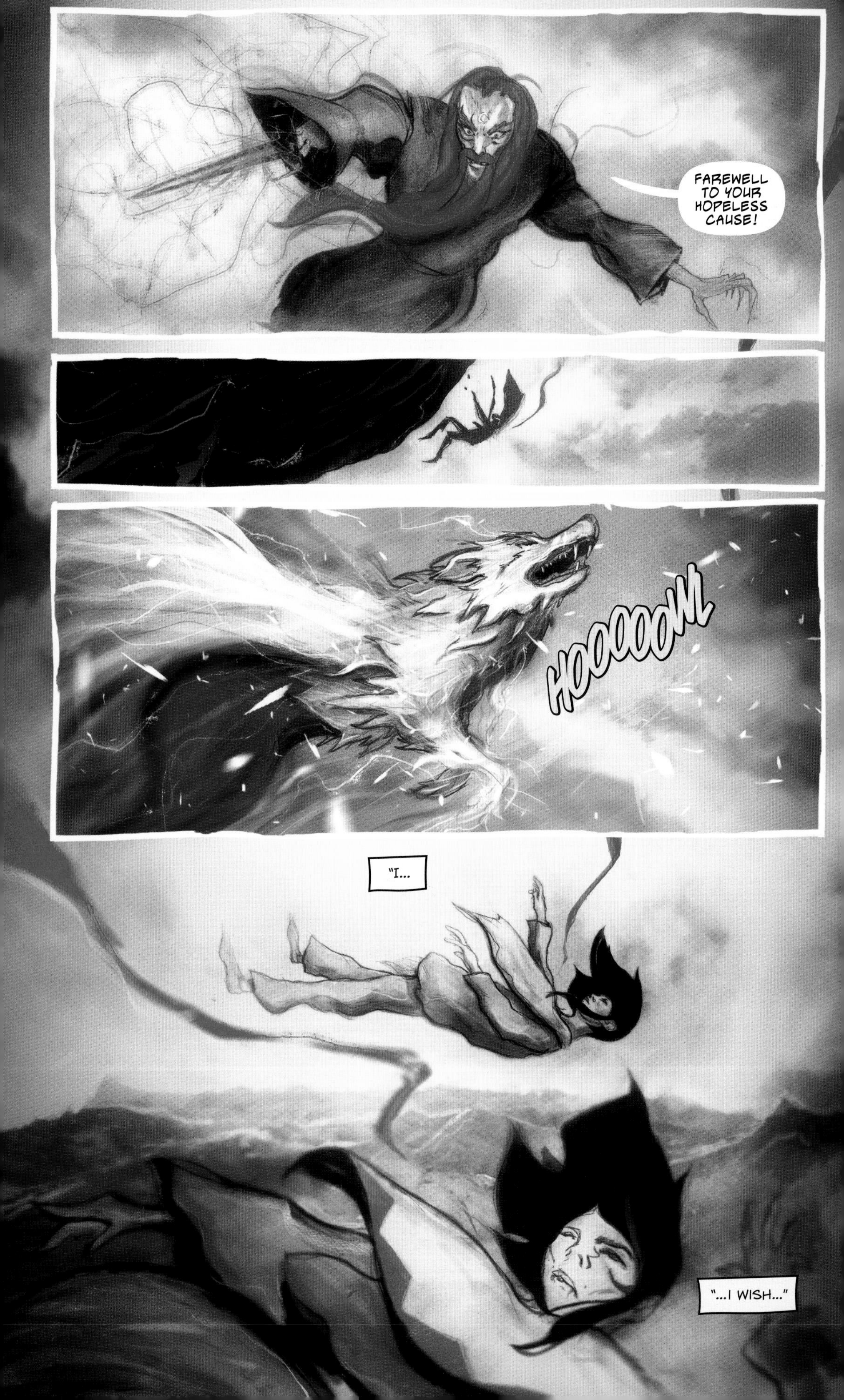
FAREWELL TO YOUR HOPELESS CAUSE!
HOOOOOWL
"I...
"...I WISH..."

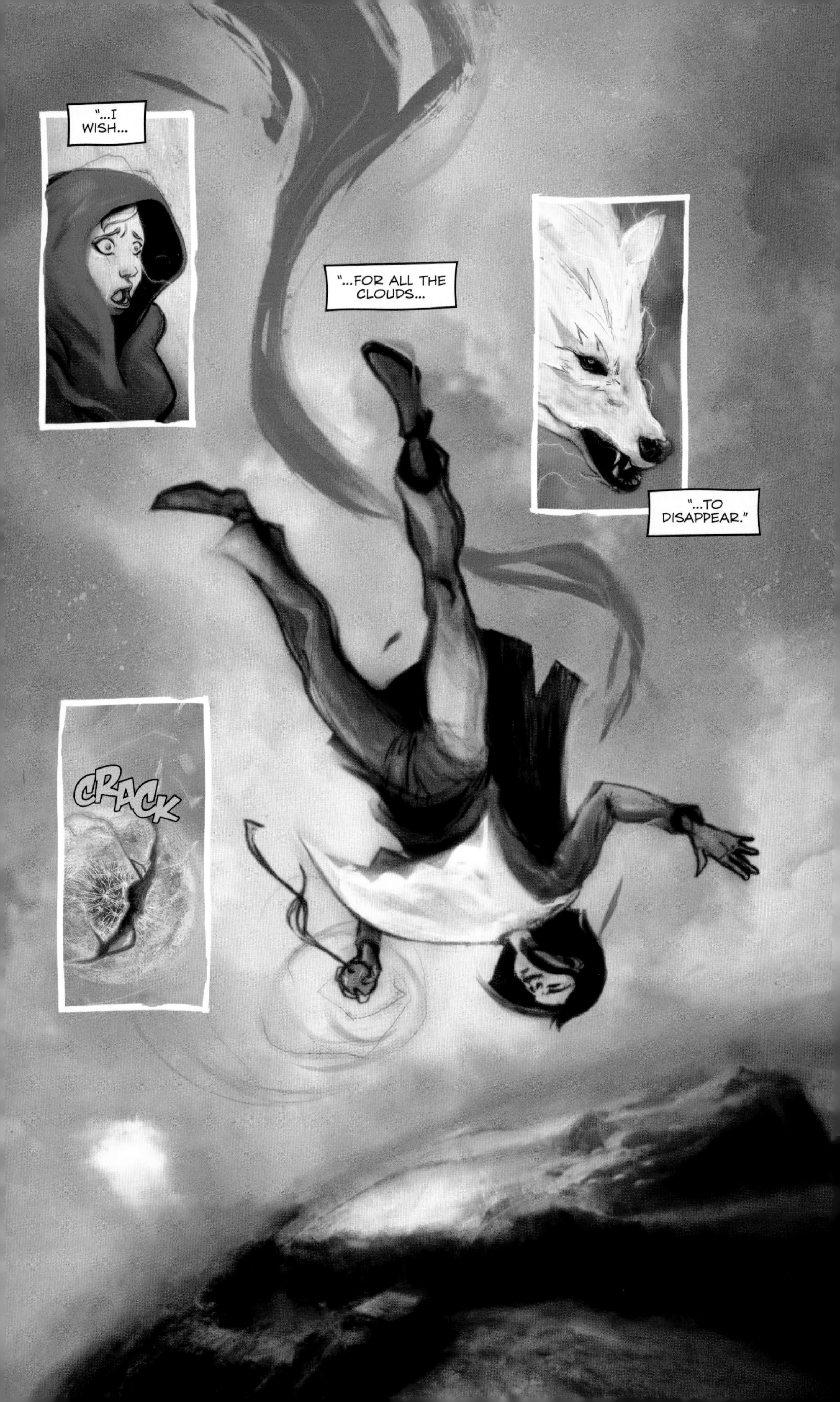
"...I WISH...
"...FOR ALL THE CLOUDS...
"...TO DISAPPEAR."
CRACK

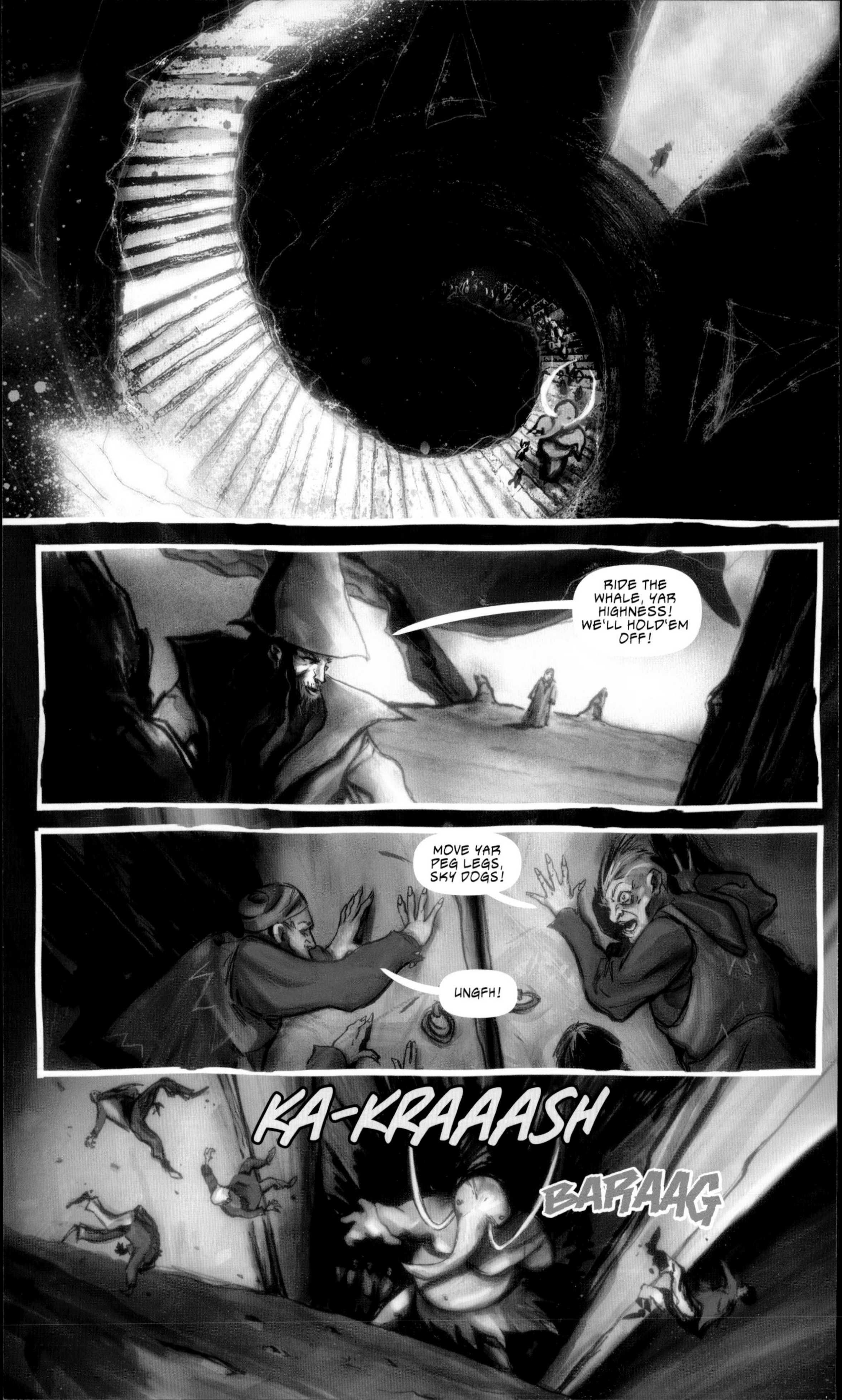
RIDE THE WHALE, YAR HIGHNESS! WE'LL HOLD'EM OFF!
MOVE YAR PEG LEGS, SKY DOGS!
UNGFH!
KA-KRAAASH
BARAAG

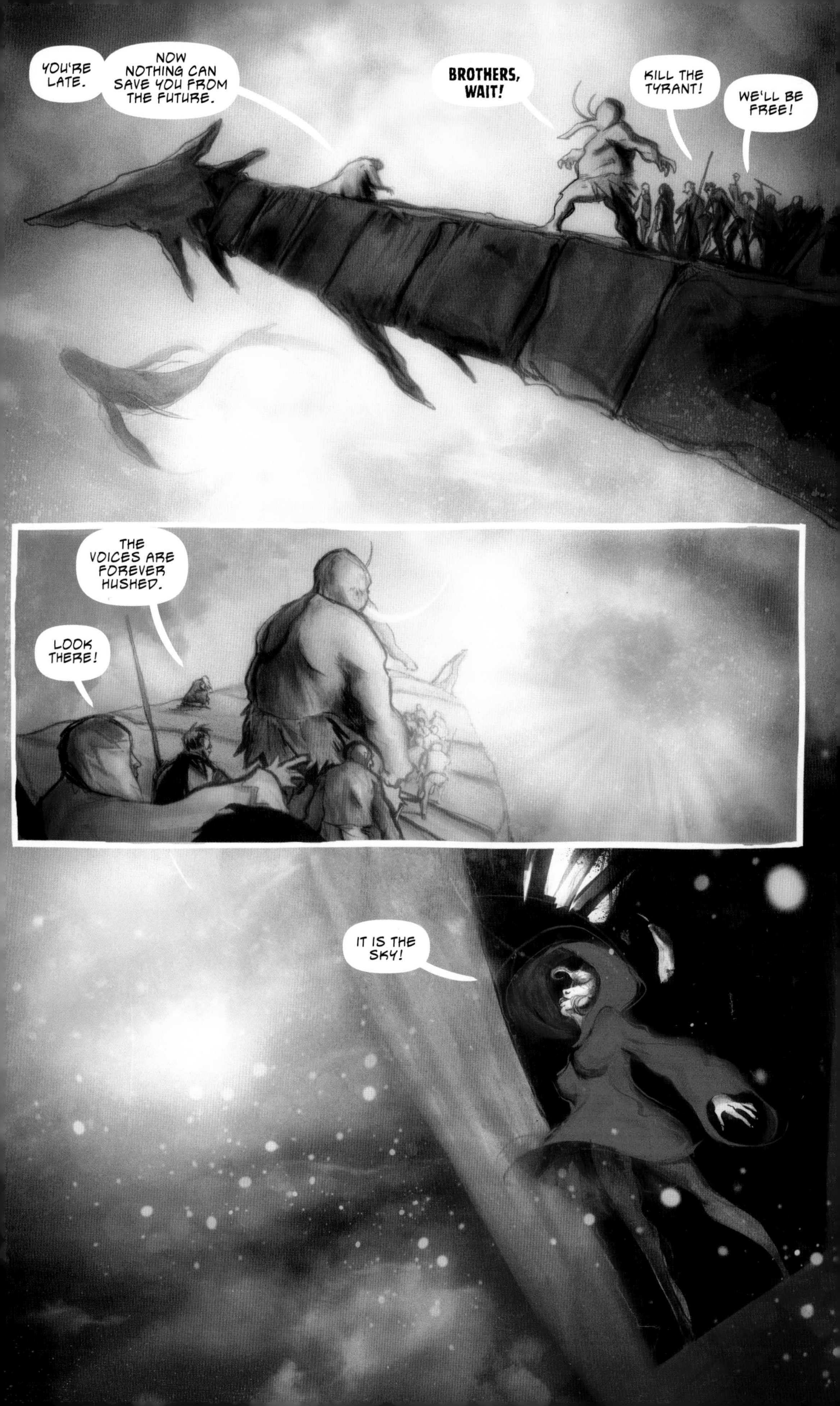
YOU'RE LATE.
NOW NOTHING CAN SAVE YOU FROM THE FUTURE.
BROTHERS, WAIT!
KILL THE TYRANT!
WE'LL BE FREE!
THE VOICES ARE FOREVER HUSHED.
LOOK THERE!
IT IS THE SKY!

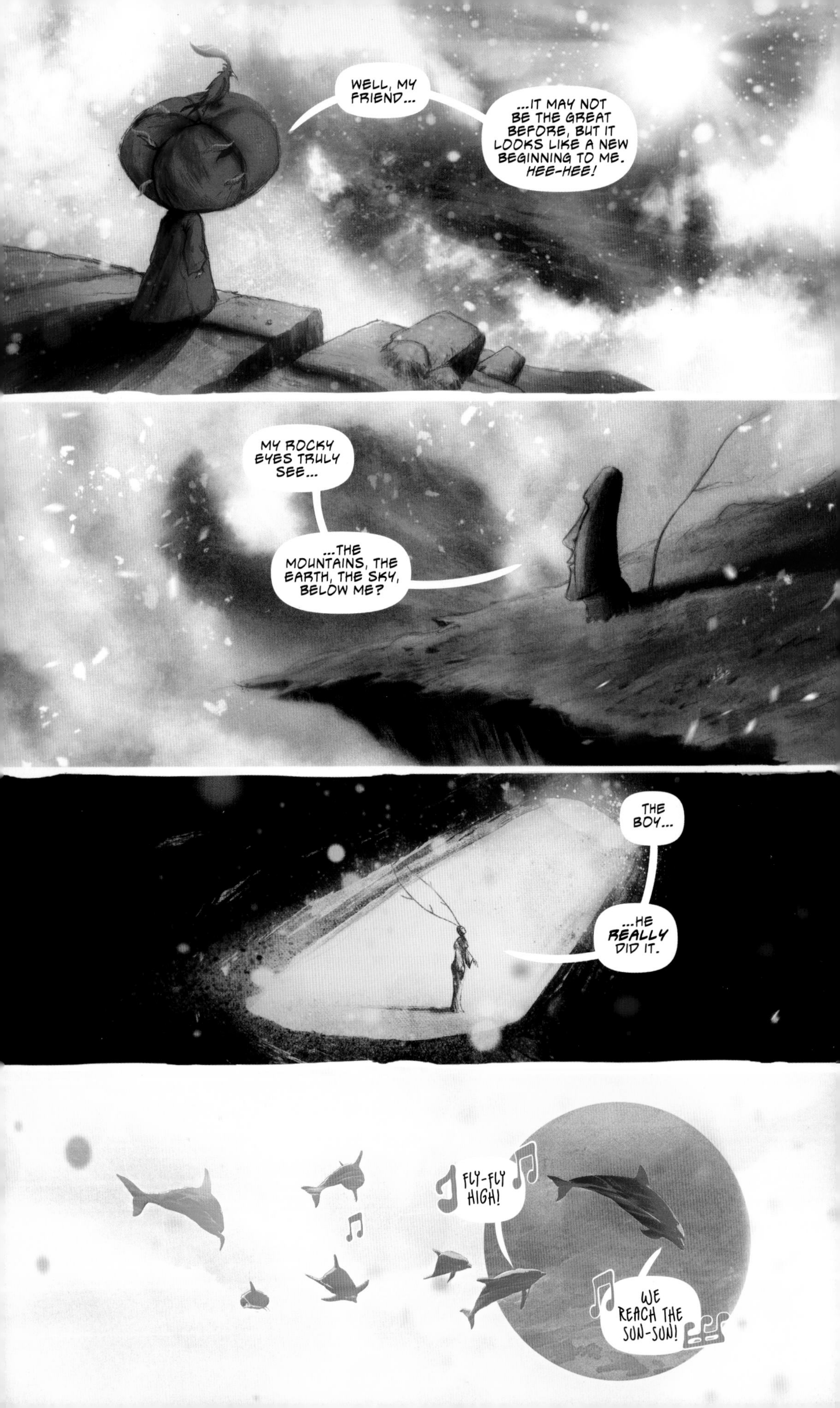
WELL, MY FRIEND...
...IT MAY NOT BE THE GREAT BEFORE, BUT IT LOOKS LIKE A NEW BEGINNING TO ME. HEE-HEE!
MY ROCKY EYES TRULY SEE...
...THE MOUNTAINS, THE EARTH, THE SKY, BELOW ME?
THE BOY...
...HE REALLY DID IT.
FLY-FLY HIGH!
WE REACH THE SUN-SUN!

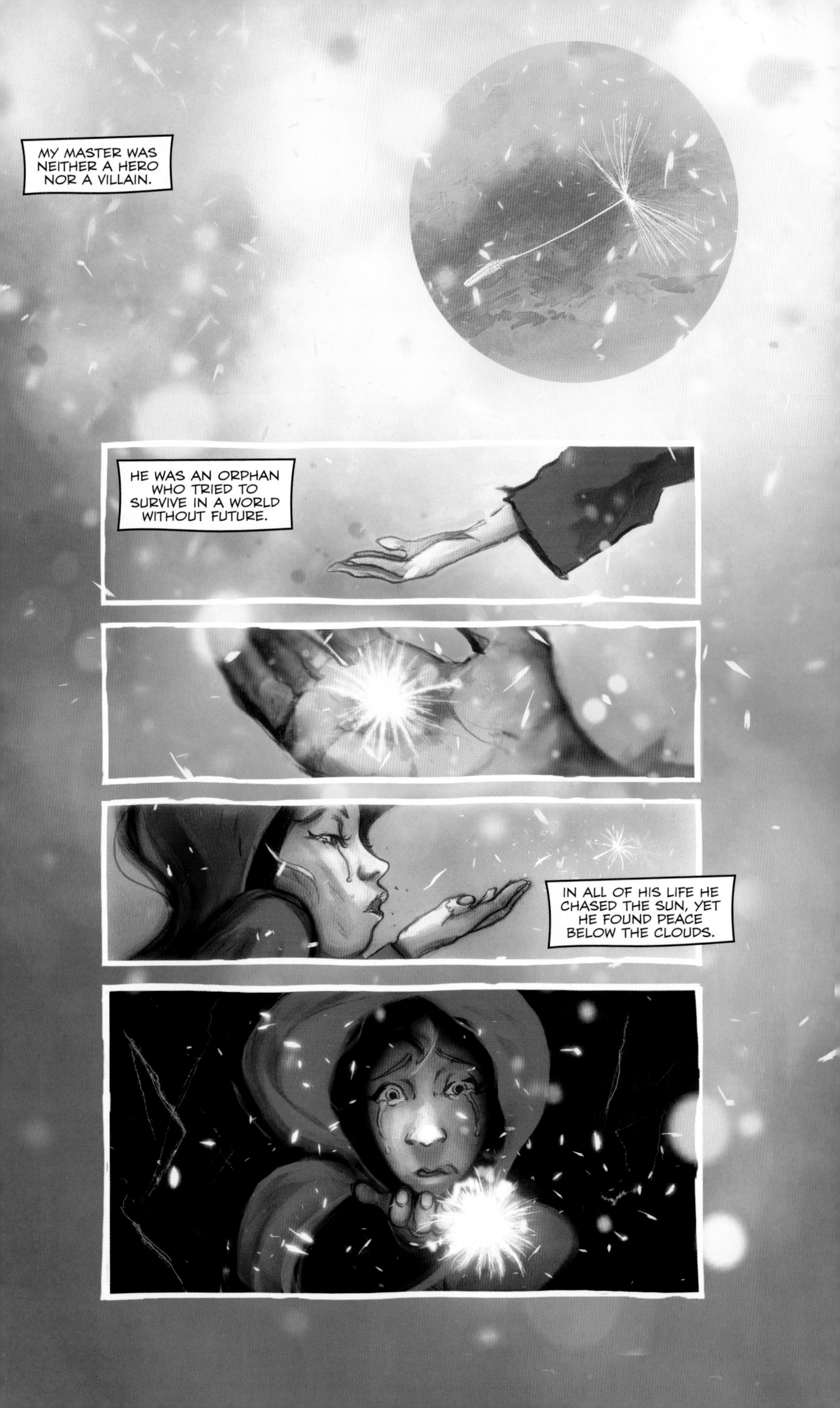
MY MASTER WAS NEITHER A HERO NOR A VILLAIN.
HE WAS AN ORPHAN WHO TRIED TO SURVIVE IN A WORLD WITHOUT FUTURE.
IN ALL OF HIS LIFE HE CHASED THE SUN, YET HE FOUND PEACE BELOW THE CLOUDS.

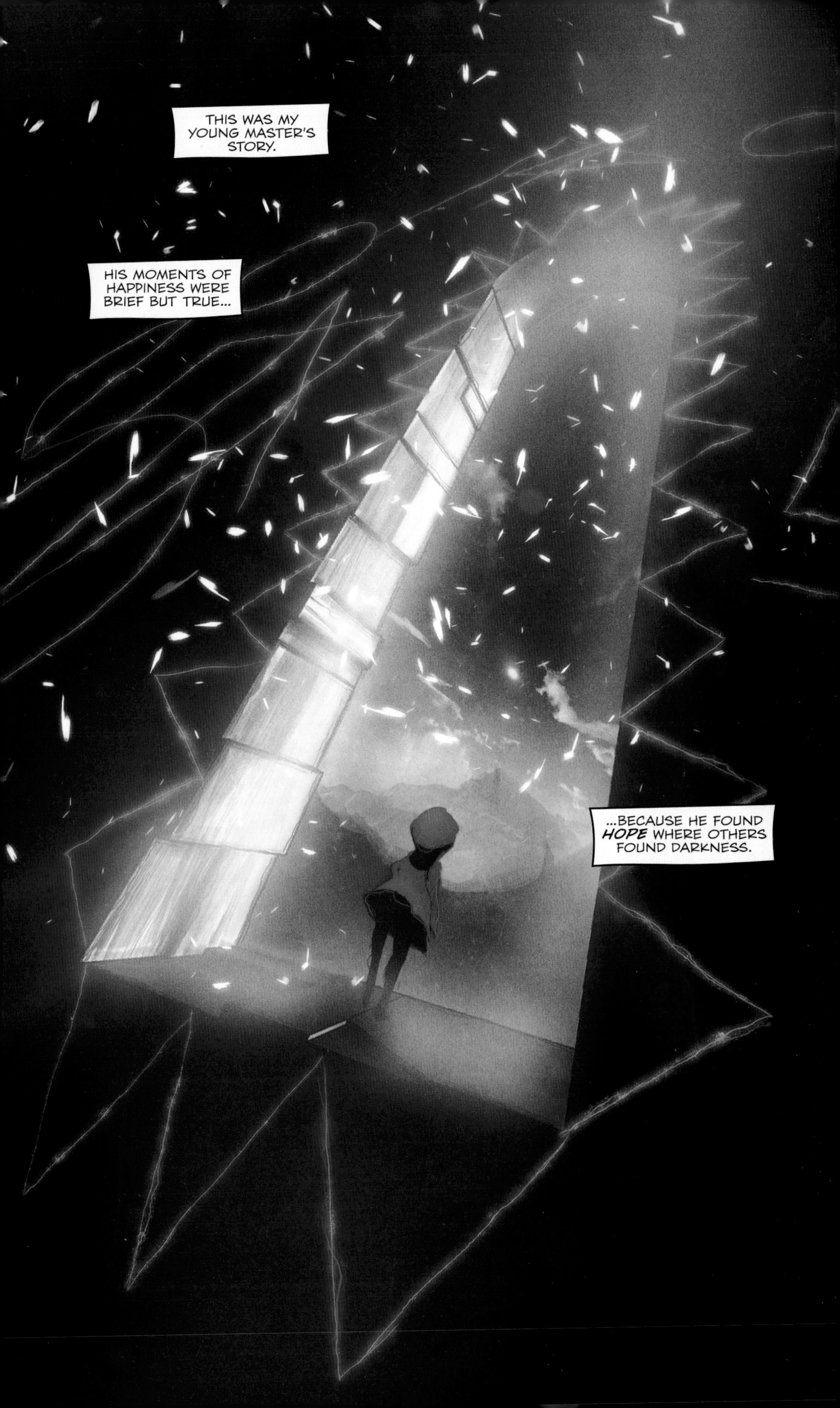
THIS WAS MY YOUNG MASTER'S STORY.
HIS MOMENTS OF HAPPINESS WERE BRIEF BUT TRUE...
...BECAUSE HE FOUND *HOPE* WHERE OTHERS FOUND DARKNESS.